THE
COMMON
SENSE
WAY

A NEW WAY TO THINK
ABOUT LEADING AND
ORGANIZING

Security Disclaimer:

This book was submitted to the Department of Defense Office of Prepublication and Security Review on April 16, 2020. It was returned with redactions on January 28, 2021, resubmitted for redaction challenges on February 12, and cleared for release to the public on March 25, 2021. The book took five years to write and over eleven months to get reviewed and cleared for release.

CLEARED AS AMENDED
Jan 28, 2021:
Department of Defense
OFFICE OF PREPUBLICATION AND SECURITY REVIEW

In an effort to protect specific organizations, operations, and/or the individuals who took part in the events covered in this book, there are a few instances where I had to use pseudonyms for people and generic names for military organizations such as the one of which I was a part. To comply with Department of Defense redactions I had to adjust some descriptions of pictures and events as well as the exact date and time they occurred. The security-instituted adjustments to this book were minor and did not affect the way the stories were written or the lessons that were learned from them.

Finally, combat is just like life, no two individuals see it or experience it the same way. The insights I share in this book are based on my perspective and the perspective or those who were with me. If a sentence or paragraph seems to be missing some level of context-specific detail the reason is more than likely to protect the operational security of those involved.

THE
COMMON
SENSE
WAY

A NEW WAY TO THINK
ABOUT LEADING AND
ORGANIZING
(BOOK II of III)

PETE BLABER

First Edition June 2021

Book Design by Alan Barnett
Copy Edited by Pam Susemiehl

www.peteblaber.com

ISBN: 978-0-578-99587-8 (hard cover)
ISBN: 978-0-578-87674-0 (paperback)

TABLE OF CONTENTS

PREFACE

Why and Where I'm writing this book

I'm writing this book from an off-the-grid cabin at 6,700 feet in the rugged alpine wilderness of the Sierra Nevada Mountains. Steep, cross-compartmented ridges cloaked in a canopy of old-growth Ponderosa and Jefferson pines surround the cabin. The terrain, altitude, and lack of road accessibility combine to provide for and protect a wildlife eco-system that has remained mostly unmolested by man and machines in modern times. Trail cameras offer my only visual evidence of its stealthy inhabitants: large, lumbering black bears, muscle-bound mountain lions, schizophrenic pigs, and condors to name just a few.

Not a day has gone by over the past six years while working on this book that I didn't pause to appreciate the wildlife, the wilderness, the land we call America, and the principle of freedom upon which they all stand.

Off-Grid Cabin in Sierra Nevada Mountains

Staring out the front window as the sun's first photons touch the tops of the tree-lined peaks, it is with the same frame of reference that I reflect on my own life and leadership journey as I write the final chapters of this book.

I am the fortunate benefactor of what I have come to believe is one of life's most esteemed privileges: that of leading fellow humans across continents, cultures and contexts.

Leadership, like life, is a privilege. Not for those we lead, rather for those of us who are fortunate enough to experience and learn from it. I've had the privilege of leading interagency and international teams while serving in the military; and leading Manufacturing, Sales, Marketing, and Research & Development teams while in Business. With privilege comes the responsibility to pay something back. If reciprocity is the currency of human interaction then knowledge is the gold standard that determines its worth. The value of what we give or what we get from any human interaction depends on the knowledge our brains learn from it.

The stories and lessons shared in this book were learned, implemented, and vetted by the living laboratory of real world leadership: from combat operations on five continents, to the boardrooms and back offices of cutting-edge Global corporations, and through the collective wisdom and knowledge of some the greatest leaders in human history. Everything I know about leadership is the byproduct of all of the brains I have had the privilege of interacting with and learning from throughout my life and leadership journey. I point this out up front to ensure I give credit where credit is due and to ensure I tell each and every one of them, "Thank you."

Although the culture of my former military Unit is one of quiet professionalism that values humility over self-aggrandizement, that same culture also instills an innate sense of responsibility to contribute to the Greater Good of our country and species. I believe that the best way to balance this tension is by sharing my experiences and the corresponding lessons on leading, learning, and living life to the fullest via this book. Accurately understanding and sharing lessons from the past is an essential step for gaining insight into and preparing for the future.

The stories that follow are mine; the lessons belong to us all.

INTRODUCTION

What is the Common Sense Way?

King Leonidas: *Then what must a citizen do to save his world when the very laws he has sworn to protect force him to do nothing?*

Queen Gorgo: *It is not a question of what a Spartan citizen should do, nor a husband, nor a king. Instead, ask yourself my dearest love, what should a free man do?*[1]

May 2003, 0330, desert hide-site just outside Tikrit, Iraq. On guard shift monitoring capture operations while standing inside the sunroof/gun turret of a specially modified SUV. Continuously fidgeting to find comfort and fend off the freeze. One of six all-terrain and undercover vehicles positioned as part of a patchwork security perimeter based on the cover and concealment potential of the surrounding sea of small and medium-sized sand moguls. Pitch black but for the crisp blinking brilliance of the stars overhead.

Desert Hide-Site

1

Movement. Human figure walking in the desert about a hundred meters straight ahead. He's heading this way. Iraqi soldier? Bedouin? Ambien zombie? Armed? Trigger aware. Thumb on safety. Thermal site centered. What the? In pitch darkness we all lose face. His silhouette, speed, and gait inform his fate.

"Hold your fire, he's friendly," I updated the others over the radio.

"Stump," I whisper-yelled, "what in the flying foxtrot are you doing walking around outside the perimeter without telling anybody?" "Sorry about that, Panther," he responded unapologetically, "a call came in for you on the Iridium Sat-Phone but the signal was too weak so I had to find some high ground...I wasn't worried because I figured you'd recognize my finely sculpted statuesque physique." Stump's 5′6″ 180-pound frame explained his name. "Who is it?" I asked. "The caller ID says *'Office of the Secretary of Defense, Pentagon'*...maybe the Secretary of Defense was watching the Predator[2] video during last night's capture mission and now he wants to know more?" In this case I knew better.

"Hello, this is Pete."

"Pete? Can you hear me, this is Tom?" Tom worked for Paul Wolfowitz who was the Deputy Secretary of Defense from 2000 to 2005. The Deputy Secretary of Defense (colloquially referred to as the Dep Sec-Def) is the second highest-ranking civilian leader in the Pentagon, essentially the "chief operating officer" for all four branches of the U.S. Military.

"I can hear you loud and clear. Go ahead, Tom," I whispered. "Pete, I had no idea you were on a mission," he whisper-responded. In combat zones whispering is common sense, like yawning it's also contagious.

"No worries, Tom, all is quiet right now, I can talk." "Okay great, I actually have two things, the first is operational, I want to know if you have any feedback you can share with me on how the Iraqi-American cultural advisors are working out for you and your teams...we're getting serious push-back from the Joint Staff[3] here at the Pentagon on the costs and the lack of usage," he added.

"I have plenty of feedback, Tom, and it's all good," I began, "but before I share it with you I need to thank you and your boss for everything you guys did to find, in-process, and then fly the Iraqi-Americans over here in time for us to take them with us before we crossed the border. Someday you'll have to tell me all about it over a beer but right now I just want to tell you how grateful me and my guys are for everything you did." "Happy to help, Pete. Do you have any examples you can share?"

"Of course," I replied, and then explained that it started with all the little things they did that made them so indispensable, whether it was reading roadway signs to help us find our way, or reading the expressions on civilians faces to help us find the enemy. Having someone with us who understands the people, the places, the history, and who can also translate that knowledge through a common cultural lens is a huge competitive advantage.

Our experiences in Afghanistan taught us to think of them as our eyes and ears as well as our voice because without our eyes, ears, and voice we couldn't make sense of what was going on around us. When we were interacting with the Iraqi people and they were with us we felt extrasensory, when they weren't we felt senseless.

"I'm sure you've heard the same thing from other units?" I added.

"Unfortunately, Pete, your guys ended up being the only ones who took the Iraqi-Americans across the border," he replied and I went speechless. My mind immediately hyper-linked to the Jessica Lynch debacle a few weeks earlier where an entire convoy of Army Supply trucks took a series of wrong turns because they couldn't read the highway signs and unwittingly drove directly into the enemy infested city of Nasiriya (March 23rd, 2003). Not only could they not understand the highway signs they couldn't understand the Iraqi people, some of who were jumping up and down and screaming at them to warn them of the hornets' nest they were obliviously driving into. By the end of the day, twenty-nine Americans were dead.

"Tom, I highly recommend you do whatever it takes to get the rest of the Iraqi-Americans attached to the key ground units A-S-A-P. My suspicion is that most of the operational commanders either had no idea they were available or no idea of how much they'd actually need them once they crossed the border. I guarantee you they do now and if given the choice they'll do everything they can to get the Iraqi-Americans attached to their units before they begin occupying the big cities."

"Will do, Pete, but at this point I'm even more concerned about Ambassador Bremer and his staff at the Coalition Provisional Authority[4] (CPA). As you've probably heard Mr. Bremer and the CPA are taking charge of the entire effort to rebuild the Iraqi infrastructure and the Iraqi government." Tom went on to tell me that the CPA plan, "did not see the need for Iraqi-American cultural advisors." According to "the plan" it would be "too much of a logistic burden to transport, house, and feed them." Tom then asked me if we could spare one of our cultural advisors to assist Ambassador Bremer and the CPA.

"Of course," I reassured him, "my guys have been advocating for the use of the Iraqi-Americans as civilian liaisons in the cities since the day we began our infiltration." I would later learn that between 50 and 100 American citizens of Iraqi descent volunteered to risk their livelihoods and their lives as cultural advisors. They came from all walks of life and many of them possessed valued professional skills and experience (e.g. city managers, engineers, bankers, realtors, and retailers to name just a few). All of those we interviewed to deploy forward into Iraq possessed the ability to translate and share those skills via their impossible-to-teach knowledge of Iraqi and American culture, language, and history.

I told Tom that even though "it was a huge operational loss for our team," we had no issues going down to one cultural advisor so the CPA could have someone to help them understand and communicate with the Iraqi people. "I'll head down to CPA Headquarters in Baghdad tomorrow with Saif (one of our cultural advisors) and then..." **Boom.**

"Mortar round, twelve o'clock, two thousand meters," one of our sentries[5] whispered with urgency over the radio.

"Call you back later, Tom," I explained as I disconnected the satellite phone and reoriented my weapon and my senses outward toward the horizon. **To Be Continued.**

REFLECTIONS/LESSONS LEARNED
What is the Common Sense Way?

We're all fugitives from the law of averages: tornados, tsunamis, and terror attacks; car crashes, crime, and cardiac arrest; asteroids, anarchy, and Armageddon. Fate rarely calls upon us at a moment of our choosing so there's no substitute for the prepared mind. In a survival situation only one thing is certain, whether we live or whether we die depends on the choices we make in the context of the moment we make them: to panic or pay attention, to fight or flee, to shoot first or question what we see. Choosing is how we humans adapt.

The rigid and non-adaptive leader making choices based on emotions, plans, or a disconnected chain of command is a disciple of death. Whether you're crossing the Iraqi desert with your team, or the hall for an urgent meeting with your boss, or a busy street with your family and friends, the argument of this book is that our individual and collective freedom to make sense of what's going on around us and sensible choices about what to do next isn't a matter of philosophy, or politics, or religion, it's a biologic necessity. Conscious awareness enables us to live, learn, and lead the Common Sense Way.

The Purpose of this book is to change the way we the people think and speak about leading and organizing. The Common Sense Way promotes a new way that can radically enhance the way we learn to adapt to complex problems and opportunities as well as the way we lead and organize to accomplish any purpose.

The stories and lessons that follow will challenge all leaders, young and old, new and experienced, high-level and low, by illuminating a provocative new way of evolved thinking based on the biologic and evolutionary underpinnings of Common Sense. It's the Common Sense Way.

What follows is an overview of the Common Sense Way and some of its key concepts as a preview of what's to come in the rest of the book:

What is the Common Sense Way? Although its framework of concepts and principles are new, the biography of this idea is as ancient as life on earth. Common Sense has been developed, honed, and validated over 3.9 billion years of intensive focus group testing also known as Evolution by Natural Selection.

How it works: Both a method and a mindset, the Common Sense Way is a pattern of human behavior naturally selected over the evolutionary eons that uses knowledge of patterns (patterns of nature, patterns of human nature, and patterns of history) to empower and enable our brains with freedom of choice to make sense of what's going on around us and sensible choices about what to do next:

Movement. Human figure walking in the dessert
about a hundred meters straight ahead.

Knowledge of patterns of nature such as light, the laws of physics, and DNA make sense of the way all life on earth survives, thrives, and evolves. What is in nature is in human nature, we are these patterns.

In pitch darkness we all lose face.

Knowledge of patterns of human nature such as how we think, how we choose, and how we behave make sense of the way our 99.5% shared DNA enabled nervous systems co-evolved with nature to survive, thrive, and evolve. And knowledge of patterns of history such as our memories, ancient recorded wisdom, and our genetic codes make sense of the way our species got to where we are today, freedom of choice and freedom of speech to make sense of the world around us and sensible choices about what to do next:

His silhouette, speed, and gait inform his fate.

The human brain operates by the same common sense principles as the universe from which it evolved. Matter can neither be created nor destroyed and no matter how hard our brains try they can't make something out of nothing. All we got is what we got. It turns out we can learn a lot. As discussed in Chapter Three every pattern we've ever learned, every face, every place, every tune, every taste, every scent and every shape is physically present in our brains as our foundational knowledge of patterns:

Stump's 5'6" 180 pound frame explained his name.

What's the biologic benefit of learning knowledge of patterns? Learned knowledge of patterns provides our brains with options and options provide us with freedom to choose between them based on the adaptive stimulus of what's going on around us:

"Hold your fire he's friendly."

The choices we make in the context of the moment are the catalysts for Natural Selection. In the process of Natural Selection when a particular response to environmental change leads to increased survival and reproduction these responses tend to spread throughout populations over time. Our ancestors chose the Common Sense Way or we wouldn't be here today.

Charles Darwin taught us, "it's not the smartest, or strongest, or most intelligent that survives, rather it's the one who adapts to changes," and one of Nature's most successful adaptive patterns is biomimicry. We don't have to be the first or fastest we only need to recognize a pattern

as advantageous then learn to adapt by mimicking it and putting it into action fast. As the stories in this book reveal the Common Sense Way provides our brains with a competitive advantage:

- It's the way our ancient ancestors successfully spread and expanded humanity across the globe.
- It's the way explorers, inventors, and entrepreneurs changed the world with discoveries, developments, and ideas that upon reflection seem like blinding restatements of the obvious (e.g. the earth rotates around the sun, washing our hands prevents the spread of disease, computers like people are smarter when you connect them).
- And it's the way thousands of generations of common sense leaders—many of whose names we'll never know—sacrificed their livelihoods and their lives to take care of their people and ensure they survived, thrived, and evolved. *It's the Common Sense Way.*

Fifteen, fifty, and 500 years from now technology, culture, and the environment will have changed drastically, yet our 99.5% shared DNA-enabled nervous systems will take thousands of years to vary in the slightest. Which is perhaps another way of saying if the way we the people choose to lead and organize our governments, our corporations, our legal, economic, and criminal justice systems is to endure to the benefit of the human species than the way must conform to our most biologically inherent human trait: *freedom of choice and freedom of speech to make sense of what's going on around us and sensible choices about what to do next.*

And here's one of the coolest things about the Common Sense Way. We don't need a special degree or pedigree to live and lead the Common Sense Way. We have everything we need etched inside each and every strand of DNA in each and every one of the 30+ trillion[6] cells that make up our bodies and brains. All that's needed to put it into practice is conscious awareness of how to access and operationalize it in the context of the moment when you need it the most.

To accomplish its purpose the book is formatted with three goals:

1. To share knowledge of a new way of thinking and speaking about leading and organizing.
2. To put the new way in context by sharing real-world stories and the common sense lessons learned from them.
3. To ensure the Common Sense Way makes sense.

1) The first goal of the book is to share knowledge of a new way to think and speak about leading and organizing. Once the human brain etches a neural pattern of thinking and behavior (e.g. when we wake, what we eat, how we get to work, whether and why we wash our hands, how we lead and organize, etc.) it can be tricky business trying to change it. Even when we intuitively understand a pattern doesn't make sense (think of dates and mates, smoking and drinking, eating and exercising) it can seem like a hopelessly Herculean battle to change or break free from it[7].

Here's the good news. The ability to learn new patterns of thinking and behaving is biologic. Anyone can do it at any time during their lives. Human learning depends on metaphor, time and feedback. To invent an atomic clock someone had to invent a sundial first. Metaphor is how the human brain learns knowledge about one kind of thing to make sense of another. Time and feedback tell us if the knowledge we learned actually makes sense.

The biology of our brains explains how it works. When new metaphors are incorporated into our prior knowledge they physically change our brains at the neural level. Words matter. They're the concept tags our brains use to recognize, encode, store, and make neural sense of what we experience. Words activate the way our brains frame the world so new frames require new words. Thinking differently requires speaking differently.[8]

To change the way our brains think about leading and organizing, the Common Sense Way proposes a transformational reframing of most traditional leadership metaphors (e.g. orders, plans, disconnected chains-of-command, etc.) by introducing the new metaphors and principles of the Language of Common Sense.

The Language of Common Sense	
The Way	**The Common Sense Way**
• Process oriented	• Purpose oriented
• Do what you're told to do	• Do what makes sense
• Stay in your lane	• Learn to adapt to patterns
• Follow plans from the past	• Freedom to make sensible choices
• Orders, Commands	• Logic of Why it makes sense
• Strategy, Plans, Disconnected Chain-of-Command	• Foundational Logic of Why (FLOW)
• Wait to be told	• Develop the Situation/Go with the FLOW
• Organizational Structure	• Organize to learn
• Get along or get out	• Collaborate, Communicate, Reciprocate
• Teach them how to follow the process	• Teach them how to think
• Stay anchored to the chain	• Build learning-feedback loops not ladders
• Need to know	• Shared Reality
• Stoic/Not fun	• Humor/Creativity

2) The second goal of the book is to support the first by putting the *Language of Common Sense* into context with an eclectic series of never-before-heard real-world stories from my leadership journey across continents, cultures, and time.

People are rarely motivated to change deeply entrenched thought patterns and behaviors by reason alone. Changing is a choice. We choose to change. The most powerful way to motivate and inspire our brains to change is through the use of story. As an example, I could tell you that "reciprocity is the currency of human interaction and the evolutionary stable pattern of behavior upon which trust and building best teams is based"; or I could tell you the story of two soldiers who fought together on the battlefields of WWI:

A soldier was hit by enemy fire and couldn't make it back to the safety of his trench so his teammate braved withering

machine-gun fire to crawl out and rescue him. He returned a
few minutes later mortally wounded and his friend whom he
carried on his back was dead. Their Commander was irate.
"You shouldn't have gone," he screamed, "Now I've lost both of
you, it wasn't worth it." Gasping for his last breaths the dying
man smiled as he whispered, "Ahh, but it was, Sir, because when
I got to him he said, 'Jim, thank God. I knew you'd come.'"[9]

As the WWI story so acutely demonstrates, the biologic benefit of
story is not to be gained from judging, adjudicating, assigning blame or
fame. The biologic benefit of story is the conceptual knowledge we learn
from it. The term "conceptual knowledge" refers to our brain's interconnected web of knowledge that enables us to understand ideas as well
as the relationships between ideas. Conceptual knowledge can only be
learned by thoughtful, reflective thinking.

The stories and lessons that follow are selected and arranged to create conscious awareness of the *Language of Common Sense*.

3) The third goal is to ensure the Common Sense Way makes sense.
Patterns of Evolutionary History reveal we humans are stubbornly skeptical of new ways of making sense of the world around us until the new
ways are verified by the science of our own senses. The term worldview
comes from the Middle Ages when it literally meant "the view of our
world (the earth) being at the center of the universe." Everyone believed
it. Then in 1543 Astronomer Nicholas Copernicus established a new
theory of the universe based on the sun, rather than earth, as its center.
No one believed him.

Until, that is, the early 1600's when Galileo perfected an eight-
power telescope and discovered multiple moons orbiting around the
planet Jupiter (you can see them today with binoculars). Although the
backlash from political and religious leaders was formidable, there was
no stopping the contagion of common sense. From shared knowledge
of this newly discovered celestial pattern emerged the logic of why the
earth-centered worldview no longer made sense.

Thanks to Galileo and his sense-enhancing telescope, people could
see it with their own eyes. The light from the sun reflected on Jupiter
and its moons the same way it reflected on Earth and our moon. It made
sense that the Earth and Jupiter both rotated around the sun. A new

worldview was born. A worldview based on scientifically verifiable sensory evidence that made sense to our senses and brains.

In 1869 Ernst Mach made making sense a universally accepted scientific principle when he declared: "we know only one source which directly reveals scientific facts—our senses." The Mach principle has stood the test of time and the scrutiny of real world feedback as the essential verification for all new scientific theories and hypotheses to this day.

To change the way we the people think and speak about leading and organizing, the Common Sense Way provides scientifically verifiable sensory evidence that makes sense to our senses and brains. We all make sense a common way. Leadership based on the common way our body's and brains make sense is the Common Sense Way.

PART I

MAKING SENSE OF LEADERSHIP

CHAPTER 1

The Journey

The Common Ground upon Which We Stand

May 2003, 0530, desert hide-site just outside Tikrit, Iraq. After three more randomly fired mortar rounds exploded harmlessly in the distant desert I asked Stump to try to reconnect me with the Pentagon. While Stump searched for a satellite signal I reflected once again on how fortunate we were to have had the Iraqi-Americans with us over the previous six weeks while developing the situation 500 miles behind enemy lines, along with all the astonishing twists and turns of fate that made it possible.

I met Paul Wolfowitz and his Deputy nine months earlier (Summer 2002) while conducting a series of presentations on newly discovered information that I was asked to share with military and civilian leaders at the Pentagon. Ironically, the original purpose of the presentation wasn't to share intelligence. The intelligence emerged as a byproduct of sharing the presentation. The original purpose of the presentation was to share unclassified lessons regarding inter-agency[10] unity of effort between military special operations forces and other government agencies such as the CIA during the search for Al Qaeda leaders in and around the border region between Afghanistan and Pakistan.

"The common pattern of all successful operations we've conducted to date is a pattern of collaboration and communication between the Military and the Agency," I began the briefing.

"What prevents you and your Agency counterparts from working together like this all the time?" Mr. Wolfowitz immediately interrupted.

"I guess it starts with a bunch of byzantine administrative policies, procedures and protocols, such as accountability of personnel, budget compensation for payroll and equipment, and who is legally responsible for whatever it is both agencies are trying to accomplish. Over the years, the men and woman of both organizations have learned to adapt to the administrative barriers but the biggest barrier to interagency unity of effort isn't administrative, or procedural, or legal, it's the way leaders of these agencies (Department of Defense, Department of State, and the CIA) think about leading and organizing." "Example?" Mr. Wolfowitz demanded.

I didn't have to think very long to come up with an answer. I simply shared what I believed then, as I do now, to be one of the most prominent and historically significant examples of our government's lack of interagency unity of effort that occurred during the first few days after 9/11.

We had no U.S. personnel on the ground, no direct contact with any Afghans on the ground, and, by proxy, no way to understand or influence what was going on in and around Afghanistan. On September 13th, 2001, the CIA was tasked by President George W. Bush to put together a team for the infiltration of U.S. personnel into the Panshir Valley of northern Afghanistan.[11] Code-named JAWBREAKER, the team's purpose was to make contact with the anti-Taliban forces in Northern Afghanistan and begin assessing the art of the possible for follow-on operations and forces.

(September 14th, 2001: JAWBREAKER Day #1) Within twenty-four hours of receiving their orders the JAWBREAKER team began brainstorming what types of men and equipment they'd need to accomplish their mission. In his appropriately titled book, First In, the JAWBREAKER team leader, now retired CIA Officer Gary Schroen, explained the first thing he and his Deputy (Rick) did to build out their team:

"During Rick's years in SAD[12], he developed an extensive network of contacts within the U.S. military Special Operation community, and he made use of those contacts to ensure we were in touch with the various military entities we might be working with in Afghanistan. I agreed with Rick's idea that we should invite the U.S. military to send a Special Operations representative as part of our team."[13]

The JAWBREAKER team leader and his Deputy had identified one of the great operational paradoxes of the way our instruments of national power are organized and resourced to conduct our country's most sensitive clandestine combat operations: The CIA has the legal charter to conduct clandestine combat operations (e.g. recruit, handle, and pay intelligence sources and foreign fighters, etc.), yet lacks both the capability and capacity to execute these same types of operations in a non-permissive/enemy occupied environment; while special operations forces have the operational capability and capacity (e.g. quantity and quality of people and equipment to infiltrate, sustain, and operate in non-permissive/enemy occupied environments), yet the military lacks the legal charter and the operational freedom to execute these same types of operations on its own.

It is exactly this ongoing paradox that makes interagency unity of effort not just a nice-to-have-option for one-off missions but an essential organizing principle for all clandestine operations in non-permissive environments. We ("the Unit") were intimately familiar with Afghanistan from the in-depth planning we conducted three years earlier (1998), which focused on developing courses of action for the infiltration and capture of UBL[14]. Additionally, we had recently conducted long-range mountain infiltration training in and around the Bob Marshall Wilderness area of Montana[15].

We shared everything we had learned with Rick, including what types of weapons, satellite radios, batteries, and sustainment items worked best in low temperature/high altitude mountainous environments. By the end of the phone call we had established a shared understanding of JAWBREAKER's purpose as well as the number and types of people and equipment the team needed to ensure they could accomplish it.

(September 15th, 2001: JAWBREAKER Day 2) Twelve hours after our phone conversation all Military Special Operations Units received an "urgent" email memo from our higher headquarters that prohibited "all direct communication between the military and Other Government Agencies until otherwise directed by a fully flushed out plan and/or a clearly established military chain-of-command."

At the time, many military and political leaders in the U.S. compared the gravitas of the moment with Pearl Harbor. There was no doubt in anyone's mind that successfully establishing a toehold in Afghanistan was one of the most important clandestine missions since WWII. It was also one of the most complex and most dangerous. Despite the fact that we had a direct phone line to our Agency counterparts that we'd been allowed to use whenever needed during peacetime, we were now no longer permitted to communicate with each other and share mission essential knowledge and operational information as we prepared to go to war.

(September 16th, 2001: JAWBREAKER Day 3) With each passing hour of inactivity our operational sense of urgency grew in tandem with our administrative sense of frustration. Someone likened it to being on the bridge of the Titanic and knowing that there's an iceberg up ahead but not being able to tell the Captain because someone in your chain of command ordered you not to speak unless you were spoken to.

The strength and power of the chain resides in the brains it constrains. When the success or failure of the mission and the survival of the men are hanging in the balance it makes sense to unleash the power of our brains—even when it requires breaking the chain.

I have no idea how it started, or who initiated it, but at some point someone simply walked outside their compound and called their counterpart on their cell phone to ask if they wanted to meet for a meal and catch up face-to-face. They used calling cards as an extra precaution to make the connection difficult to track and/or trace. I explained to Mr. Wolfowitz that "these were not the actions of individuals motivated by impulse, impatience, or inexperience," nor were these the actions of deep-state political partisans with an axe to grind.

These were the actions of seasoned operational leaders motivated by an innate sense of duty and responsibility to do the right thing for the success of the mission and the survival of the men without regard for any potential rewards or repercussions to themselves. These men weren't undermining their leaders or the mission; instead they were doing everything they could to ensure they accomplished it.

(September 17th, 2001: JAWBREAKER Day 4) Late in the afternoon on day four we finally received approval to reestablish communication with JAWBREAKER. Despite the bureaucratic friction that had slowed things to a standstill during the first few days, we had made significant progress in properly preparing our people over the previous twenty-four hours. Thanks to the all-night, all-hands-on-deck effort by our support teams we were within a few hours of having everything in order for our guys to get out the door in time to join JAWBREAKER for their departure on September 19th.[16]

What happened next is best described by the JAWBREAKER team leader in his book *First In*:

> *"Although the memory of many events leading up to the nineteenth remains a blur, one thing that remains clear in my mind was the issue of having a U.S. military Special Operations officer accompany the team. Rick had been working the phones steadily for two days, talking with his Delta Force contacts at Fort Bragg in North Carolina, with the Special Operations Command and U.S. Central Command Headquarters in Tampa, Florida… although Rick's contacts were enthusiastic and more than willing to participate. The bottom line was that no SpecOps personnel would accompany JAWBREAKER into Afghanistan. The official reason given was that without search and rescue (SAR[17]) helicopters nearby, the mission was considered 'too dangerous' for military personnel."[18]*

During the days and weeks that followed, the JAWBREAKER team was able to successfully accomplish their initial purpose: "to make contact with the Northern Alliance and lay the groundwork for follow-on special operations forces." However, the lack of interagency unity of effort prevented the U.S. from getting sufficient special operations personnel and equipment on the ground and into the fight for another 6–8 weeks.

The bureaucratic delays and lack of interagency collaboration proved disastrous at Tora Bora (see map), a mountain range in Eastern Afghanistan where Osama bin Laden[19] and his foreign-fighter security detail went into hiding after 9/11. When a small, hastily patched-together team of U.S. military special operations personnel finally arrived on the ground in Tora Bora (around December 10, 2001) they didn't have enough troops, time, situational awareness, or operational freedom to prevent UBL and his henchman from escaping across the border into Pakistan a few days later.

CIA officers who were on the ground at the time believed that "Osama bin Laden could have been captured if the U.S military had committed more troops into the battle in early December."[20] Most military personnel who were on the ground agree. A few more troops and a few more days would have made a significant difference. However, what the CIA officers did not mention, or weren't allowed to mention, in their books was that the CIA had reliable intelligence that UBL had moved to Tora Bora in early September.

Whether the intelligence pin-pointing UBL's location in Tora Bora wasn't shared with the military because the phone lines were cut off on September 15th, or whether the CIA decided the source of the intelligence made it too "sensitive" to share with the military, we'll never know. What we do know is that in early October 2001 the U.S. Military deployed massive amounts of men and machines into the region to conduct two highly complex air assault raids on empty targets instead of deploying straight to the Tora Bora mountain range. Once on the ground we would have had more than enough personnel, equipment, and time (8–10 weeks) to use common sense and develop the situation in order to capture and/or destroy UBL and his foreign-fighter entourage. It would take an additional ten years of death and destruction to accomplish the same purpose we could have accomplished in the first ten weeks.

I concluded my presentation by telling Mr. Wolfowitz that despite all the built-in bureaucratic friction, "one of the most remarkable and redeeming aspects of our American interagency system is that it's chock-full of common sense people." No matter how senseless things get, freedom-loving people, like life, always have and always will find a way. "I agree," he conceded, "but we shouldn't have to depend on a safety net of common sense people to watch over us like sentinels, we need to find a way to bring the sentinels out of the shadows and make common sense the way the entire Federal Government operates."

He stuck out his hand to shake mine but I had to leave him hanging for a second while I finished scribbling down what he said about sentinels guarding against senselessness. After the meeting adjourned Mr. Wolfowitz's Deputy, "Tom," introduced himself to me as we walked out of the office into the bustling E-ring hallway. Likely in his mid-30's he looked as if he was in his just-out-of-college 20's. A boy wonder in every sense of the word, he was PhD smart, emotionally intelligent, patriotic, and full of out-of-the-box ideas on every operational topic (his favorite was Inkblot theory). I later learned he was one of the youngest civilian executives in Pentagon history.

"If you and your guys ever run into barriers like you did after 9/11 please don't hesitate to give us a call," he offered while pushing his black horn-rimmed glasses up on his nose. "Thanks, Tom, and likewise, if you ever need on-the-ground information or have a question on any operational topic no matter how seemingly mundane, please don't hesitate to call me wherever I am or whatever I'm doing. If I don't know the answer I'll do everything I can to connect you with someone who does." "Sounds good, Pete," he replied while handing me his business card.

"My personal cell phone number is written on the back," he pointed out as both of us started to laugh. "Does this make me a sentinel?" he posited. "Only if the caller ID reads 'pre-paid calling card,' and only if you answer the call," I responded as we continued to walk and talk. "What time is your briefing with the Secretary of Defense?"[21] he asked. I told him it was in ten minutes and asked if he had any advice for me. He smiled and seemed to choose his words carefully, "He asks a lot of questions and he'll want to know more about how you and your agency counterparts actually discovered the information on UBL's current location in Pakistan."

"Got it," I responded as we shook hands and went our separate ways. Before I walked into the Secretary of Defense's office I paused in the middle of the hallway and carefully placed Tom's business card inside a hidden fold of my working wallet. I had no idea when, or if, I'd ever actually use it but I also had no doubt about its potential value as an option for the future. Just like the late-breaking intelligence I was about to share with the Secretary of Defense, the option emerged as a byproduct of sharing knowledge. The term "knowledge is power" implies that hoarding knowledge is what gives a person power. As I prepared for what would be my ninth presentation in the last twenty-four hours I realized that the most potent power of knowledge comes from sharing it. It's common sense/knowledge of patterns.

"Psssst, Panther, you awake?" Stump whispered while waving the satellite phone in front of my face, "We have a strong signal and you're reconnected to the Pentagon." I hadn't thought about the concept of common sense sentinels or its practical application until that moment in the desert. "Hello, Tom? How much did you hear me say about the Iraqi-Americans before we lost the connection?"

Only then, while whispering to Tom on the satellite phone, did I realize that everything we had accomplished up to that point in Iraq we had accomplished off the chain. From sharing knowledge about interagency unity of effort with the Deputy Secretary of Defense; to requesting and coordinating for the inclusion of Iraqi-American cultural advisors with his staff; to sharing satellite phone numbers that linked us with our British, Australian, and U.S. Special Forces counterparts; to getting approval for the delivery and attachment of ten M1A1 Abrams Tanks by first sharing the logic of why it made sense with the Commanding Generals aide-de-camp.[22]

No one told us how to organize, so we self-organized.[23] No one had to remind us of our purpose, our purpose was said out loud and shared by all. We didn't have a roster, or organizational structure, or a flag, or a chain-of-command. All we had was common ground on common sense.

When the success of the mission depends on working together as one team it's common sense to break down and/or go around bureaucratic barriers that prevent it. When searching for something in enemy territory that you've never stepped foot in before, it's common sense to share knowledge via open and free flowing communication channels instead of compartmentalizing it. When you're 500 miles behind enemy lines and under constant threat from enemy attack it's common sense to collaborate, communicate, and reciprocate with your fellow teams (U.S. and International) instead of competing against or ignoring them. Positive feedback, over time, reinforced these patterns of behavior as common operating principles for all high-performing teams.

"I think I heard everything you said about the Iraqi-Americans," Tom whisper-responded. "Just in case we lose the connection again, let's get the administrative thing out of the way first. It will only take a second." "Okay, go ahead, Tom."

"It's good news, Pete, we just received word that you've been accepted into the Secretary of Defense's Corporate Fellowship Program," he paused but I had no idea what he was talking about so I stayed silent and waited for a clue. "I just need to know which company you want to go to." Now I knew.

During the same briefing I conducted at the Pentagon nine months earlier, Mr. Wolfowitz asked me what my academic background was and I told him I had a Masters degree in National Security, and an MBA. A former Professor at John Hopkins University, it was immediately apparent by his reaction that we had found common ground. He enthusiastically described an obscure Department of Defense program called the Secretary of Defense's Corporate Fellowship.

Established in 1981, the original purpose of the program was to exchange leadership and management best practices between military and corporate leaders by sending eight military Officers (two from each service) to work for one year on location at some of our country's most successful corporations. "What a cool idea," I thought.

I read the program brochure his aide slid in front of me and was impressed by the names of the participating companies, as well as the fact it was an alternative to attending one of the military "War Colleges," but that was the last I heard or thought about it. Until that moment in the desert. "What are my choices?" I asked him.

"Well there's only eight slots each year for all four services and five slots have already been filled, your choices are Microsoft, Du Pont, or a biotechnology company called Amgen... I know this is a big decision so if you need more time I can probably put them off another two or three days."

"No need, Tom, I'll go with the biotechnology company Amgen,"[24] I replied. "That's a great choice, Pete, I'm actually a closet microbiologist...someday you'll have to tell me why you chose it. Amgen it is, okay now let's get back to the Iraqi-Americans and your upcoming meeting with Ambassador Bre..."

"Hello? Tom, are you still there...?" Nothing heard. Once again the call dropped and once again we reconnected but not until two days later after I drove down to Baghdad with my Iraqi-American cultural advisor "Saif" to meet with Ambassador Bremer.

Unaware of it at the time, but crystal clear through the rear-view lens of hindsight, the choices I made over the satellite phone in the context of the dark desert moment in Iraq not only changed the situation for me and my teams on the ground at that time, they also changed my life's future trajectory in ways that I am only now beginning to fully comprehend and appreciate.

Six weeks after the phone call I was standing in a line under a sign that read "Access Badges" while pondering the answer to a personable HR woman's question of whether I wanted people to call me Peter or Pete. "We generally recommend you go with one syllable because it makes it easier for people to read and pronounce," she explained. Life is only surreal if you have a metaphor for real. In this case I didn't, so I told her, "thanks for the suggestion, I'll go with 'Pete,'" and "it's a real pleasure to meet."

Along with twenty or thirty other new employees, I was in-processing at Amgen, one of the world's first and largest biotechnology companies. Located in Thousand Oaks, California, Amgen's open air and architecturally avant-garde campus was what the military refers to as my place of duty for the next twelve months.

This was Amgen's first time participating in the Fellowship program so there was no protocol for what to do with me. Since I was neither a part-time nor a full-time employee the friendly HR woman wasn't sure what color and type of access badge to issue me. "Would you say that what you're going to be doing is kind of like a consultant?" she asked with a hint of angst in her voice. "Yes, I think you could say that," I answered without a clue. "Okay, I'm just going to give you a green consultants' badge, she replied as she selected, sealed, and handed it over to me. "Congratulations, Pete, you now officially have access," she said with a smile. I thanked her for her time and the access, as I would repeatedly over the weeks and months that followed.

The very next day I was meandering around campus with a green consultant's badge on my belt and a campus map held up in front of my face. I was searching for an obscure conference room that no one I asked seemed to have ever heard of, where I was scheduled to attend a meeting with people I had never met, to discuss a topic I knew next to nothing about. I was genuinely looking forward to it. If I could only find the conference room.

Like a lot of other big companies Amgen was heavily dependent on consultants to handle most of their problem solving and productivity enhancing efforts. McKinsey was the consultant company of choice at that time and their consultants were well-respected, hardworking, and everywhere on campus. Thanks to my green consultant's badge I quickly learned that I could walk into almost any meeting on almost any topic and no one would ask me who I was, why I was there, or why they had never seen me before. They simply assumed I was another consultant, so all they wanted to know was how I could help. I never turned down a project. Undercover and anonymous I spent most of my time working with cross-functional teams to accomplish a common purpose. Instead of feeling out of place I felt right at home.

I'm often asked what it was like going from a year-and-a-half in Afghanistan and Iraq, to a corporate campus in California. My answer then, and now, is the same—it wasn't any big deal and I loved every minute of it. The best thing about it was that I was meaningfully engaged in something I had never experienced before. Life teaches and our brains learn to adapt. Crisscrossing the globe over the previous thirteen years with my Special Operations colleagues taught me that when we enlighten our brains with something new (traveling to new places, meeting new faces, learning a new language, a new culture, a new way of operating, etc.) we see the world in a different and more revealing light.

Twelve months to the day after arriving at Amgen I transitioned once again. This time from the corporate civilian world to the corporate government world in Washington DC, where I was asked to serve in the newly established position of special projects officer for the Global War against terrorists. My job had no formal description, no history or protocol for what I was supposed to do and thanks to all of the above, no objections from me on performing it. My place of duty was the Pentagon. My boss: my fellow common sense sentinel, Tom. My purpose: to support and assist the civilian and military leadership in the Pentagon on all matters concerning ongoing combat operations in Afghanistan and Iraq.

I spent half of my time interacting with other government agencies (DoD, CIA, Dept. of State, etc.) in and around Washington D.C., where I had the opportunity to learn firsthand how our instruments of national power make decisions, solve problems, and organize to accomplish their purposes. The other half of my time was spent going back and forth to Afghanistan and Iraq conducting security assessments of the situation on the ground in both countries.

Going back and forth between combat and corporate, civilian and government, international and national leadership contexts, turned out to be one of the most foundational learning experiences of my military career. It would also turn out to be one of my last.

In 2005 I chose to retire from the military. We never make major life choices based on one single variable. Whether the choice involves changing jobs, changing houses, or changing relationships, major life choices are never just about one thing. Instead they are always about a whole bunch of things. Choosing to retire from the military after twenty-two years was prima facie of this principal. We live our lives and make choices about what to do next like we manage our calendars, through multiple context lenses: family, friends, professional, personal, spiritual, social, etc. The choice that makes the most sense is the choice that coheres across the most contexts of our lives and adapts to what's going on around us in the context of the moment. My decision to retire from the military and explore new frontiers made sense across all contexts of my life.

As fortunate as I was to lead some of the finest interagency and international teams ever assembled for the complexities of combat, fortune found me once again in business. I returned to the biotechnology industry where I had the opportunity to assess, select, and lead common sense people and teams that spanned every functional area of the company (Commercial, Research & Development, and Manufacturing) while interacting with Healthcare professionals and Scientists located all across the U.S. and Europe.

There is no adjective I can use that would do justice to the impact these relationships and the knowledge I learned from them had on me as a leader as well as the stories and lessons that follow. When leaders connect and share knowledge about leadership they always learn to lead better. To this I can attest. Sharing what we've learned from our experiences over time enables evolutionary learning. Over time a common pattern emerged.

Whether boundary-spanning across bureaucratic borders with my clandestine counterparts, discussing the art of the possible with Iraqi or Afghan freedom fighters, or brain-storming solutions with my biotechnology business partners, I learned through experience and confirmed with feedback that whenever we ask our people to rely on logic and common sense instead of outdated policies, plans, or disconnected chains of command we always get better, faster results with less resources expended and more job satisfaction for our people.

After using the term common sense to describe the way I lived and led for most of my adult life, this was the first time I actually paused to ponder what common sense actually is and why people seem to recognize, respond to, and appreciate common sense leadership whenever they experience it.

To find the answer to any question in life whether it's how to cure cancer, how to find our car keys, or what the relationship is between leadership and common sense, success or failure depends on where we focus our search. I was fortunate to focus mine in the living laboratory of real world leadership while learning from fellow soldiers, citizens, scientists, and businesspeople. As it turned out the answer was both all around and inside of me. It's not political, or religious, or philosophic. It's biologic. Biology reveals that life always finds a way. It's the Common Sense Way.

REFLECTIONS/LESSONS LEARNED
The Common Ground upon Which We Stand

What's is the relationship between leadership and common sense and why do people seem to recognize, respond to, and appreciate common sense leadership whenever they experience it?

What is Leadership? Most of us think we know what leadership is until someone asks us to actually define it. Then we usually find ourselves at a loss for words. It's not because we don't know what leadership is, rather that, like common sense, leadership is completely contextual. How do we know? When we think about leadership in the context of one of our own specific life circumstances (whether in combat, corporate, country or community), most of us can describe in so many words the attributes and behaviors of both great and not-so-great leaders. We know good and bad leadership when we see, hear, or feel it. Why is that?

Leadership isn't about where we went to school, or what degree we earned, or what we look like, or how tall we are, or our gender, and you'll likely never hear any of these qualities used to describe the attributes of great leaders. What you will hear, sooner or later, in every description of every great leader is common sense. Have you ever known a great leader that wasn't a common sense leader?

The Origins of Leadership: Leadership is an evolutionary pattern of human behavior that emerged the moment the first few members of our Homo sapiens species breathed their first few breaths.[25] The first leaders weren't Kings or Queens, Presidents or Prime Ministers, Sirs or Ma'ams. They were parents.

First Homo sapiens leaders were parents

English philosopher Thomas Hobbs described their hunter-gatherer lives as nasty, brutish, and short. They lived their lives in the moment because every moment presented a survival choice. They either found something to eat or for heat and shelter, or they starved, froze, and/or were eaten by something else. Find or fail, eat or be eaten, work together or perish.

The purpose of our ancient-ancestor parents was crystal clear to them: to do whatever it took to ensure they and their offspring survived, thrived, and evolved. Success or failure as leaders and parents depended on their ability to take care of their people. Time and feedback teach our brains what works. To accomplish any purpose it makes sense for modern day leaders to follow the same instinctive pattern as our ancient ancestor parents, to take care of the people we lead. Not rule them.

How do we know? Each and every one of us alive today carries knowledge learned by our ancestors that was passed on to us via our DNA. Our DNA was there, and by proxy they are here with us today. Our species evolutionary history exists as patterns of amino acids in our DNA. Every living thing on our planet (that we know of) has DNA. Whether you're a Hippo, a Head of Lettuce, or a Human, your DNA, and its elegantly simple double helix design carries hereditary knowledge across time and evolution using patterns of amino acids known as our genetic code.

What is our genetic code? Genetic means relating to, caused by, or controlled by Genes. A code is a pattern of letters, numbers, or symbols used in a system to mark, represent, identify, or communicate something (e.g. language, equation, message, etc.). Our genetic code is the biologic language our DNA uses to store and communicate knowledge. Its alphabet consists of just four letters: A, G, C, and T, which represent the first letters of their amino acid names.[26] How do we make sense of it?

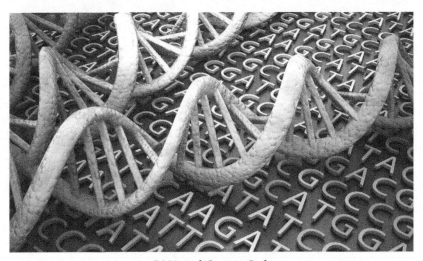

DNA and Genetic Code

Just as the words earth and heart have the same letters and different meanings, it's not the letters themselves that give biological meaning to our genetic code. It's the patterns and relationships of the amino acid letters that make biologic sense of the knowledge stored in our genes. Thanks to one of Humankind's greatest intellectual achievements (Decoding of the Human Genome, 2000), we can now read the patterns of amino acids in our DNA and understand the story they tell.[27]

It's the story of who we are, where we came from, and how to create a sense-making survival organism. Our capacity to make sense of the world around us is already determined by the time we are born. Every member of our species who has ever lived is born with a nervous system[28] that is generally capable of seeing light within the same range of wavelengths, hear sound waves within the same range of frequencies, and can taste and smell the same range of molecules and chemicals.

Our 99.5% shared DNA-enabled nervous system ensures that humans all make sense a common way. Which is why we all have two eyes, two ears, a nose, a mouth, a brain and a spinal cord packaged inside a body eloquently wrapped in skin. Evolution won't let us make sense any other way, not without becoming a new species.

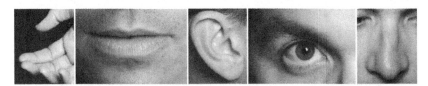

Our Common Senses

Question: What does every bit of good advice you've ever gotten or given have in common? (e.g. "Look both ways before you cross the street," "Don't talk to strangers," "Always tell someone when you're heading out into the wilderness," "A bird in the hand is worth two in the bush," "A penny saved is a penny earned," "Do unto others as you would want them to do unto you," etc.)

Answer: They're all considered common sense and they're all based on learned knowledge of patterns. Not just any patterns. Patterns that enhance our own and our ancestors' potential to survive, thrive, and evolve.

The Saber-toothed tiger hunts the family watering hole on moonless nights.

Recognition that life experiences are informed by patterns and relationships is thus built into us at the most basic neural level. In the human brain it is transformed from neural axiom into a never-ending quest to make sense of what's going on around us and sensible choices about what to do next.[29]

> *It makes sense for the family to stay away from*
> *the watering hole when the moon is away.*

What is a Pattern? A pattern is a combination of things such as atoms, events, shapes, colors, and behaviors that form a consistent or characteristic relationship. Every thing in life emerges from patterns. The things we sense around us and for which we have names such as, stars, planets, and weather; proteins, cells, and people; plants, animals, and air; are all to a greater or lesser extent stabilized patterns of atoms.

There are three common pattern recognition principles baked into our brains: 1) patterns emerge from the relationship of their parts, 2) patterns combine to make sense, and 3) patterns repeat.

> *Sunrise, light, warm, safe; Sunset, dark, cold, dangerous.*

Patterns are nature's way of naturally selecting the most adaptive way for life on earth to survive, thrive, and evolve. To be a common sense leader we must be able to recognize patterns. We can teach ourselves to recognize patterns.

Patterns Make Sense of the Way
the Real World Works

Our choice of concepts and metaphors depends on the extent to which they help us organize and retrieve knowledge. Rather than thinking about patterns as independent features, think of them in the context of the patterns of life that highlight three comprehensive categories: patterns of nature, patterns of human nature, and patterns of history as the key interacting ingredients for making sense of what's going on around us.

When the days shorten, the trees lose their leaves,
the birds head elsewhere, and life-threatening cold
and hunger always follow close behind.

Patterns of Nature, Patterns of Human Nature, and Patterns of History. The patterns of life are omnipresent. Constantly combining, connecting, and coalescing to create the adaptive stimulus we know as the "context of the moment" every moment of our lives. The context of the moment informs our perception of the reality of the situation as it is going on around us. As such, its our constant catalyst for change:

Should we stay or should we go?

It depends. On what? On our purpose and the adaptive stimulus of what's going on around us in the context of the moment. Context is the set of facts or circumstances that surround a situation or event. Moment refers to a slice of time that's never happened before and will never happen again. The patterns of life are never static. No two moments are ever the same. Stepping your foot in a river now is to step in a different river than a moment ago or a moment from now. The context of the moment emerges from the relationship between the patterns of life as they coalesce.

The birds always leave before it gets cold
and return when it gets warm.

Think of the patterns of life in the context of the moment like sensory clues. Remnants of who, what, when, where, and why things happened in the past and precursors of what is likely to happen in the future. Individual clues don't do much good on their own, yet when we combine and connect them with the knowledge we learn over time they provide our brains with context and options to make sense of what's going on around us and sensible choices to prepare for the future.

*Drying corn and meat for the harsh winter ahead is
a survival option discovered and developed by our
ancestors based on learned knowledge of patterns of
seasons, patterns of human metabolism, and patterns
of their own weather-related survival history.*[30]

When we have options we have freedom to choose between them
based on the adaptive stimulus of what's going on around us:

It makes sense to gather up the family and the food and follow the birds.

Anticipating the future is how we stay out of harm's way. The term
"Premonition" literally means, forewarning. Instead of thinking of pre-
monitions as extra-sensory visions of things that haven't happened yet,
think of them as our brain's capacity to recognize patterns and relationships as they are coalescing (e.g. weather patterns, family health patterns, food supply patterns, etc.), and extrapolating the patterns forward
to reveal what is likely to happen in future:

Dark sky, heavy winds, temperature drop, big storm is on the way.

Although patterns aren't predictive they are highly directional.
Conscious awareness of the patterns of life as they coalesce in the

context of the moment is how our brains make sense of what's going on around us so we can anticipate the future and make sensible choices about what to do next.

What's the benefit for Common Sense Leaders? Most leaders aren't consciously aware of the power they have to shape the present and influence the future as it unfolds in front of them. This power comes from the power of choice. The choices we make in the context of the moment—big and small, public and private, individual and collective— not only shape our paths in the present, they also influence our potential to accomplish our purpose in the future.

How's the temperature in the room you're sitting in? Like touching a rolling ball, when we choose to interact with the patterns of life in the context of the moment we irrevocably influence their future trajectory. Are you and your people falling asleep because the room's too hot? The only way our brains can influence anything in life is by learning to adapt to it by choosing to interact with it. Open a window and you'll see.

We can't control the future because it hasn't happened yet, but we can influence it by shaping the present via the choices we make. Time and feedback teach our brains whether the choices we make are sensible or senseless. Choosing to open the window a few seconds in the past, changes the temperature of the room in the present. You and your people can sense the difference. It feels cooler. Your people no longer feel sleepy. The choice makes sense. A sensible choice is a choice that coheres with our purpose: to make the room temperature more comfortable for our people, and adapts to what's going on around us in the context of the moment: a hot room and a cool breeze outside. A coherent-adaptive choice is a sensible choice.

What is the relationship between leadership and common sense? Leadership isn't about status, rank, title, degree, pedigree, and/or similarity to me. Leadership is common sense/knowledge of patterns. The most successful leaders across the ages take care of their people by following the same pattern as the most successful parents from our ancient past: freedom of choice to make sense of what's going on around us and sensible choices for the purpose and the people we have the privilege to lead.

Conscious awareness is how we live and
lead the Common Sense Way.

CHAPTER 1 SUMMARY OF KEY CONCEPTS

- **The first common sense leaders** weren't kings or queens, presidents or prime ministers, Sirs or Ma'ams, they **were Parents.**

- Our 99.5% shared DNA-enabled nervous systems ensure we humans all make sense a common way, via learned knowledge of patterns and their relationship to events. **Which is why it's called common sense.**

- A pattern is a combination of things such as atoms, events, shapes, colors, behaviors, etc. that form a consistent or characteristic relationship.

- 3 Principles of Patterns:
  - ► Patterns emerge from the relationship of their parts.
  - ► Patterns combine to make sense.
  - ► Patterns repeat.
    Sunrise, light, warm, safe; Sunset, dark, cold, dangerous.

- 3 Types of Patterns:
  - ► Patterns of Nature *(e.g. gravity, time, weather, DNA, etc.).*
  - ► Patterns of Human Nature *(e.g. the way we think, choose, and behave, etc.).*
  - ► Patterns of History *(e.g. Patterns of Nature and Human Nature that occurred in the past).*

- **The Patterns of Life** is a unifying metaphor for understanding the infinite patterns that inform the behavior of the world in which we live.

- *Patterns of Nature + Patterns of Human Nature + Patterns of History = Patterns of Life*

- The Patterns of Life are omnipresent, constantly combining, connecting, and coalescing to create the adaptive stimulus we know as **the Context of the Moment** every moment of our lives.

- The Context of the Moment is our constant catalyst for change.

- Common Sense/knowledge of patterns is the common ground and common language that connects all humans across the planet all across time.

- The most successful leaders across the ages take care of their people by following the same instinctive pattern as the most successful parents from our ancient past: freedom of choice to make sense of what's going on around us and sensible choices for the purpose, place and the people we have the privilege to lead. **Leadership is Common Sense**

CHAPTER 2

What's Wrong With the Way?

Central Iraq, May–June, 2003: Twenty-four hours after my phone call with Tom I drove down to Baghdad with my Iraqi-American cultural advisor Saif to meet with Ambassador Bremer at the newly established Coalition Provisional Authority (CPA) Headquarters.

CPA Headquarters was located in a place formerly known to the people of Iraq as Saddam Hussein's Presidential Palace. Saif was a 40-something square-jawed realtor from California who also served in the Iraqi army as a private before immigrating to the United States of America in 1991. Dressed in desert khaki pants and top, desert boots, floppy hat and AK-47 vest, he looked like what he had become over the past six weeks. One of us. As we walked under the obtrusively opulent palace entry-arch it was Saif who was first to say what both of us were thinking, **"this doesn't feel right."**

Entry Way to Saddam Hussein's Palace[31]

Although most of Saddam's palaces were bombed and looted in the days leading up to and following the invasion, the surgical precision of satellite-guided munitions resulted in the physical structures themselves surviving relatively intact (other than a few new skylights and basement trenches).

The CPA was established by the leaders of the Coalition which consisted of the United States, Britain, Australia and Poland. The newly anointed leader of the CPA was a career State Department Officer named Paul Bremer who also assumed the title of U.S. Presidential Envoy. Although Mr. Bremer had arrived in Iraq for the first time only a few days earlier, UN Security Council Resolution #1483 instantly anointed him with sweeping executive, legislative, and judicial decision-making authority over essentially everyone and everything inside the country. Most notably, UN Resolution #1483 permitted Mr. Bremer to rule by "decree."

Unprecedented in modern times a decree is a rule of law and/or order that is issued by a head of state such as a Monarch, Dictator, or omnipotent Military Commander. Although he had never lived or worked in Iraq, Mr. Bremer issued his first decrees a few days after he arrived: CPA Order #2 decreed the dismantling of the Iraqi Army which put over 100,000 mostly Sunni soldiers out of work and out on the streets in search of something to do and some way to feed their families. One less controversial yet perhaps equally impactful decree involved the annexing and repurposing of all of Saddam Hussein's former palaces and properties throughout the country for use as CPA housing and military headquarters.

After we passed through the security checkpoint, the guard pointed us toward one of Mr. Bremer's assistants who was busy counting boxes, checking his clipboard, and barking out orders. A thin, balding, and bespectacled man with a gray ponytail, he seemed stressed out so I quickly introduced myself and Saif and explained the purpose of our visit: "to offer Saif's services as a combat-tested Iraqi-American cultural advisor to advise and assist Mr. Bremer and his staff in the rebuilding of the Iraqi infrastructure and the new government," I added that he "could call the Deputy Secretary of Defense Paul Wolfowitz if he needed any background information or a reference."

The Assistant, who like Ambassador Bremer was also a career State Department employee, waited for me to finish before looking up from his clipboard and over his reading glasses. "Listen, bub, I know who Paul Wolfowitz is, he's D-O-D, but this is a State Department show now and we're not using Iraqis or Iraqi-Americans to rebuild the infrastructure or the new government, it's not part of the plan." He paused as a couple of workers walked between us carrying cartons full of air conditioners.

"I can give your boy here sixty bucks a day to help us as a translator but that's it…now if you'll excuse me I got a lot of work to do," he exhorted as he turned to talk to one of his workers. Saif stared at me with a look of dread and disbelief, "How they going to rebuild the country with outsiders who don't understand the history and can't communicate with the people?" His question memorialized the moment for me, as the first time in my life I felt weirdly embarrassed for my own country.

"Can you just point me to Mr. Bremer's office?" I asked dispassionately. "Sorry, bub, but he's in the middle of an important meeting and his schedule is packed solid for the next two weeks." *"Two weeks? Don't charge the machinegun nest, go around it."* I looked around and saw a magic marker written sign that read "Conference Room" with an arrow pointing down the long mahogany-walled marble hallway. "Let's go, Saif. Thanks for your help, bub," I added over my shoulder as we headed down the hallway in search of some sense. "Hey, you can't go down there. You don't have an access badge and they're in the middle of an important meeting," he whined while he followed us a few steps behind.

"What's the meeting about?" I asked over my shoulder. "What day of the week to begin garbage pick-up. Why do you care?" he scoffed. "What day should they pick up the garbage?" I asked Saif while we continued to walk. "Any day except Saturday,"[32] Saif replied incredulously, "just pick it up as soon as possible, some piles are ten feet high and it stinks very bad. It's a serious health problem but all you have to do is pay the neighborhood men to pick it up and bring it to central locations. They will do it for next to nothing if somebody of authority just asked them…this is kind of thing I can help you with, Mr.…." Saif implored as the assistant stared off in the distance and pretended to ignore.

"Is this guy for the real?" Saif asked me in frustration "I don't think so, Saif, but since he's pretending he doesn't hear you let's just pretend he isn't here." "You got it, Boss," Saif agreed as we arrived outside the thirty-foot high, ornately carved conference room doors.

I wiggled the giant knobs but the doors were locked so I stuck my eye up to the gaping crack to see what was going on inside. "You aren't cleared to look or listen to what's going on in there," the assistant warned. "You hear something, Boss? Maybe it's just the wind, sometimes it blows really hard around here," Saif deadpanned. "Well done, my friend," I complimented as the assistant stormed off in search of someone to tell.

"Thanks, Boss, I don't like making fun of 'the man' but this is very frustrating for me as American and as Iraqi. The Iraqi people know how much work there is to do, they know what needs to be done, and they are willing and able to do it. If someone else start making all the choices for them they will think it's just another version of Saddam. Those of us that know Iraqi history and the history of this region know the only way a country can rebuild itself, is to rebuild itself."

Patterns of world history are littered with proof positive of Saif's common sense rebuild principle. From 1950 forward the U.S. has engaged in fourteen "nation-building" efforts. In only two such efforts, Panama and Grenada, was democracy sustained ten years after departure of U.S. forces.[33] It made me realize once again how fortunate we were to have Saif on our team, and it doubled my sense of urgency for getting him imbedded with the leaders of the CPA.

Through the crack I could see twenty to thirty people sitting around a massive rectangular table. I saw lots of suits but not a single Iraqi or Iraqi-American. "Let's just wait here until the meeting ends," I said to Saif as we sat on one of Saddam's over-stuffed velvet sofas. "*After all, how long can a meeting to decide what day to pick up the garbage last?*"

Four frustrating hours later as the sun began its decent toward the dusty desert horizon, I realized we could wait no more. With Martial Law in place and a couple of night-time capture operations on deck we had no other option but to get back to our inner city safe-house and off the roads before darkness set in. Although disappointed, I figured we'd try again another day. "Maybe once they get settled in they'll come to their senses," I encouraged a clearly disillusioned Saif as we drove.

We made multiple attempts to offer Saif's services to the CPA over the next few weeks but instead of getting "settled in" the CPA seemed 100% focused on getting comfortably "sequestered in" instead. "Come back later," "we're too busy," "we don't have time." All of Saddam's former palaces across the country were beehives of activity as private contractors worked around the clock to remodel and refurnish the interiors while simultaneously enlarging and reinforcing the walls and barricades[34] around the exteriors.

As the number and lethality of car and suicide bombings increased, so too did the height and thickness of the walls and barriers. Force Protection became the CPA's primary and self-perpetuating purpose. More enemy attacks meant more troops and more weapons were needed to combat them. Which meant more staff officers and administrators were needed to command and control them. Which meant a proportional increase in office/living/storage space to house them, as well as food, water, vehicles, and medical supplies to sustain them. Which meant more guards and bigger barriers to protect them. On and on it went.

Within a few weeks the CPA and their massive military and civilian staffs around the country were safely ensconced inside their impenetrable palatial Headquarters. To celebrate the completion of work at Saddam's main palace in Baghdad they threw a barbecue at the newly refurbished presidential pool.

Outside the walls there was no power, no water, no plumbing and no one to talk to about how to fix any of it. In those first few weeks after the Saddam government fell you could drive almost anywhere you wanted in Baghdad, which we did in armored SUV's as we searched for Saddam and his henchmen. We spent twelve hours a day driving in and around the city to meet with potential intelligence sources and follow up on the leads that they provided. To help the people and the economy get back on their feet we tried to eat as many meals as possible in the restaurants and open-air cafés that dotted the city streets.

We were always armed, but to blend in and find common ground with the Iraqi people we wore civilian clothes (e.g. lightweight, earth tone pants and long sleeve, loose fitting shirts). Most every Iraqi we talked to knew what needed to be done. The shop owners, the elders, and the kids, all you had to do was ask and then give them an ear. Without any Iraqi-Americans there was no way for the CPA to understand the problems the people of Iraq were struggling with and tragically no way to listen to and take advantage of their on-the-ground solutions. Perhaps most frustrating for the people of Baghdad, there was no consistent or credible source of information to update them on how much longer they would have to hang on without water, power, plumbing, and supplies (e.g. food, medicine, fuel).

Humans can endure unimaginable hardships as long as they have reason to believe things will get better in the future. Survivors from sinking ships can swim superhuman distances as long as they believe there's an island or a rescue ship up ahead. Without any reason to believe things will get better in the future, hopelessness quickly sinks in and so too does the swimmer.

Three weeks after the CPA meeting to decide what day to pick up trash the piles had grown into rat-infested mountains that blocked vehicle access on most residential streets. Neither the infrastructure nor the people were working. With the onset of another blazing hot Baghdad summer (average temp 107 degrees F), the Iraqi people's patience simmered just below the boiling point while suicide bombings and the enemy insurgency steadily picked up steam. When populations of people are oppressed and/or denied their freedom to participate and have a say in their own destiny they will always inevitably rise up against the source of their oppression.

No one knew what the right thing to do was in the early days of post-Saddam Iraq. To make sense of any situation our brains require context. The only way to get context is to learn from, adapt to, and interact with what's going on around us. Outside the palace walls the feedback was both immediate and pronounced.

Former Maj. Gen. James "Spider" Marks who headed intelligence for U.S. ground forces in Iraq before and after the invasion, as well as former Iraqi General, Abu Omar, both say that "the insurgency was not inevitable." Both point to the initial decree issued by the CPA in May 2003 to disband the Iraqi Army and throw hundreds of thousands of mostly Sunni soldiers out of their jobs and onto the streets in search of a way to feed themselves and their families.[35] Deputy Secretary of Defense Paul Wolfowitz believed it was "the CPA's decision to establish an occupation government instead of handing sovereignty to Iraqis at the outset." It could also be argued that *not* using Iraqi-Americans as civilian liaisons—think learning-feedback loops—with the Iraqi people was equally impactful. All of the above lessons are antecedents of the same time-tested guiding principle:

"The only way a country can successfully rebuild
itself (structurally and politically) is to rebuild
itself." It's the Common Sense Way.

Success or failure in any situation depends on the choices leaders make in the context of the moment they make them. Cordoned off from the people of Iraq by their impenetrable walls, barriers, and organizational cultures, the senior leaders of the CPA and the Military had no way to make sense of what was going on around them, and, by proxy, no way to make sensible choices based on the purpose, place, and the people they were given the privilege to lead. When our brains can't make sense of what's going on around us we make senseless choices.

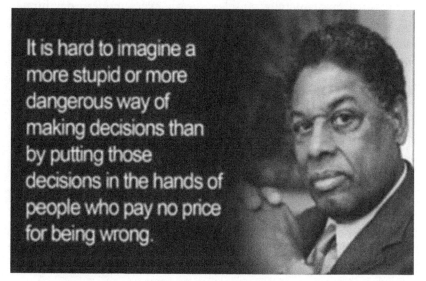

It is hard to imagine a more stupid or more dangerous way of making decisions than by putting those decisions in the hands of people who pay no price for being wrong.

Thomas Sowell

REFLECTIONS/LESSONS LEARNED
What's Wrong With the Way?

So how can it be that common sense is the common ground and common language that connects us all? Yet the way we currently choose to think about leading and organizing (e.g. strategy, plans, and hierarchical chains of command) doesn't make sense?

With the exception of the individual choices we make to shape our own destinies, the choices made by the leaders we interact with throughout our life journeys have the most profound impact on every aspect of our existence. On the battlefield, the survival of our soldiers, and, by proxy, our citizens and our society; in business, our job satisfaction, our productivity, and our company's, country's, and kinfolk's potential to thrive; and over time, the success or failure of our species in our ongoing quest to evolve. The way we choose to lead and organize ourselves irrevocably influences our potential to survive, thrive, and evolve. **Leadership Matters**.

Or does it? After thousands of years of trial and error with man-made dogma, doctrines, formulas and fads (e.g. monarchies, theocracies, bureaucracies, etc.), each of which history has exposed as either suboptimal or shamefully senseless, nearly every modern day human who has worked in any type of organization continues to complain about virtually the same things our parents, grandparents, and frontier forbearers did when it comes to the way we're led and organized today:

Out of touch, outdated, out to lunch; micromanages,
misses the point, all messed up; doesn't listen,
doesn't care, doesn't make sense.

The list is only limited by the amount of time we spend interrogating our experiences. Which leads to the self-evident truth so important for all future common sense leaders and organizations to internalize: The way most public, private, profit, and non-profit human social systems are led and organized today is outdated, misguided, and in most cases simply does not make sense.

Where did the current way come from? The current way emerged from people, processes, and environments that no longer exist. Vestiges of authoritarian leadership methods and mindsets that trace their origins back to the days when the survival of both individuals and societies depended almost entirely on forced physical labor such as the planting and plowing of fields, the movement of dirt, rocks, and trees, and the construction of shelters, walls, and fortifications.[36]

Over the past five hundred years the mechanical/industrial revolution and its foundational principles such as cause-and-effect (one action or event causes another), and Newton's First Law of Linear Motion (a body at rest will remain at rest unless acted upon by a force), ushered in breathtaking change and advancements that transformed the way we, the people, thought and talked about our lives.

Just as language drifts across populations, countries, and continents (think of Latin, Spanish, and English), language also drifts across different contexts of our lives (e.g. the use of sports metaphors in the military, the use of military metaphors in business, and the use of all of the above by new leaders). Somewhere along the way the language of machines drifted across contexts of our lives to define the language of leadership.

Although most of us aren't consciously aware of it, nearly all of our modern day leadership metaphors (e.g. orders, plans, hierarchical chains of command, etc.) are byproducts of machine-based thinking that presupposes the organization as the machine and the humans that make up the organization as the individual parts. If each individual part does precisely what it's told to do when it's told to do it, the machine will accomplish its purpose. It makes sense to treat a machine this way because that's the way machines work. Unfortunately it's not the way our DNA-enabled nervous systems are biologically hard-wired to learn from, adapt to, and make sense of the world around us.

Nowhere else in nature are living organisms taught to ignore the reality of the situation going on around them and instead defer to an order, a plan, or a disconnected chain of command.

To survive, thrive, and evolve, our nervous systems are biologically hardwired to make sense of our experiences based on patterns and relationships of the way things happen. Every instinctive survival behavior to any type of stimulus such as the scent of a predator or possible prey, feeling the on-set of life-threatening cold or heat, or the sight of an alluring and available mate, developed as our nervous systems evolved incrementally over the eons based on learned knowledge of patterns and their relationships to events.[37]

The fundamental role of patterns in making sense of nature and human nature is best illuminated by one of the simplest and most comprehensive scientific theories of our time: Complexity Theory. Definition follows:

The universe we live in is made up of systems (solar systems, weather systems, human social systems) and these systems are made up of infinite number of independent variables (atoms, events, people) that interact with each other in an unpredictable manner and with accelerating frequency (transportation, communications, technology). The key to making sense of any complex system is understanding the patterns and relationships that inform its behavior.[38]

As Complexity Theory underscores, learned knowledge of patterns and their relationship to events is the biologic way our brains evolved to make sense of the world around us. Yet despite a treasure trove of tragedies, miscalculations, and unintended consequences—such as those made in the early days of Iraq—the use of machine-based metaphors as the language of "the way" has grown to dominate the Western World's way of thinking and speaking so thoroughly that it has surreptitiously morphed into "the only way" our schools, our businesses, our military, and our politicians think and speak about leading and organizing today.

"Listen, bub...we're not using Iraqis or Iraqi-Americans to rebuild the infrastructure or the new government, it's not part of the plan."

What specifically defines the way and how do we recognize it when we see, hear, feel or say it? We recognize the defining symptoms of the way as patterns pervasive across all contexts of leading and life. The paragraph below lists a few of the most prominent. To see whether or not you think the way makes sense simply say the sentences that follow out loud, while thinking about those early days in Iraq, and you'll see.

Forcing people to follow plans from the past that fly in the face of present facts and forfeit our freedom to affect the future. Organizing teams based on antiquated administrative policies, procedures and proportionality protocols instead of the strengths of our people and the purpose we are trying to achieve. Making complex, life changing choices based on hunches, haste, and hierarchical hubris instead of the adaptive stimulus of what's going on around us. Selecting and electing leaders based on criteria such as status, rank, title, degree, pedigree, and similarity to me, instead of character and characteristics such as collaboration, communication, competence, and common sense. And critically oppressing instead of enabling the source of our species' most biologically human trait: our brain's freedom of choice to make sense of what's going on around us and sensible choices about what to do next.

"The way" plays no favorites. It treats all humans with equal derision. The conflicts that cause the most friction across all contexts of leadership and life are the contradictions between the way we the people, are told to do what we do, and the way the reality of the situation going on around us reveals we should do. Whether the mechanical way of thinking about leading and organizing ever made sense is debatable, whether it does now is not.

In one of the largest most comprehensive leadership studies ever conducted, the Gallup organization polled over one million employed workers and revealed what almost all of us already knew but couldn't express as factual: "the number one reason employees quit their jobs is their leaders."[39] *People don't leave bad companies. They leave bad leaders.*

The most common leadership complaint from employees is to be stuck in a job working for a micromanager who doesn't care and doesn't provide opportunities for growth or advancement. Micromanaging is oppressive, fosters anxiety, and creates a high stress work environment. Gallup also found that poorly led teams are on average 50% less productive and 44% less profitable than well-led teams. Bad leadership is bad for productivity, bad for profits, and bad for attracting and retaining the best people to build the best teams. **Bad leadership matters, too.**

Yet many other studies, authors, and individuals throughout history have sounded similar alarm sirens to warn whoever was paying attention of the senselessness of "the way." Which begs the question: if the way has always been messed up and we the people always knew the way was messed up, why haven't we done something about changing the way?

The answer is Common Sense. The same reason one of mankind's most monumentally mindless leadership methods and mindsets—aka the Monarchy—survived as the way for so many centuries prior to 1776. Our ancestors simply knew no other way.

That is until a freedom-loving Colonist from Philadelphia named Thomas Paine shared knowledge of a new way by publishing a series of three pamphlets, the first of which was appropriately titled, *Common Sense*. Thomas Paine understood what cutting-edge cognitive science confirms today, "to motivate our brains to change deeply entrenched thought patterns we must first understand the logic of why it makes sense to change." Paine used *Common Sense* to share common knowledge of patterns, that when read or said out loud revealed the logic of why it made sense for we the people to change. Here's how he did it:

> *"Perhaps the sentiments in the following pages are not yet sufficiently fashionable to procure them general favor; a long habit of not thinking a thing WRONG gives it a superficial appearance of being RIGHT and raises at first a formidable outcry in defense of custom. But the tumult soon subsides. Time makes more converts than reason."*

Patterns of Nature: "*...there is something very absurd, in supposing a continent to be perpetually governed by an island. In no instance hath nature made the satellite larger than its primary planet, and as England and America, with respect to each other, reverses the common order of nature, it is evident they belong to different systems; England to Europe, America to itself.*"

Patterns of Human Nature: There are "*two ancient tyrannies in the English constitution, the monarchical and aristocratic tyranny of the king and peers who rule by heredity and decree and contribute nothing to the people.*" "*There is something exceedingly ridiculous in the composition of Monarchy; it first excludes a man from the means of information, yet empowers him to act in cases where the highest judgment is required. The state of a king shuts him from the world, yet the business of a king requires him to know it thoroughly...*"

Patterns of History: "*These are the times that try men's souls. The summer soldier and the sunshine patriot will, in this crisis, shrink from the service of their country; but he that stands by it now, deserves the love and respect of all men and woman.*" "*We have it in our power to begin the world over again.*" "*The cause of America (Freedom[40]) is in great measure the cause of all of Mankind.*"

Often read out loud in town squares and under candlelight in town taverns it is believed that every colonist either read *Common Sense*, heard it read, or was told about its contents. Fellow Colonist and future President John Adams told others he expected *Common Sense* to become the common language of all free people.

Common Sense changed the way the colonists thought about leading and organizing. It was the first time that ordinary people realized they were free to have a say in their own destinies. The Colonists could choose to do nothing and continue to live their lives under the Crown. Or they could choose to launch a common sense revolution to bring the crown down. The Colonists chose Common Sense. The rest is history.

The Declaration of Independence was published less than one year later. Its linkage to the foundational logic of why illuminated by Thomas Paine was eminent: "We hold these truths to be self-evident, that all men are created equal, that they are endowed by their creator with certain unalienable Rights, that among these are Life, Liberty, and the pursuit of Happiness. That to secure these rights, Governments are instituted among Men, deriving their just powers from the consent of the governed. That whenever any Form of Government becomes destructive of these ends it is the Right of the People to alter or to abolish it."

> *"The most important thing for leaders to take away from the self-evident truths of the Declaration of Independence is that they are biologically, universally, and permanently true."*

Other societal problems such as over-population, illegal immigration, terrorism, water conservation, and pollution can never see the light of progress unless we first fix the way we're currently led and organized. If we care about the survival of our social systems and species we must learn a new way and **the new way must make sense.**

CHAPTER 2 SUMMARY OF KEY CONCEPTS:
What's Wrong With the Way?

1. It's not based on the way the real world going on around us works. Complexity theory explains it: *The universe we live in is made up of systems (solar systems, weather systems, human social systems) and these systems are made up of infinite number of independent*

variables (atoms, events, people) that interact with each other in an unpredictable manner and with accelerating frequency (transportation, communications, technology). The key to making sense of any complex system is understanding the patterns and relationships that inform their behavior.

2. It's not based on the way our 99.5% shared DNA-enabled nervous systems are biologically hard-wired to make sense of the world around us and sensible choices about what to do next: *To survive, thrive, and evolve our nervous systems evolved to make sense of experiences based on patterns and relationships of the way things happen. Every instinctive survival behavior to any type of stimulus such as the scent of a predator or possible prey, feeling the on-set of life-threatening cold or heat, or the sight of an alluring and available mate, developed as our nervous systems evolved incrementally over the eons based on learned knowledge of patterns and their relationships to events.*

3. The language of the way such as strategy, plans, and orders from disconnected chains of command, inhibits instead of enables one of our species' most potent evolutionary advantages: *Our freedom of choice and freedom of speech to make sense of the world around us and sensible choices about what to do next.*

CHAPTER 3

The Journey (Part II)

The Biology of Sense-Making

Directly transitioning from combat operations in Afghanistan and Iraq to a high-tech Biotechnology company in California made me appreciate what my International experiences and my colleagues in the Unit had taught me about the cohesiveness of common sense. No matter the continent, country, or culture you can always find common ground with the common language of common sense/knowledge of patterns. Think safety and security, health and happiness, family and friends. Common sense/knowledge of patterns is the common ground and common language that connects us all.

My first job at the company was leading a team of process improvement specialists on a project that's purpose was to provide recommendations to the CEO and other senior leaders on how to improve decision-making and problem solving throughout the company.

What is a Biotechnology company? Biology is the the study of life. The basic unit of life is the cell. Biotechnology uses computer technology to study the biology of both diseased and healthy cells. The ultimate purpose of a Biotechnology company is to use knowledge of the cell's own chemistry to discover, develop, manufacture, and market breakthrough medicines that make a meaningful contribution to the lives of patients. To accomplish this purpose, biologists, chemists, doctors, engineers, and business specialists must work together, make good decisions, and solve complex problems involving both nature and human nature. Herein lies the challenge.

As the CEO described it to me, The results of the three previous company-wide "Climate Surveys"[41] had identified "decision-making and problem solving" as the company's highest priority issue and the number one source of employee dissatisfaction. "Our employees are telling us we don't make good decisions and we can't solve the simplest of problems. We've paid millions of dollars to consultants and academics who used all the best known process improvement techniques, yet after all that money and all that time all they produced were a couple of hundred power-point slides that are cool to look at but don't tell us whether the problem is our processes or the people who are in charge of the processes. Your background and experience make you uniquely qualified to lead this project and it's a great opportunity for you to learn how the company works."

I thanked the CEO for the opportunity and for his leadership. Instead of listening to high priced consultants and their power-point cut-and-pastes, he was listening to what his people were telling him and taking decisive action to remedy it.

A few hours after meeting with the CEO, I met with my newly formed process improvement team which consisted of three highly experienced problem-solving specialists from different functional areas across the company. Their areas of expertise included Six Sigma, Lean, and Root Cause Analysis (the same problem-solving techniques the CEO referenced to me). Each of my team-mates had between five and twenty years of experience using these techniques so when I mentioned what the CEO said about wasting millions of dollars on consultants and their complicated processes, they all had the same question: "what other decision-making and problem solving technique can we use?"

After thirteen years of dropping into the middle of chaos, calamities, and complex situations all across the globe I learned the key to successful decision making and problem solving rarely comes from detailed strategies, plans, or processes. The most valuable decision-making/problem-solving asset my fellow Unit members and I brought to the table was the common sense/knowledge of patterns we had in our heads. Summed up by three of the Unit's most foundational and time-tested guiding principles:

"Pay attention to what's going on around you."
"Blend in anywhere."
"The only failure is a failure to try."

Sometimes abbreviated as Learn, Adapt, and Interact, these three guiding principles were taught to us by senior Unit members, consistently referenced and repeated as part of our common language, and continually reinforced by feedback from real world missions. Over time, the three guiding principles morphed into one. We called it Developing the Situation, abbreviated as D-T-S.

Develop means to bring out the possibility or potential of something. Situation refers to what's going on around us in the context of the moment. As a method, Develop the Situation means to bring out the possibility and potential of what's going on around us in the context of the moment. As a mindset, we bring out the possibility and potential of something when we take time to think about it.

As mentioned in my first book, Developing the Situation is the common sense course of action we recommended for capturing Osama bin Laden in Afghanistan in 1998. The inspiration for the concept came from Lewis and Clark, or the Corps of Discovery as they were called by President Thomas Jefferson when he commissioned them in 1803.[42] The purpose of the Corps of Discovery was to survey the unexplored western half of the United States from the Mississippi River to the Pacific Ocean. The expedition lasted over two years. Along the way they confronted harsh weather, unforgiving terrain, treacherous waters, injuries, starvation, disease, and both friendly and hostile Native Americans. Nevertheless, the approximately 8,000-mile journey was deemed a huge success and provided new geographical, ecological and social knowledge about the previously uncharted western half of North America.

The Corps of Discovery provides an apt metaphor for any team that is dealing with complex decision-making and/or problem solving. Think about it, they didn't have any detailed maps, plans, or satellite connectivity to distant chains-of-command. All they had to make decisions and solve problems was their biologic instincts and the knowledge they had in their heads. To survive one of the most complex and dangerous expeditions ever attempted, the Corps of Discovery didn't plan, they prepared. They used time and their minds to learn from, adapt to, and interact with what was going on around them. The Corps of Discovery used common sense and developed the situation.

I applied the concept of developing the situation to most every mission I participated in from 1998 forward. In 2001–2002 we used it in Afghanistan when we had no other guidance for what to do or how to organize our teams; in 2003 we used it to infiltrate and operate undetected, 500 miles behind enemy lines in Iraq; and in 2006 I used common sense and developed the situation to figure out what I wanted to do with my life after I got out of the military. Up to this point all I knew was that developing the situation made real world operational sense. What I was about to learn from my scientific colleagues was that it also makes biologic and evolutionary sense.

Biology is the study of life on earth. The Evolution of life on earth refers to the development of populations and species over time (e.g. how primitive protozoa changed into the complex cornucopia of species we know as life on earth today). The three main elements biology contributes to the development/evolution of human behavior are: self-preservation (survive), reproduction (evolve), and pleasure (thrive).

Since our brains are formed by life experiences, and since an individual doesn't keep doing what doesn't work (we learn through trial and error), evolution has reinforced the behaviors and values that help us survive and reproduce. When a behavior enables us to stay alive (survive) and spread our genes (evolve) our emotions reinforce the behavior by releasing neurochemicals that make us feel good so we (thrive) as human beings. Our common human emotions reinforce behaviors (positive/negative, pleasure/pain) that enable our species to survive, thrive, and evolve.

The term Evolutionary Stable Strategy (ESS) was coined in the early 70's by a Naturalist named John Smith to describe how Evolution by Natural Selection acts on different kinds of survival behaviors.[43] The old idea had been that Natural Selection inevitably favors organisms to act aggressively. Smith showed that this isn't necessarily true and that Natural Selection doesn't care whether the behavior is aggressive or non-aggressive only whether the behavior increases survival and reproductive success. An evolutionary stable strategy is defined as a strategy that cannot be bettered, provided everyone else in the population is doing it. What are these evolutionary stable patterns of behavior?

Harvard Psychologist Robert White coined the term "affectance motive" to explain what he described as our instinctive drive to develop competence through exploring and influencing our environment.[44] He defined competence as "the ability to interact effectively with the environment." Developing competence is "almost as basic a need as food and water except it's a constant presence in our lives because we are always interacting with our environment." Unlike biologic motives such as hunger and thirst, competence motives are never really satisfied so our brains never stop developing the situation.

Manifested in the moment as curiosity, we see this instinctive pattern of behavior in children who develop brain connections by using their senses to interact with the world around them; in teenagers whose appearance, behavior, and language continuously changes in consonance with the friends and social circles in which they cavort; and in adults, motivated by what Einstein called the "passion for comprehension," like the scientist, the explorer, and the philosopher, hypothesis testing, pushing out into the frontier, and asking Socratic questions. All driven by their genetic quest to learn from, adapt to, and make sense of the world around them and sensible choices about what to do next.

To Develop the Situation is to bring out the possibility
and potential by learning from, adapting to, and
interacting with what's going on around us.

Anyone who has ever worked on any type of problem, whether simple of complex, has experienced the non-linearity of this instinctive process. When the lights go out in our house at night we don't light a candle so we can come up with a step-by-step plan for what to do next. Instead, we immediately begin learning from, adapting to, and interacting with what's going on around us. We try the lights in different rooms of the house and learn they don't work either, so we adapt by looking outside to see if the other houses in our neighborhood have lights. When we see the other houses around us have lights we adapt again by checking the fuse-box and circuit breakers, etc. The more complex the problem, the more we need to learn from, adapt to, and interact with it to have any hope of coming up with a solution. Developing the Situation is the Common Sense Way we humans are hard-wired to make decisions, solve problems, and accomplish any purpose.[45]

To better understand and learn about the decision-making/problem-solving processes at the company, my team and I began *developing the situation* by conducting one-on-one interviews with leaders from all levels, and all functional areas of the company (Manufacturing, Research and Development, Commercial, Administration, etc.). After six weeks and over 100 interviews a number of common patterns emerged. What follows are a few of the most prominent:

"The only time we do well with decision-making/problem solving is during a crisis."

"Whenever there's a crisis pressure starts building from above until an anything-goes mentality takes over. That's when bureaucratic boundaries & barriers fall, information flows freely, and the people who actually understand the problem from all different areas of the company get together and figure it out."

"We can't make quality decisions because the people that make the decisions don't understand all the facts."

"We can't make timely decisions about the future because we have no institutional memory of the past."

"When someone comes up with an innovative solution there's no way to get the idea to the key decision makers."

"When we try to tell our leaders that something isn't working, or that we figured out a new way to make it work better, they tell us to 'stay in our lane' or 'go see Schmedlap,' or 'put some time on my calendar.'"

"No one knows what they are supposed to do because we have too many chains of command. We have our standard chain of command made up of people who were formally selected to leadership positions, and then we have our shadow chains of command—HR, Finance, and Legal—who aren't part of any formal chain of command and have no operational authority, yet drive all our decisions even though they can't tell you the first thing about the business."

The more feedback we accumulated the more I began to realize that the issues and problems described to us weren't peculiar to one specific leader, or one specific company, or one specific Industry. Rather these were common symptoms of the way most Corporations, Schools, Government agencies, and individual leaders are taught to think and speak about leading and organizing. The mechanistic metaphors of the way (e.g. strategy, plans, disconnected chains of command, etc.) are as common and as counter-productive in the corporate world as they are in government and the military. Go online to any corporate, government, or military blog site and you'll see similar complaints on every site. We humans all make sense the same way so it makes sense that we all recognize senselessness the same way too.

With only a few weeks left before we were scheduled to present our findings and recommendations to the CEO and his staff, we transitioned from interviewing home office personnel to interviewing people in the field sales force. Most companies refer to their field sales force as the tip of the spear because they are the primary points of contact between the company and the people who determine whether or not the company will accomplish its purpose. In the military we know them as the guys on the ground.

A Biotechnology Salesperson's primary purpose is to provide information about the medications their company makes so that physicians can decide whether or not the medication makes sense for their patients. Biotechnology Salespeople don't make direct sales and they aren't involved in monetary transactions. To accomplish their purpose they have to rely on clinical knowledge of their products and the diseases that their products treat (cancer, arthritis, diabetes, etc.).

The best way to learn from the guys on the ground is to hang out with the guys on the ground. I spent a couple of days with each of the company's ten most successful salespeople, conducting what is known as ride-alongs with them as they visited their customers. I learned a lot from each of them, yet it was my very first ride-along that would have the most foundational impact on the way I framed my final recommendations, and ultimately the way I would make decisions, solve problems, and lead my teams over the next ten years.

Tucson Arizona, 0750: Brad picked me up at the airport and introduced himself to me as I jumped in the front seat of his Cactus Green Ford Taurus. "We have a jam-packed schedule today," he explained as he handed me my copy of the time schedule. "Our first appointment is in ten minutes and our last appointment is at 6 PM," he added as he straightened his tie while looking at the rearview mirror. Likely in his late 30's, Brad had thick brown hair, an always-on smile, and the prominent facial features of a character actor. He carried himself with the confidence and credibility of a person who is at the top of their profession and is 100% focused on staying there.

"My manager told me you're leading a project to improve the decision-making and problem-solving processes for the field sales force so if there's anything in particular you want to talk about just let me know. Also if you have any suggestions, or critiques regarding the way I'm interacting with the doctors and nurses that we meet with today please don't hesitate to tell me."

"Okay, will do," I told him, even though I was pretty sure I'd be in total listening silence mode for most of the day. I had zero first-hand knowledge of how a biotechnology salesperson is supposed to interact with healthcare professionals, and because I had been in the military and overseas for the last twenty years I didn't have much first-hand knowledge or exposure to civilian doctors, clinics, and hospitals. Since we were getting ready to walk into our first doctor's office of the day I figured I'd wait for a better time to tell him.

As we walked into the office we were met with a chorus of "Hi Brads." Every member of the office staff knew Brad's name and Brad knew the name of every member of the staff. After exchanging pleasantries with each of them he went right to work providing the doctor with clinical information that she had requested during Brad's previous visit. Brad was what Malcolm Gladwell calls a connector. Someone who attracts and connects people with knowledge. If a doctor had a question that Brad couldn't answer he would connect the doctor with someone who did. Even if that someone was a doctor who worked at another practice in another town. He did the same thing with the nurses and office administrators. Reciprocity is the currency of human interaction; we get what we give in life. It was obvious to me that Brad's successes as a salesperson were underpinned by the strong mutually supportive relationships he had built with his customers over time.

Over the next eight hours we visited hospitals, clinics, doctors' offices, and pharmacies all across Tucson. While driving between locations we reviewed what we learned from our last appointment and then went over what our objectives were for the next. During these discussions Brad began preempting many of his comments with, "as you know better than anyone," or "as only salespeople like us can understand." Once again I wanted to tell him I'd never had a sales job before and was relatively new to biotechnology, but, selfishly, I didn't want to interrupt him and the amazing flow of insights he was sharing with me as we drove.

It was an eye-opening experience. Prior to that day I took our healthcare system for granted. It's definitely not perfect, however, if you understand the immense number and throughput of patients, the clinical complexity involved in treating them, and the monumental administrative complexity involved in getting approval and reimbursement for medications, treatments, and hospitalizations, you realize that our American healthcare system actually works amazingly well.

The best way to understand just how well it works is to see it in action from the perspective of those that deliver it (the doctors, the nurses, the physician assistants, the pharmacists, the officer managers, and their staffs, etc.). These are the guys on the ground for our healthcare system, which is why they should be a primary source of knowledge and feedback for any type of future healthcare crisis (e.g. pandemic or healthcare reorganization).

At dinner that night I asked Brad how the decision-making and problem-solving process works between the home office staff and the field sales force. My timing was good because we were on our second beer. He smiled and answered rhetorically, "Do you really want to know? I've been with the company for eleven years and I don't think I've ever followed a single sales strategy or plan." I almost spit my beer back into my glass. It was as if I was looking at and listening to the biotechnology version of a small-unit commander operating on the frontier of Afghanistan.

"Don't get me wrong," he continued, "the reason I don't use the strategies and plans that the home office spends millions of dollars and thousands of hours on isn't because I don't think they make sense. It's because our physicians and patients don't think they make sense. If it doesn't make sense to our physicians and patients then it doesn't make sense for us to continue trying to use it. Which is why I spend $150 a month of company money on a storage locker that's filled from floor to ceiling with unused binders, trifolds, and pamphlets."

"What does the home office say when you tell them their strategies and plans don't make sense to your patients and physicians?" I asked. "They say a different version of the same thing every time, 'you don't understand the big picture,' or 'this is what the data is telling us,' or 'just do what you're told to do.' After eleven years and hundreds of failed strategies and plans I learned the secret to success in this business comes down to one simple principle." He pregnant-paused as I reached for my pen: "When you always choose what's in the best interests of the patient you'll always choose what's in the best interests of the business." I wrote down what he said under the heading "Golden Rule of Sales" then sat back and contemplated the sense-making simplicity of it.

When you always choose what's in the best interests of the patient you'll always choose what's in the best interests of the business.

"It sounds overly simplistic but that's the beauty of it," he continued. "It allows me to make choices much faster and much more effectively because it's always the right thing to do. 'The best interests of the patient' is my constant purpose so no matter how different the problem or opportunity, the patient-focused purpose always paves my choice of paths. Best of all it keeps me out of trouble because when you always make choices based on what's in the best interests of the patient your choices will always make legal, moral, and ethical sense. That's it. That's the secret to all my successes. It's not rocket science it's good ole fashioned common sense," he added for emphasis.

"Now I understand why you're so successful, Brad. Hey, there's something I've been wanting to tell you all day but couldn't find the appropriate time."

"Oh boy, please don't tell me you're actually from HR and now you're going to fire me for telling you I don't follow strategies and plans," he replied with a smile and a hint of uncertainty.

"Do I look like I'm from HR?" I responded (with no negative connotation meant toward being in HR). "What I wanted to tell you is that I'm not a former sales guy I'm a former Army guy."

Now it was he who almost spit his beer back in the glass. "Well I'll be a monkey's uncle" (his actual words because Brad never swears), "HQ finally sends someone out to ride-along with me and ask me what I think about the business and it turns out to be an undercover Army guy."

I explained that the only reason I didn't tell him about my background was that I didn't want to interrupt our conversation and I didn't want to distract him from his focus on his customers.

"One of my best friends is in the Army Special Forces and he never talks about what he does either so I'm guessing you were in Special Forces?" He asked. I took another sip of my beer as I contemplated how to answer. "I should have known," he blurted, "you even look like a Special Forces guy." "I'll take that as a compliment, Brad, especially after being told I looked like I was from HR" (once again with no negative connotation meant toward being in HR).

"Can you at least tell me if you were in Afghanistan or Iraq so I can say thanks?" he asked. "I was in both," I replied. In addition to being a world-class biotechnology salesperson Brad is also a world-class patriot. He spent the rest of the dinner thanking me for my service, laughing about what happened, and teaching me about the business.

Two weeks later I passed my findings and recommendations to the Senior Vice-Presidents in charge of the Commercial Organization. One of the most prominent patterns that emerged from our interviews and the one that drew the most attention during my presentation was the number of people who described the way the company operates during a crisis as the best example of the way the company should operate all the time. "Why is that?" they asked me.

If you want to understand the decision-making/problem-solving power and potential of Developing the Situation simply observe how your organization operates during a crisis. Think of NASA during Apollo 13, New York City after 9/11, and families and communities before, during, and after any type of natural disaster. Even when we don't have anyone or anything to tell us what to do or what to choose, we always have our instinctive capacity to bring out the possibility and potential by learning from, adapting to, and making sense of what's going on around us. It's the common sense way we're hard-wired to make decisions and solve problems.

My final recommendation for how to improve decision-making and problem solving in the company was to teach people how to use common sense and develop the situation. The senior leaders who sponsored the project agreed. Although I didn't realize it at the time, saying you're going to use common sense and develop the situation to make decisions and solve problems is the easy part, putting it into practice is much more difficult. I had plenty of experience applying both concepts with my military teams in Afghanistan and Iraq, however, my lack of context-specific experience leading biotechnology business teams made it difficult for me to describe with words how to put common sense and develop the situation into practice throughout the company.

Learning is an iterative process. It takes time, context-specific experience, and feedback to learn. A capstone learning opportunity emerged a few months later when I was given the opportunity to select, develop, and lead a large (120-person), geographically dispersed sales team in preparation for the worldwide launch of a new breakthrough medicine.

The war for leadership talent is real, and
organizations with the best leaders will win.

In any endeavor (e.g. combat, business, sports, etc.), your success or failure as a leader is directly influenced by how well you select and develop your people. Although I had zero experience selecting biotechnology sales people, I had over thirteen years of hands-on experience selecting elite operators and developing high-functioning teams at the Unit.

One of the closest held secrets in the Unit has nothing to do with technology or tactics. It's the secret "formula" for selecting the best people and building the best teams. Only a handful of key leaders and Unit psychologists have ever been told what the secret formula actually is. During one of our semi-annual Selection and Assessment sessions I asked one of our most highly respected Unit psychologists, "Larry," if he could share the unclassified version of the secret formula with me. Without hesitation here's what he told me: "the key to selecting the best people and building the best teams is to always use common sense." **To Be Continued.**

REFLECTIONS/LESSONS LEARNED PART I
How to use common sense to select
the best people and build the best teams

To select the best people and build the best teams the first thing common sense leaders must do is teach their people how to see themselves and those around them through the common lens and language of common sense/knowledge of patterns.

Don't allow yourself or your people to be duped by man-made-up categories such as: status, rank, title; race, creed, degree; politics, pedigree, and/or similar to me. It's not the man-made-up categories that matter. It's the character and characteristics we've learned from our life experiences that matter most (e.g. competence, communication, courage, compassion, and common sense, etc.). It's what's inside our heads.

Our 99.5% shared DNA-enabled nervous systems all make sense a common way, via learned knowledge of patterns and their relationships to events. Common sense/knowledge of patterns is the common ground and common language that connects us all. What we learn from the sense we make is what differentiates us.

As patterns of evolutionary history continue to reinforce, sometimes the knowledge of patterns we're taught and told to accept as common sense turn out to be senseless.

The earth is flat; the sun rotates around the earth; our species evolved into different races, religions, and nationalities.

Carl Sagan wrote in 1995, in *The Demon-Haunted World: Science as our Candle in the Dark:* "One of the saddest lessons of history is this: If we've been bamboozled long enough, we tend to reject any evidence of the bamboozle. We're no longer interested in finding out the truth. The bamboozle has captured us. It's simply too painful to acknowledge, even to ourselves, that we've been taken."

We've been lead to believe that the concepts of race, religion, and nationality are solidly grounded in present-day biology and evolutionary fact. Yet if we brought together 500 of the world's most esteemed geneticists they would unanimously explain to all of us that human DNA is on average 99.5% the same.[46] Of that tiny 0.5% difference, 94% of the variation is among individuals in the same populations (e.g. same race, religion, and nationality).[47] To the extent that there is genetic variation among humans most of it is between individual people, not individual populations of people.

As Charles Darwin was first to illuminate with the theory of Evolution by Natural Selection, diversity and mutation are the evolutionary spice of life. Without that tiny 0.5% pinch of difference our species would be incapable of adapting to the changes that life continuously throws our way (such as disease, weather, natural disasters, etc.) The survival of our species depends on that 0.5% difference. This is not to say that we are all cookie cutter the same. There are approximately seven billion humans alive today and no two of us share the exact same physical characteristics (facial features, body shape, hair, skin, etc.). Where do all these differences come from?

Our Homo sapiens species evolved in what biologists refer to as genetic clusters.[48] Each genetic cluster consisted of various sized populations of people who were separated from other populations of people by mountains, rivers, oceans, continents, and sheer distance. Over hundreds of thousands of years these genetic clusters and their offspring lived together, adapted to their local environments together, mated together, and sometimes moved on together. Today when genetic testing companies tell us our DNA is *"48.3% North African, 27.2% Eastern European, 11.6% Asian, 9.2% Native American, and 3.7% Western European,"* they are referring to the location on the globe where some of our ancestors lived during different periods of time in different genetic clusters.[49]

As Spencer Wells who heads the joint National Geographic-IBM Genographic Project explains: "the kinds of differences that people notice such as skin pigmentation, hair color, limb length, and eye shape, are basically 'surface features' that have been naturally selected based on the specific environments in which our ancient ancestors lived for long periods of evolutionary time" (e.g. lots of sun vs. little sun, high temperature vs. low, abundance of plants, animals, fish vs. few, etc.).

According to Wells, "when geneticists peer beneath the surface at the underlying level of genetic variation between people they discover we humans are all much more similar than we appear to be. There are no clear, sharp delineations." If we asked our 500 esteemed geneticists to give us a genetic definition of race, they wouldn't be able to do it. Our genes are 99.5% the same. There is no genetic basis of race, religion, or nationality. Is this biologic fact the result of some recent scientific breakthrough?

Astoundingly it is not. As far back as 1950, the United Nations Educational, Scientific and Cultural Organization (UNESCO) issued a statement asserting that "all humans belong to the same species and that concepts such as 'race' are not a biological reality but a myth." The UNESCO statement was based on a summary of the findings from an international panel of anthropologists, geneticists, sociologists, and psychologists. Since that time enormous amounts of scientific evidence has reinforced their findings culminating with the successful sequencing and verification of the human genome in the year 2000.

The Human Genome Project revealed there is no genetic pattern in our DNA that makes sense of human racial categories. The common/ matching patterns of our genetic code is what makes us a species. We now have physical proof that "human races" are not natural genetic groups; instead they are culturally constructed, made-up categories.[50]

Modern scholarship overwhelming regards race as a social construct or idea through which social categorization is achieved.[51, 52, 53] While partially based on physical similarities within groups, the construct of race is not an inherent physical or biological quality.[54] Like the constructs of religion, and nationality, the construct of race only exists as a concept inside our heads.[55] Where did the concept of race come from?

Etymologists tell us the concept of race was first used to refer to people who spoke different languages (e.g. Greek was a race).[56] As humans continued to explore the continents and conquer the oceans they encountered populations of people who possessed distinctively different surface features (e.g. color of skin, eyes, and hair; shape of nose, eyes and heads, etc.). Somewhere around the 17th century people began using the concept of race to refer to differences in the way other people looked, sounded, and behaved (phenotypes).[57] Over time and across generations, the language that our 18th, 19th, and 20th century ancestors used to describe each other (e.g. White, Black, Asian, etc.) became part of theirs, and eventually our, cultures.

How does culture influence the way we think about each other? Culture is a complex concept with many different components. Essentially, it is a pattern of learned beliefs, language, and behaviors that are shared and passed on by clusters of humans (e.g. Ethnic groups, Nations, Religions, Families, Friends, Communities, Teammates, etc.) This includes habits and routines (aka patterns of behavior) such as how they greet each other, how they dress, and the way they think about and describe the world around them (their worldview).

In a Harvard Magazine article titled: "Race in a Genetic World,"[58] author Duanna Fullwiley, who is a Professor of Anthropology at Stanford University describes how culture influences different people's perception of her race as she flies around the world to do fieldwork.[59] "I am African American," says Duana Fullwiley, "I take a plane to France, a seven- to eight-hour ride. My race changes as I cross the Atlantic. There, I say, *'Je suis noire,'* and they say, 'Oh, okay—*métisse*—you are mixed.' Then I fly another six to seven hours to Senegal, and I am white. In the space of a day, I can change from African American, to *métisse (mixed)*, to *tubaab* (white/European)."[60]

Today we live in an interconnected and interbred Global society that enables us to expose the man-made illusion of surface features as indicators of race in a matter of decades instead of millenniums. The examples are all around us. At the time of this writing there is a world famous athlete whose father was of African-American descent and whose mother was of Asian descent. The world famous athlete (and son of these parents) married a woman of Nordic/European descent who gave birth to two beautiful children of all of the above descents. What "race" would you call the children? How would you categorize their surface features? White? Black? Asian? Nordic? All of the above? How about none of the above?

As children all around the world enable us to see with our own eyes, and as scholars across the globe continue to confirm with their research: There is no genetic basis of race, religion, or nationality. Humans are humans. We are one.

When I first read the research papers from the authors and scholars referenced above I wondered why I'd never heard any of this before. Shouldn't this knowledge be taught at every level of our school systems and shouldn't it be considered foundational knowledge for our civil, legal, economic, and political systems? Critically, if there is no genetic basis of race, religion, and nationality how do we get people to stop perpetuating the myth of race and its nefarious offspring racism?

> *"You want to know how to end racism in America?*
> *Stop talking about it."* Morgan Freeman[61]

Shared knowledge that there is no genetic basis of race, religion, or nationality is the first step toward getting people to stop talking about it. We are one. Say it out loud so others can begin to see. Once we humans stop talking about race we can begin listening to what our children have been showing and telling us all along: when we view the world through the unfiltered biologic lens of common sense/knowledge of patterns we are blind to skin color, eye shape, religion, and nationality. Conscious awareness that there is no genetic basis of race reveals there is no genetic basis of racism either.

To see for yourself, imagine you and your loved ones are stranded high on Mt. Everest with no ropes, no supplies, and no knowledge of how to get down. The last words you heard on your radio before the batteries ran out were the words of the rescue team leader who said, "We're on our way." As you huddle together holding your loved ones for warmth and what may be your final embrace, you understand with crystal clarity that time, temperature, and altitude are all working against you. All you have left is hope. Hope that the members of the rescue team are up to the challenge. Take a moment to think about your rescue team and make a mental list of the character and characteristics you are hoping they possess?

Was anyone hoping for a team of handsome men or beautiful women? How about whether they are tall or small? Black, Brown, or White? Rich, poor or related to royalty? What about whether or not they went to your alma mater? When our lives and the lives of those we lead are on the line it's not the surface features or man-made categories that matters, it's the character and characteristics such as competence, courage, compassion, and common sense.

What do all of the above characteristics have in common? Just like race and racism they are all learned. Character is an autobiography of the characteristics we learn from our life experiences. We humans aren't born with competence, we learn it through practice and feedback. We aren't born brave, we learn to overcome our fears with logic and experience. We aren't born with compassion, parents teach their children to share, to help others, to say I'm sorry, and to do unto others as we'd want them to do unto ourselves.

Whether waiting on top of a frozen mountain for the people who will rescue you, or waiting in an office for the doctor who will diagnose and treat you, or waiting to interview the job applicant who may work with or for you, it's the character and characteristics of the person not the criteria that matters most.

> *I have a dream that my four little children will one day live in a nation where they will not be judged by the color of their skin, but by the content of their character.* Martin Luther King Jr.

If we spread the word and stop talking about the concepts of race and racism they will gradually fade into irrelevancy in much the same way as the concept of Royalty has. Those who choose to continue perpetuating the man made-up concept of race should be thought of the same way as those who continue to perpetuate the man made-up concept of Royalty. Senseless.

You can't be racist if you don't believe in races.

What's the benefit for Leaders?

- To select the best people and build the best teams, teach your people how to see themselves and those around them through the common lens and common language of common sense/knowledge of patterns.

- Common sense leaders don't waste time trying to change their people or to make all their people the same. Recognizing the 99.5% similarity of the people we select, develop, and lead, enables common sense leaders to reinforce the similarities and celebrate the differences in the same way our DNA does.

- That 0.5% difference in our DNA is not only the key to the survival and success of our species, it's also the key to the survival and success of our companies, communities, and countries.

- It's not the surface features or man-made categories that matter. It's the character and characteristics (e.g. competence, courage, compassion, and common sense, etc.) that we've learned from our life experiences that matter most. It's what's inside our heads.

- To select the best people and build the best teams select for what's inside their heads: *It's Common Sense/Knowledge of Patterns.*

Part II: After ten weeks and over 100 individual interviews I had the distinct privilege of selecting and hiring eleven District Managers, and then assisting each of them with the selection and hiring of their own 7–10 person teams. Common sense leaders begin developing their people by teaching them how to see themselves and the world around them through the common lens and common language of common sense/knowledge of patterns. There's nothing new about this technique. After all learning to recognize patterns and trends is one of the keys to success for any businessperson in any business. *"It's not rocket science it's good ole fashioned common sense."*

With only a few months left until the worldwide launch of our new medicine we brought the entire team together for a weeklong pre-launch meeting. We spent most hours of every day listening to clinical information about the medicine, learning about the different disease states the medication was approved to treat, and talking amongst ourselves about how to translate that information to healthcare professionals in twenty-four different states. We had a lot to learn and not a lot of time to learn it.

To learn something new our brains follow the same sense-making principles as the universe from which they evolved. Matter can neither be created nor destroyed and no matter how hard our brains try they can't make something out of nothing. It takes knowledge to make knowledge and one of the best ways to manufacture knowledge amongst new teams is to use the same techniques our ancient ancestors used: bring people together—usually around a rock, tree, fire, or table—and start talking.

In human social systems the primary means of evolving toward higher levels of order, competence, and progress is the communication of knowledge (e.g. how to make a fire, find food and water, how to speak and how to lead, etc.). What's the biologic benefit of sharing knowledge? Learned knowledge of patterns provides our brains with options and when we have options we have freedom to choose between them based on the adaptive stimulus of what's going on around us (cold, hunger, thirst, a new team, new competitors, etc.).

Get a group of people together for the first time and they will initially mingle around in a state of very low order sometimes referred to as small talk (e.g. weather patterns, traffic patterns, sports patterns, behavior patterns aka gossip.) Small talk is the incremental way our brains build trust. The first person shares knowledge and the other person(s) reciprocates. Once the individuals within the group begin trusting each other it's only a matter of time before they begin searching for common ground (e.g. my name is, where are you from, why are you here, security, hunger, thirst, comfort, etc.)

Once the group finds common ground on purpose they instinctively begin making choices together to accomplish it *(Should we let them know we're here? Who wants to go first? Do you want to get something to eat/drink? etc.).* It is at this point that the group begins evolving toward higher levels of order, competence, and progress as a team.

This time-tested method of human learning and problem-solving was common amongst our ancient ancestors yet usually has to be relearned by people who've spent their entire professional lives attending and hosting top-down driven discussions, meetings, classes, and off-sites, where the individual leader running the meeting always has an explicit and/or hidden agenda.[62] *It makes sense to be suspicious of people who have an agenda. When we say it out loud we can see.* For this reason we chose to call our free-thinking meetings "agenda-less."

An agenda-less meeting is a meeting that has no personal or hidden agendas. The purpose of an agenda-less meeting is to find, learn, or reaffirm your common purpose as well as all the key patterns and principles you've learned to accomplish it. The best way to facilitate this type of learning is through authentic dialogue and the open exchange of thoughts and ideas. Agenda-less means you can start anywhere, go anywhere, and end anywhere that makes sense. I kicked off our first agenda-less meeting by asking the question: "what's our purpose and what do we need to do to accomplish it?" Then I sat down and let the team leaders start talking.

Each of our eleven managers had a geographically-unique perspective based on the twenty-four different states in which their people worked (the Western half of U.S.), and the different policies and laws that governed the healthcare systems within those states. It's critically important to have someone write down and/or illustrate the key thoughts and ideas in a way that enables everyone who is participating to visually acquire them (e.g. on a white-board, chalkboard, butcher paper, projection screen, etc.). When separate elements of a problem or opportunity are experienced together we maximize our brain's ability to contrast, cohere, and assess how they stack up against each other so we can prioritize them based on our purpose.

When it was my turn I talked about using common sense as the common way our geographically dispersed teams should make decisions and solve problems. To provide a real-world example I shared the story of my ride-along with Brad and the time-tested sense-making principle he shared with me: *"When we always choose and do what's in the best interests of the patient we always choose and do what's in the best interests of the business."*

Crickets.

Since it was the first operational comment I'd made to the entire team I wasn't sure whether or not it made any sense to them. Then one of them raised her hand. "Julie" was the District Manager of a ten-person team spread across Utah, Montana, Idaho, and Colorado. She was a single mother of two, super smart, super fit, and a fiercely independent thinker. She was also a data whiz who spent many hours of her personal time teaching me and the rest of the team how to use spreadsheets to recognize and make sense of sales patterns.

"I like the patient focused purpose," she began, "but if all 120 of our people are going to be using it shouldn't we come up with some common driving factors we can all use to ensure we're on the same sheet of music regarding what the best interests of the patient actually is?" She was looking at me when she asked her question so I just stared back at her with my best "please answer your own question because I have no clue" look. It must have worked because she stood up and walked over to the white board to better illustrate her point.

"Think of driving factors like you think of the laws of physics," she began as she wrote the words Gravity, Energy, Time on the white board. "No matter how different the location or situation we can always make sense of it with the same laws of physics. What goes up must go down applies anywhere at any time. The speed of light is constant. Time only moves in one direction. If a driving factor can't produce consistent results it can't be credible." "Consistency is credibility," someone else added out loud as all eleven team leaders got up out of their chairs and gathered around the white-board to begin discussing and building on the idea.

I looked on in awe and likely some self-congratulatory pride, as I realized that using common sense to select and develop your people works just as well in the corporate world as it does in the military. It takes common sense people to operate the common sense way.

After thirteen years of leading at various levels in the Unit, I was used to leading people who had more context-specific knowledge and technical competence then I did. All of my biotechnology team leaders were aware of my military background and leadership experience because I explained it to them during their hiring interviews. I also explained that I was confident in and depending upon them to help me fill in the knowledge gap as quickly as possible. *Which they did.*

No matter how much experience we have as leaders we never stop learning to be better leaders. For me, this was another in a long line of lessons learned regarding leadership vulnerability. Far from being a sign of weakness, when leaders acknowledge their own vulnerabilities (such as lack of context-specific knowledge) they are also acknowledging their trust and confidence in the knowledge and competence of their people. Sharing vulnerabilities builds trust.

After a few hours of discussion the team unanimously agreed on our foundational purpose—*"to always choose to do what's in the best interests of the patient"* (thank you, Brad). Then we re-focused our attention on identifying and agreeing on the common driving factors that would enable us to accomplish it.

Even the most complex problems and opportunities have an identifiable or underlying pattern to them (such as the laws of physics.) These underlying patterns are what Julie referred to as driving factors. **Driving Factors are the key patterns and relationships that influence whether or not we accomplish our purpose.** If you understand your purpose and pay attention to what's going on around you, you'll learn what the driving factor patterns are when you see, hear, feel, and experience them.

Julie and the rest of the team leaders came up with five driving factor patterns that they referred to as the "5C's." The 5C's stood for: Clinical, Cost, Control, Convenience, and Compliance. Here's how they explained these driving factor patterns to someone who at that time didn't know much about how our healthcare system works (that someone was me):

- **Clinical** = Safest and most effective medicine for the patient. To be in the patient's "best interests clinically," means the medicine has to be the safest and most effective for the patient's specific condition/disease.

- **Cost** = Lowest out-of-pocket cost to patient. To be in the patient's best interest the medicine has to provide the most benefits to the patient for the least out-of-pocket cost. One of the main drivers of a medicine's cost is the pathway used to access it. There are two primary pathways available to patients for accessing injectable medicines such as this one. The first and most common is called Part D, also known as the Retail pathway because it requires the patient to travel to, pick up the medicine from, and pay for it (~$100 for this medicine) at a retail pharmacy. The second access pathway is known as Part B which means the medicine is delivered to, billed through (~$0 for this medicine), and administered by the patient's doctor.

- **Convenience and Control** = Simplest/most convenient method for the patient to receive the drug. To be in the patient's best interests, with few exceptions, the most convenient way for any patient to receive a biologic medicine like this one is from their own doctor who is also able to control the administration and timing of the injection.

- **Compliance** = The dosing regimen required to maximize the drug's effectiveness (e.g. daily, weekly, monthly, semiannually, etc.). To be in the patient's best interests the compliance required to effectively dose the medicine must fit the patient's lifestyle, condition, tolerance, etc.

Even though I didn't have much sales or biotechnology experience to compare it to I had plenty of experience as a patient so everything they said about the 5C's made sense to me. Organizational Learning is an iterative process. We start with an idea or hypothesis like the "Best Interests of the Patient principle" and the "5C's"; we say it out loud to see if it makes sense; and then we put it into action and pressure test it in the living laboratory of real world experience.

Setting up the new processes and systems that hospitals, doctors' offices, and clinics needed in order to request, receive, administer, and get reimbursed for a Part B medicine required a lot of extra time and effort by our customers and our teams. None of this had ever been done before so there was no template or guarantee it would work. The only thing we knew for sure was what our doctors, nurses, and office administrators continued to tell us every step of the way: "accessing this specific medicine through Part B (in the doctor's office) is in the best interests of their patients."

How do we know if the choices we make and actions we take in situations such as this one make sense? Over time, feedback emerges (positive/negative, pleasure/pain) that reveals how well an idea/solution holds up under the weight and gravity of real world circumstances. And ultimately whether or not the idea makes sense. In this case the results spoke for themselves.

Our patients and physicians loved the new medicine but only if they could access it through Part B. As a result, our team was one of two (out of eight total) to make our goal for the first year after launch (we would go on to extend that streak to every quarter for the next five years). We were 13% of the business unit driving 28% of total revenues. Our teams won every award, incentive, and contest the company offered. Extrinsic rewards and compensation are always appreciated, yet the three accomplishments I was most proud of were intrinsic. Our team had the highest retention rate and the lowest turnover rate in the company for four straight years; we had the highest promotion rate in the company, and we had the highest Customer Satisfaction Survey results in the three separate years the survey was issued.

One year after the worldwide launch of our new medicine we were exceeding the standard in every category the company measured (e.g. revenue growth, market share, customer satisfaction, highest retention rates, lowest turnover, and highest job satisfaction, etc.). While our team and one other continued to exceed our goals and expectations, the other six teams continued to struggle. There was a lot of pressure on them from the home office chain of command to fix it.

My colleague, "Judd," who had twenty-five years of experience in the pharmaceutical industry and whose teams were also exceeding all of their goals, suggested we bring all seventy-five Team Leaders from across the nation together for a couple of days so they could share knowledge and learn from each other's successes and problems. Sharing knowledge between individuals and teams seemed like a no-brainer to me. Unfortunately, the home office chain of command was dead-set against it.

Their official response came the next day via an email addressed to "all field-facing personnel." The chain of command decided to put all the people who were under-performing on "performance plans" (the corporate version of probation). *Why keep them isolated, fearful, and flailing around in search of a solution, when we can bring them together and share knowledge of successes and solutions from the people who actually learned them?*

Think about where our species would be in evolutionary terms if we couldn't communicate and share knowledge with each other. If the first person that discovered how to make a fire wasn't allowed to share, explain, and teach what he/she learned with others, it could have taken hundreds if not thousands of additional years for every individual human across the globe to discover how to make a fire for themselves.

> *Matter can neither be created nor destroyed and no matter how hard our brains try they can't make something out of nothing. It takes knowledge to make knowledge. Once our brains learn about one kind of thing we can make sense of something else.*

After I read the email I asked Judd what he thought about it. "I've seen it at every company I've worked at." (He had worked at three of the largest pharmaceutical companies.) "Ego is the enemy of executive decision-making and this decision is just one more example." "But what does ego have to do with not allowing individuals and teams who've already figured out how to achieve success, from helping out other individuals and teams that haven't?" I interrupted.

"The home office chain of command loves the results our two teams have achieved but not the way we're achieving them so they don't want us to share what we're doing or how we do it with the other teams."

"I don't get it."

"Everything comes back to money, including ego," he explained, "their end-of-year bonus works just like ours, it's based on what they are able to quantify on their end-of-year performance reports. If a successful strategy or plan didn't come from their desk before being approved by HR, Finance, and Legal, then they can't quantify and claim credit for it on their end-of-year performance report. By proxy they can't get paid for it," he emphasized.

"What if someone just explains to them that it's not about who gets credit for the strategy or plan, it's about doing the right thing for our patients, our physicians, our people, and ultimately the future of the company?" I asked incredulously. Instead of going along with or agreeing with me, Judd, who was both a good friend and a good mentor laughed out loud and then said something I didn't initially understand: "Oh the innocence…the best way to answer your question is to ask it yourself."

Curious, I decided to use my monthly update meeting at the home office to ask my boss, "Biff," (not his real name) what, if anything, the problem was?

"It's not what you're doing that's the problem, Pete, it's what you're not doing that's causing all the issues." He began.

"I don't understand, Biff, can you give me an example?"

"You're not following the strategy," he barked.

"The strategy?" I asked with genuine W-T-F obliviousness.

"Yes the strategy," he responded as he got up from his chair and walked over to his desk to grab a folder. "The new strategy is called 'pharmacy first'" (e.g. the patient should be encouraged to access their medicine from a retail pharmacy or Part D first). "We spent a lot of time and money putting this strategy together and getting approval from HR, Finance, and Legal," he added as he threw a paper copy of a power-point presentation titled Pharmacy Phirst Strategy on the coffee table in front of my seat. The spelling of the word "first" as "phirst" wasn't a typographical error. It was the marketing way we were told to spell "first" whenever we wrote it on an email or a power-point slide in order to help the Pharmacy Phirst Strategy catch on. "Oh boy, the Strategy," I said to myself while thinking about Brad and the small unit commander in Afghanistan.

My conversation with Biff about strategy was eerily reminiscent to many conversations I had in the military where otherwise sensible leaders, and sometimes entire organizations, refuse to believe things that they can see, hear, feel and make sense of with their own senses over man-made-up strategy's, plans, and e-mails from disconnected chains of command. To make sense of something our brains require some sense to make it with. Time and feedback teach the best response to people who aren't making any sense is to try to talk some sense into them.

"It's not that our teams aren't following the Pharmacy Phirst Strategy, Biff. It's that our doctors and patients aren't following it. The reason they're not following it is because the Pharmacy Phirst Strategy doesn't make sense to *them*," I explained while pulling out a copy of the most recent company-funded customer survey results.

"Doctors, nurses, and hospital administrators across the country are telling us that patients make their medication choices based on what their physicians, their bodies, and their pocket books tells them 'makes the most sense,'" I read verbatim from the survey. "Patients don't know our strategy exists nor do they care unless it's in their best interests and that's the main problem with the Pharmacy Phirst Strategy," I added.

"The Pharmacy Phirst Strategy proposes the patient access their medicine from their local retail pharmacy at an average out-of-pocket cost to the patient of over one hundred dollars. Versus accessing it in their doctor's office or local hospital for free, or zero dollars. The Pharmacy Phirst Strategy inconveniences patients (elderly females) by requiring them to pick-up the medicine at the pharmacy, then take it home and keep it in cold storage until they can transport it to their doctor's office for their next visit. Versus having the syringe delivered directly to their doctor's office where the doctor and/or office staff controls the storage and ensures the patient receives their injection on time which keeps the patient compliant.

"Clinical, Cost, Control, Convenience, and Compliance," I summarized. "A strategy always has to be in the best interests of the patient, Biff, otherwise it can't and won't ever be in the best interests of the business," I concluded.

Biff flashed a half-hearted, half-second smile then responded: "Great discussion today, Pete, and you brought up some interesting points to think about, but here's the 'teachable moment' I want you to take away from all this. Even though your 'best interests of the patients' principle might seem like it 'makes sense' to you and your teams, I've been doing this for over thirty years and have probably sat in on a thousand brand planning sessions and in all those years and all those planning sessions I've never once heard anyone use 'makes sense' as a strategy. In the business world when we tell our people what to do we tell them by using the language of strategy, and as far as I know there is no language of 'making sense.' Now I need you to make sure every member of every one of your teams understands that the strategy is to send the patient to the Pharmacy Phirst and they need to start following it or there will be consequences."

This was the moment everything crystallized for me. I didn't think of what Biff said as an example of a clueless or greed-mongering corporate executive doing whatever he/she can to exploit and profit off of patients. Instead it was an object lesson in the stifling bureaucratic senselessness of "the way." Not only did the Best Interests of the Patient principle make more legal, moral, and ethical **sense** then the Pharmacy Phirst Strategy, it also made more **cents.**

The disconnected chain of command could see it with their own eyes yet they couldn't break free from the doctrinal prison of the strategy and plan. I may have lost my corporate innocence that day but I gained a valuable insight: The conflicts that create the most friction between leaders and their teams (e.g. combat, business, sports) emerge from the contradictions between the way leaders tell their people what to do (e.g. strategy, plans, disconnected chains of command) and the way the adaptive stimulus of what's going on around us in the context of the moment reveals we should do (in this case the best interests of the patient and the 5 C's).

What's the source of these contradictions? It's not an individual, or a government, or a religion, or a philosophy. It's the word-metaphors (strategy, plan, and hierarchical chains of command, etc.) that enforce its fate.

The status quo of "the way" is protected by its vocabulary. As an example, even though we all recognize things that make sense (like "always choose what's in the best interests of the patient") work better than things that don't (like "strategies and plans created by disconnected chains of command"), it's difficult to convince ourselves or others of this because there is no historic or scientific basis for the concept of making sense. By proxy, it's also difficult for sensible leaders to put into words why the way is more often than not, so senseless.

If we want to expose the senselessness of the way we need a new vocabulary that enables us to make sense of sense-making.

Each of the terms and concepts introduced in the chapters that follow started as ideas, insights, and/or observations that I wrote down over the years from my experiences. It wasn't a quest to come up with something new or to write a research paper or a new book. My motivation was, at its roots, mostly self-centered. I was simply trying to learn to be a better leader for the purpose and the people I was given the privlidge to lead. A few months after my conversation with Biff, I chose to leave the company to write this book.

REFLECTIONS/LESSON LEARNED
The Biology of Sense-Making

In this section you'll learn: 1) How our nervous systems make sense of what's going on around us; 2) What it means to make sense; and 3) The three benefits of conscious awareness: a) Recall b) Surety c) Evolutionary Learning.

The only things we know about the world around us come from knowledge of patterns we learn from our senses. So how does our nervous system convert physical patterns (e.g. light waves, sound waves, aromas in the air, etc.) into information that our brains can make sense of? This is a problem of coding, and nature solved the brain's coding problem thousands of years before modern humans ever even thought about inventing a computer.

The 2004 Nobel Prize in Physiology or Medicine was awarded for the discovery and verification that our nervous systems use a common combinatorial coding process to recognize, encode, store, and retrieve knowledge of patterns of/from our senses.[63] Human Intelligence is a pattern-recognition process designed to make sense of real world problems and make sensible choices about what to do next.

How it Works: Our brains make sense of real world problems by comparing and contrasting sensory patterns from the adaptive stimulus of what's going on around us *(the sound of a breaking branch, the sight of something moving behind a bush, the smell of something pungent in the air)* to previously learned knowledge of patterns stored as memory *(that looks, sounds, and smells like a bear[64] behind the bush)*. Combinatory code patterns enable our nervous systems to learn from, adapt to, and make sense of the world around us. Stay calm, DTS.

In his superb book, *Harnessing The Windmills Of The Mind*, author Abraham Thomas describes the pivotal significance of the combinatory code discovery as threefold:

1. The Mystery of how the human brain makes sense solved.
2. One of Mankind's most magnificent mysteries—the location of memory—solved.
3. Everything we've ever learned, every sight, sound, smell, taste, and touch is physically present in our brains as combinatory codes for lightning quick sense-making and problem solving with plenty of room left over for more.[65]

1) Solving the Mystery of How the Human Brain Makes Sense: The discovery of combinatory coding patterns makes sense of how neurons (nerve cells in our brains) identify the subtle differences between millions of sights (e.g. letters, words, faces, places), sounds (e.g. footsteps,  screams, rustle of leaves), smells (e.g. smoke, gas, food), and temperatures (e.g. hot, warm, cold, just right). Our nervous systems are capable of recognizing, recalling, and making sense of a virtual infinity of patterns and relationships by using combinatory codes stored as simple molecular matrices that the **researchers** liken to the colors on a patchwork quilt.

Odorant receptors	1	2	3	4	5	Description
Odorants						**Description**
A					●	rancid, sour, goat-like
B	●					sweet, herbal, woody
C	●			●	●	rancid, sour, sweaty
D	●				●	violet, sweet, woody
E	●			●	●	rancid, sour, repulsive

Combinatory Codes Stored
as Simple Molecular Matrices

Nobel Prize winner Linda Buck showed that the olfactory sense-making process[66] begins with the analysis of microscopic molecules floating in the air. Whether it's the scent of coffee brewing, or wildflowers blooming, or a bear with digestive problems, the things we actually smell are tiny molecules released into the air by the things around us (e.g. plants, animals, humans, etc.).

When we breathe in these tiny molecules they temporarily attach to receptor cells high inside our noses, causing structural changes to occur that **create** simple combinatorial code patterns (See Chart Above: E1 + E4 + E5 = large smelly animal) which are sent to the brain as electrochemical impulses.

2) **What does it mean to make sense?** To make means to combine, connect or create something (e.g. combinatory codes, letters, words, stories, feelings, DNA, a child, etc.). Sense refers to knowledge of/from our nervous system's five primary senses (sight, sound, smell, taste, touch).[67] To make sense our brains combine, connect, and create knowledge of patterns from our senses. The most fundamental tool of our Intelligence is our nervous system's capacity to make sense of what's going on around us:

"What was that?"

Our ears hear patterns, our nose smells patterns, our skin feels patterns, our eyes search for patterns and our brains combine, connect, and create knowledge of patterns to make sense of what's going on around us. Our nervous systems make sense by forming learning-feedback loops with the world around us at the molecular level.

"I think there's something outside the cabin, Caution."

Our senses work independently and together to enable our brains to recognize, respond to, and make neural sense of what's going on around us. Combinatory codes provide the common language that enables our senses, our emotions, and our motor controls to interact:

It makes sense to pay attention to what our senses are telling our brains.

Note: The above two pictures were taken a few minutes apart by a motion-activated trail camera outside of my cabin. The sequence began one morning while I was inside the cabin writing this book. I randomly stopped writing, stood up, and walked over to the front windows to look outside. Not sure what I was looking for I decided to take an early break and go for one of my daily treks around the property. When I walked out the front door I did something I'd never done before, or since. I drew my Smith & Wesson revolver from my chest holster and tactically cleared the corner of the cabin. I felt proud of myself for rehearsing my draw which I was trained to do before every combat operation. I then switched to a one-handed carry as I walked down the steps and up the path before re-holstering my weapon and finishing my two-mile walk. I never saw the black bear or knew it was just around the corner when I walked outside the cabin. Until I downloaded the pictures from the trail camera later that evening and saw it with my own eyes. Believe in and trust your senses.

We need our senses to make sense of what's happening in the world around us. If we lose or are deprived of one, or more, of our senses we lose much of the experience of being alive. Which is why one of the worst punishments that can be given to any human, anywhere on the planet, at any time in human history, is depriving them of sensory information from the outside world. Also known as solitary confinement.

> *It is the brain's capacity to combine, connect, and manufacture sense that is responsible for all knowledge we have about the world in which we live. If it doesn't make sense to our senses it's nonsense. Consciously saying or doing things that aren't based on our senses is senseless.*

3) The three benefits of conscious awareness.

A) **Recall:** Conscious awareness that complex sensory patterns (e.g. sight, sound, smell, taste, touch, etc.) can be recognized, stored, and recalled by nerve cells using simple combinatory code patterns enables our thinking brains to comprehend the galactic storage and recall capacity of our DNA-enabled nervous system.

> *Which way did the front door open at the house you lived at ten years ago?*

To find the answer simply ask your brain some questions: the current date minus ten is what year? What were you doing for a living that year? Where did you live? Can you see the front door? Which way does it open? Well done.

Everything we've ever learned from our life experiences, every sight, sound, smell, taste, touch, including the way the front door opened in our house ten years ago is physically present in our brains as combinatory codes with plenty of room leftover for more. How is it possible to store that much information?

Each and every strand of DNA in your body contains about a thousand times as much precisely-coded digital information as a laptop computer.[68] If you unraveled and connected every six-foot strand of DNA in each and every one of the thirty-two trillion cells that make up your body and brain, they would on average stretch from earth to Pluto and back at least 12 times.[69] An almost incomprehensible thought comparable to infinity. Yet its value goes beyond banal cocktail party trivia. Your brain is capable of storing and retrieving everything you've ever learned.

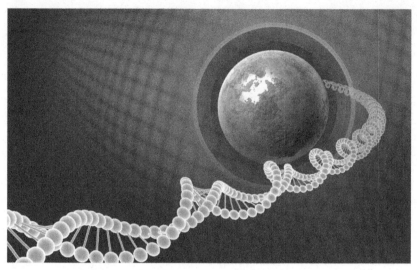

Learned Knowledge of Patterns = How our Brains Make Sense

What kind of car did George Washington drive? How did you know the answer? Most likely you instantly recognized that there were no cars when George Washington was alive (1732–1799). But how did you make sense of it without even thinking about it? Intuition is an exquisitely simple sense-making algorithm[70] that uses a yes/no process of elimination to logically search and retrieve the best-match answers from our brain's massive neural knowledge base.[71] Combinatory codes enable our intuition to extract precisely the knowledge we need before we can consciously think of it.

Context is identified through the process of elimination. All nerve cells are tuned to recognize combinatorial code patterns. Those cells that are unrelated to your current concern become inhibited since they fail to recognize a linking pattern. If the delivery boy hands you a bag you instantly recognize it's not the pizza you ordered because pizza comes in a box.[72]

> *"The cognitive guys think it's impossible to throw everything*
> *you got into the next computation every time. But that's exactly*
> *what the brain does. Consciousness is about bringing your*
> *entire life history to bear on your next step, your next breath,*
> *and your next moment." Walter Freeman, Neurobiologist*

Our brains obey the same laws of physics as the universe from which they evolved, matter can neither be created nor destroyed and no matter how hard our brains try they can't make something out of nothing. It takes knowledge of patterns to make knowledge of patterns.

"Why would we keep them isolated, fearful, and flailing around to find solutions when we can bring them together and make them smarter by sharing first-hand knowledge of successes and solutions from the people who actually learned them?"

B) **Surety:** Learned knowledge of patterns such as: how to crawl, walk, and run, what goes up must come down, "look both ways before you cross the street," and "always do what's in the best interests of the patient," aren't just ephemeral concepts or ghostly apparitions floating around inside our heads. Instead they are physically present in the form of combinatory codes and neural circuitry that combine and connect like mesh fibers to form a neural foundation of knowledge in our brains.

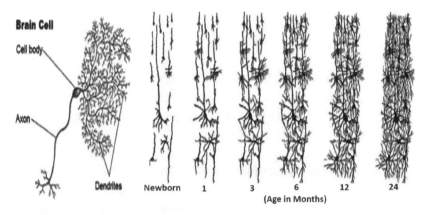

Learned Knowledge of Patterns + Time + Feedback (+/−) =
Foundational Knowledge of Pattern (e.g. laws of physics, weather patterns,
speech patterns, best interests of the patient pattern, etc.)

To make sense of any type of life challenge, whether simple or complex our brains must have knowledge of something foundational to pivot off of. Foundation means the basis upon which a thing stands and/or is supported. The phenomenon of one learned response forming the foundation or basis for another is called secondary conditioning. Secondary conditioning is an iterative process. Over time, with feedback, the patterns we learn and reuse successfully become our foundational knowledge of patterns.

c) **Evolutionary Learning:** Essentially, the choices we make today and in the future are a function of the foundational knowledge of patterns we've learned from our past experiences. We adapt to what's going on around us by learning from the consequences of our actions. Things that worked well in the past we reuse, while things that didn't work so well we avoid. Time and feedback teach our brains what works. Touch your hand to a hot stove and you won't touch it again any time soon. That's a learning-feedback loop. From birth to last breath our individual and collective brains never stop building and remodeling our foundational knowledge of patterns.

> *Copernicus's theory of the solar system led to Galileo's astronomical discovery that the earth rotates around the sun, which paved the way for Newton's theory of universal gravitation, which led to Einstein's theory of relativity...*

Our Foundational Knowledge of Patterns provides our brains with options and when we have options we are free to choose between them based on the adaptive stimulus of what's going on around us.

The dilemma of choice lies not so much on making the choice as the basis or foundation of knowledge upon which it stands. **"Taking a stand," "Standing up for others,"** and **"Standing our ground"** are all timeless metaphors for choosing to do the right thing. To do the right thing our brains require a strong structurally sound **foundation of knowledge** that can support the weight and gravity of the choices we make on it:

> *"There is no genetic basis of race, creed, or nationality. We are one."*

> *"When we always choose what's in the best interests of the patient/customer/people we always choose what's in the best interests of the business."*

*"Common sense is the common ground and
common language that connects us all."*

This simple idea that the way we think and speak about leading and organizing should be based on the common way our brains are biologically hard-wired to make sense of what's going on around us and sensible choices about what to do next, forms the basis or foundation of knowledge upon which the Common Sense Way stands.

CHAPTER 3 SUMMARY OF KEY CONCEPTS

- There is no genetic basis of race, creed, or nationality. We are one

- Human Intelligence is a pattern recognition process designed to make sense of real world problems and sensible choices about what to do next.

*What's going on around us + What we know =
How our brains make sense*

- Our nervous systems use a common combinatorial coding process to recognize, encode, store, and retrieve knowledge of patterns of/from our senses. (Nobel Prize, 2004)

- To make means to combine, connect or create something (e.g. combinatory codes, letters, words, feelings, DNA, a child, etc.). Sense refers to knowledge of/from our Nervous systems five primary senses (sight, sound, smell, taste, touch). To make sense our brains combine, connect, and create knowledge of patterns from our senses. *That's a Bear behind the bush*

- To assist our brains in making sense humans have discovered, developed and invented sense enhancers (e.g. microscopes, telescopes, stethoscopes, computers, etc.). In summary, there are three general ways to make sense: 1) directly using our five primary senses, 2) indirectly, by using sense-enhancing technology, or 3) by using our imagination to create a mental model that we can pressure test to see if it predicts things. All three methods are based on using our senses.

- Everything we've ever learned from our life experiences, every sight, sound, smell, taste, touch, including the way the front door opened in our house ten years ago is physically present in our brains as combinatory codes with plenty of room left over for more

- Intuition is an exquisitely simple sense-making algorithm that uses a yes/no process of elimination to logically search and retrieve the best-match answers from our brain's massive neural knowledge base.[73] Combinatory codes enable our intuition to extract precisely the knowledge we need before we can consciously think of it.

- Over time, with feedback, a pattern can be thought of as foundational if it has been applied to a real world solution at least three times.

- Driving Factors are the key patterns and relationships that influence whether or not we accomplish our purpose.

- When we always choose what's in the best interests of the patient we always choose what's in the best interests of the business.

- Common sense is the Common ground and Language that connects us all.

PART II

BUILDING ON OUR FOUNDATION OF KNOWLEDGE

CHAPTER 4

Learning Emotional Intelligence from the School of Fish

*"You will continue to suffer if you have an emotional reaction to everything that is said to you. True power is sitting back and observing everything with logic. If words control you that means everyone else can control you. Breathe and allow things to pass." **Bruce Lee***

Walking with short, precise, powerful steps Sister Michael Thomas silently glided down the aisle between the desks. A smidge over five feet tall and somewhere around 200lbs of solidly proportioned muscular mass, she moved as if she was balancing a stack of books upon her head. She was smooth, stealthy, and strong as an ox. She was also a strict disciplinarian best known for dishing out some of the most monumentally memorable corporal punishments in school history. For minor infractions she would simply whack us on our hands with the ruler she carried around with her at all times. Her specialty was mopping the floor up with a student by holding onto one leg (the mop handle) and then sashaying the body back and forth across the floor while she walked backwards around the room.

Like the rest of the Sisters at the school she dressed in the Traditional Dominican Nun motif known as the "habit." The habit consisted of a heavily starched, black-and-white, full-body robe with "coif" that covered the top of the head and attached to a long black veil that hung down her back like a cape. The only parts of Sister's body that were ever visible were her face and hands. I always wondered what color her hair was.

Photo of a Nun wearing the traditional "Habit"

While the rest of the students in our class were outside for physical education or PE, six of us were sitting in the classroom to makeup a class we missed due to absenteeism. The topic of the day was written in capital letters on top of the chalkboard "THE HISTORY OF MANKIND." There were pictures of Adam and Eve and a caveman pinned to the bulletin board off to the side. I wanted to ask why Adam and Eve didn't have hair all over their bodies like the cavemen, but as would be the case throughout most of my scholastic career I kept it to myself to avoid the potential embarrassment of asking a stupid question.

St. Edmunds School, Oak Park, Il
(Classroom is located on first floor right corner)

The Sister began the class from the front of the room as she always did, by emphasizing the importance of *paying attention.* Then she turned toward the chalkboard and tipped up on top of her toes as she spelled out words and narrated what she wrote. The chalk never lasted more than a few sentences due to the explosive pounding she gave it as she underlined, underscored, and added exclamation points for emphasis. Over time we learned that her thick flowing headdress and veil covered more than just her hair, it also covered her ears. Combined with the noise from the chalk she could barely hear a thing that was going on behind her.

Sitting in the desk behind me in the back of the room was Eileen Brennan. With long dark hair and an always-on gap-toothed smile Eileen was funny, popular, and one of two, or maybe three, girls I secretly hoped to someday ask to couple skate with at the local ice skating rink. "What did you guys think about the Sister's horrible hot chocolate this morning?" she whispered loudly, followed by a pantomime "gag." On frigid winter mornings the Sister often made hot chocolate in the convent and then served it to us out of a large spaghetti pot with a ladle as we filed past her on our way into the classroom. "Mine tasted like muddy water," someone else added. "Pay attention please," the Sister barked over her shoulder as she pounded out another word and another piece of chalk.

Turning around so I could get in on the fun I added, "Mine was so watery I threw it out the window while she wasn't looking." "Way to go, Pete," Eileen responded.

It was the first time she ever said my name and the first time we ever made up-close eye contact. I struggled to respond. It wasn't like I was trying to say something witty. I was just trying to say something. Rolling my tongue around my mouth in hopes of sopping up a hidden drop of saliva, I managed to spit out a question, "How did yours taste, Eileen?" Unfortunately, whenever Eileen had something funny to say she usually upped the decimal level as part of her delivery.

"Mine tasted like it was made from boiled water with a bunch of brown crayons mixed in," she blurted. Besides being a blatant breach of classroom etiquette (talking without raising your hand), Eileen had just openly criticized the Sister's hot cocoa.

"Eileeeeeeeeen," the Sister screeched. Silence serenaded the situation. Until I broke it. **"Not on me you don't,"** I said out loud while still staring at Eileen.

I thought what I said was pretty funny and expected Eileen would say the same. She didn't say a thing. She didn't need to. Her face said it all. *Danger. Please stop looking at me. That was a really bad move. You shouldn't have said that.* I was back in the moment and it was a moment of dread. Made worse by the fact I was the only one in the class not looking at the Sister. I could feel her eyes burning a hole in the back of my head.

I slowly untwisted my trunk to turn back toward the front of the room. There stood the Sister. Arms flared to her sides with clenched fists resting high on top of her hips. Her face began to flush in darkening shades of vein-popping purple. I wanted to tell the Sister I was sorry and that my sarcastic play on words had nothing to do with her weight and that I was only trying to make Eileen laugh. Unfortunately, the Sister's body language was telling me I'd be better off not saying anything at all. So I tried my best to look sorry instead.

Most of us had witnessed her primal pre-attack ritual many times in the past. Like looking at a sky filled with dark clouds, I didn't know exactly what was going to happen next but I was pretty sure it was going to be something bad.

Her cheeks slowly inflated in preparation for the violent discharge of her verbal displeasure. **"Bold as the day is long,"** she bellowed as she began barreling down the aisle like a charging rhino heading straight for my desk. I had taken plenty of pummeling's from her and the other Sisters in the past, and in fairness to all of them I believed then, as I do now, that my actions warranted most of what they dished out. Yet what happened next surprised even me.

Her Holy mass rammed into my little person desk with a force of impact that momentarily stunned my fifty-nine-and-a-half pound frame. With the speed and precision of a rodeo cowboy she attached one of her powerful paws under the back of my shirt collar and the other under my belt near the small of my back. Then in one fluid yank she surgically extracted me from my chair.

Carrying me like a bucket of water about to be tossed onto a flaming fire she speedily shuffled toward the front of the classroom. I thought she was taking me to the Principal's office until she stopped near the classroom door directly in front of the 100-gallon fish aquarium. Before I could figure out why she was stopping or what she was going to do next my head was under water.

If W-T-F had been in my vocabulary back then I would have used it, but it wasn't, so I went with the elongated version instead. Screaming it underwater as bubbles of bewilderment blew out of my furiously flapping jaws. The water was cold. Worse than that it stunk. *Goldfish turds.*

After a few seconds underwater, she yanked my head out and began shouting at me. Something about learning a lesson, but between gasping for air, trying to tilt my head to get the water out of my ears, and the shock of the whole drowning thing, I didn't really get the gist of what she was teaching. My classmates were in stitches. I could only think about one thing. My hair was messed up.

The worst thing that can happen to a ten-year-old in any social setting is embarrassment. It was happening to me at that moment. Before I could feel any sorrier than I must have looked she dunked my head in a second time. Once again I wasn't expecting it and hadn't fully oxygenated my lungs. *I'm drowning, damn it.* Indignation induced panic was setting in. I wiggled my body and arched my back in a frenzied attempt to break her powerful grip but my feet were off the floor so my body had nothing foundational to pivot on. My spastic efforts were futile.

She yanked me out of the water once again while screaming something about learning a lesson but all I cared about was not drowning. I flashed back to all the times my older brother had dunked me at the public swimming pool. He was much bigger and way stronger than me and I hated the feeling of helplessness more than I disliked being deprived of air. When the lifeguard saw what was happening he blew his whistle and made my brother get out of the pool and sit under his chair for ten minutes. After asking me if I was okay the lifeguard told me, "if it ever happens again, the most important thing you can do is stay calm and think." I never forgot that advice.

I gasped for as much air as I could get before she dunked me in a third time. "Stay calm, think," I mantra'd to myself as I went under. This time I opened my eyes and discovered I could see. Not just underwater, but through the aquarium glass. There was Eileen, wide-eyed and wooden. She looked worried. I wanted to make her smile but before I could make eye contact the Sister squatted down in front of the aquarium and eclipsed my view.

Separated by a sheet of aquarium glass and a few floating fish turds, I could see the Sister's lips moving. *What was she saying?* Her mouth and tongue moved with a familiar rhythm. As soon as her lips stopped moving she stood up straight and yanked me out of the water once again. "You have five seconds to tell me what lesson you learned today young man or you'll be right back in."

"That's it, she's counting seconds, and she's keeping track of how long I'm underwater. She's not trying to drown me," I realized with relief while gasping for as much air as I could get. A couple of seconds later I was back in again.

This time I counted too, while I wondered whether or when she was going to stop. The last time the Sister mopped the floor up with one of my classmates she didn't stop until the entire classroom was clean. "It's all about learning lessons and some lessons take longer than others to learn," she lectured the onlookers.

Whether or when she was going to stop the dunking wasn't that big of a deal to me. What was a big deal was the potentially monumental embarrassment I'd be saddled with for being the kid who suffered the most humiliating punishment in school history. I had to figure out a way to turn this thing around. Five seconds later I was out of the water again. Instead of trying to answer her question about the lesson I kept counting seconds; it helped me to stay calm and think. Underwater for five seconds, out of water for five seconds. Then back in again.

One-one thousand, I was starting to get used to it and it seemed as if the goldfish were as well; *two-one thousand, they were swimming right up to my face; three one-thousand, the way they moved their mouths made it look like they were talking to me; four one-thousand, I wondered, what were they saying? Five-one thousand*—as the Sister yanked me out of the water one of my friends yelled "hang in there, Pete" and someone else shouted, "Stop it, Sister, you're hurting him." I wanted to tell my friends not to worry and that I was okay but before I could open my mouth the Sister screeched, "SILENCE," over her shoulder and then dunked me back in even deeper. Now upside down with my feet sticking straight up in the air, it was almost as if she was using my body as a human exclamation point.

"I need to let my friends know I'm okay—one-one thousand—here comes the goldfish again—two-one thousand—maybe I should try talking back to them by imitating their fish mouth movements—three-one thousand—hey, my friends are starting to smile again, they must think it's funny—four-one thousand—how 'bout I add wide open eyes and darting head movements...?"

Before I could see what my friends thought of my full-face fish imitation the Sister squatted down and eclipsed my view once again. My submerged, upside-down, fish-imitating face was staring eye to eye with the Sister's right-side up, totally fed-up with a smart aleck[74] student stare. Just as her lips began to mutter "five-one thousand" she briefly glanced over her shoulder at my classmates then turned her attention back to me. For just a split second I could have sworn her scowl softened ever so slightly and her lips cracked upward in the hint of a smile. Then, as if catching herself, in one fluid motion she stood straight up, yanked me out of the aquarium, and lowered me down gently until my feet touched the floor.

Sopping wet, with a piece of seaweed hanging off my ear, she finally released me from the prison of her powerful paws. My classmates stared at me with open-mouth awe. My white shirt was see-through wet and on sideways. My black pants and underwear were hiked up high above my hips in what was then, as it is now, universally known as full wedgie mode. Lucky for me, kids didn't have camera phones back then.

The Sister leaned in within whisper distance of my face, "Now what was the lesson you learned from this incident today young man?"

As much as I wanted to come up with an acceptable answer, or any answer for that matter, I couldn't think of anything except the excruciating pain emanating from my crevasse. I genuinely had no idea what she wanted me to say. All I wanted to do was reach down and un-wedge my underpants. However, as a veteran of both giving and getting wedgies, I had learned from experience, and confirmed over time, that the funniest part of a wedgie is watching the victim try to get un-wedged. I figured I had already provided enough laughs for my classmates so I decided to suck up the pain in my pants and wait until I was in private instead.

"I'm not sure, Sister," I mumbled feebly.

"Then why don't you think about it on your way to the Principal's office? And make sure you stop off at the boy's bathroom on the way, I don't think the Principal would appreciate you getting aquarium water all over her office floor."

"Yes, Sister," I replied with all the respect and remorse I could manufacture. As I turned to walk away, she grabbed my collar again and pulled me back in close to her face, "then you get right back to your desk or so help me Saint Vitus[75] I will be all over you like white on rice." "Yes, Sister."

With a slight hitch in my step and a trail of aquarium water in my wake, I sucked up the pain as best I could and staggered out the door.

Over the years I recounted the fish tank story many times to both my friends and my family. There was something about that incident that kept it churning around in my mind. Always flashing back to the Sister's quixotic question: "what was the lesson I learned?" Many years later while writing this book I finally began to understand.

The fish tank story is a metaphor for life. We can be cruising along swimmingly when without warning the situation going on around us changes and we find ourselves struggling to keep our heads above uncharted waters. We either make sense of what's going on around us and sensible choices about what to do next or we're going to go down fast. Those who depend on a manual, a plan, or a disconnected chain of command to bail them out are disciples of death.

The first instinctive survival behavior of all sentient beings is to make sense of what's going on around them. The only way the human brain can make sense of any situation, whether it's the sound of a stick snapping in a nearby bush or the intentions of a teacher standing forebodingly in front of a classroom, is to pay attention to it. **What was that?**

The biologic way our brains pay attention is by engaging our neocortex. You're doing it right now otherwise you wouldn't be able to make sense of the words on this page. Up until recently, science wasn't sure what the evolutionary benefit of the neocortex was because it's slower to react than our older unconscious brains. As I learned from the "school of fish," and you'll learn from the pages that follow, we now know the neocortex provides a significant evolutionary advantage to our species. Perhaps the most important one.

REFLECTIONS/LESSONS LEARNED
Learning Emotional Intelligence from the School of Fish

Want to learn how to keep cool in a crisis? How to vanquish anger, fear, panic, and despair? How to access the part of your brain that enables you to be who you really are? Your capacity to influence what's going on around you requires conscious awareness of what's going on inside you first. Learning about the way our brains think and make decisions (metacognition) enables us to make better decisions and think better thoughts.

One of the best ways to learn how our brains influence our thoughts and behaviors comes from neuroscientist Paul MacLean who came up with the Triune Brain metaphor to describe the three distinct evolutionary stages in the development of the human brain. The triune brain metaphor provides an easy to understand and scientifically verified way to make sense of how our brains process sensory information.[76]

Brain Evolution

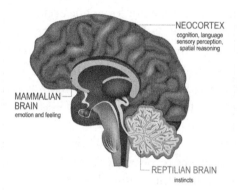

"In contrast to the engineer, evolution does not produce innovations from scratch. It works on what already exists, either transforming a system to give it a new function or combining several systems to produce a more complex one." Francois Jacob

Our three interconnected brains sit one on top of each other in order of evolutionary development. All three systems interact with each other to influence different aspects of thought and behavior so to truly "know thyself" you have to know about all three.

The Reptilian or Primal Brain is responsible for our primal instincts such as self-preservation, preservation of family, and reproduction (e.g. survive, thrive, and evolve). As the first and oldest part of our brain, it also monitors and controls our most basic survival functions such as heart rate, breathing, metabolism, and body temperature.[77]

At the most basic level the Reptilian brain helps us **identify familiar and unfamiliar things.**

Familiar things such as faces, places, favorite food, feeling well, our family, our friends, people who look like us, and the route we take to work each day, are usually seen as safe and preferable; while unfamiliar things such as new places and strange faces, lack of food, water, and oxygen, extreme heat and cold, violations of our personal space and/or social status, and getting trapped or lost, are treated as potential threats. When exposed to any of these unfamiliar triggers the reptilian brain follows a fixed program of behavioral responses. These include but are not limited to: fear, anger, aggression, territoriality, ritual displays, and panic.

A common everyday example of a reptilian brain trigger and response occurs when a friend or loved one accidently steps on our toe or bumps into us: *"Owww W-T-F was that,"* we scream. That's our reptilian brain's automatic, unconscious, and irrational reaction to the unfamiliar. In this case the unexpected pain and perceived violation of our personal space and/or social status. On the highway we call it road rage. It is for these reasons that the reptilian brain is said to be very primitive and animalistic in its nature.

The reptilian brain is neither good nor bad. Staying alive (survive) and spreading our genes (evolve) are instincts common to all humans. My initial response to getting dunked in the fish aquarium was 100% reptilian. Without this behavioral program operating as part of our subconscious we wouldn't have lasted very long here on earth. The problem arises when people choose unconscious reptile mode as a way of being (e.g. tyrannical leaders, mobs, rioters, and partisan political pundits). **Caution:** The reptilian brain doesn't understand language, has no memory, no conscience, and is incapable of learning from its experiences. The more the reptilian brain is stimulated the more animalistic a person will become. Conscious awareness of our reptilian brain triggers and responses enables our thinking brain to watch out for them.

The primary way our reptilian brains perceive the world is through images. Even though the reptilian brain doesn't understand language the use of catch phrases repeated over time can also be used to create vivid imagery in our reptilian brains. Repetition breeds recognition. Because the reptilian brain has no conscience and is incapable of learning from its experiences it's also easily manipulated.

Advertisers, Political Pundits, and the Main Stream Media are all aware of, and adept at, using vivid imagery and repetitive catch phrases as reptilian brain triggers to manipulate human behaviors. Understanding how vivid imagery, edited videos, and the echo chamber of fake news can be used to manipulate our individual and collective behaviors enables us to take action to neutralize them. One of the simplest and most effective techniques is to consciously ignore and/or dismiss them.

At the next level **the Mammalian or Emotional brain** evolved to enhance the function of our reptilian brain by enabling our ancestors to learn from their experiences. The way the mammalian brain accomplishes this is by attaching emotions to our memories. All emotions do the same thing in different ways. They encourage us toward things associated with pleasure *(eating, drinking, sex, collaboration, social status, progress, etc.)* and steer us away from potential pain *(embarrassment, guilt, failure, thirst, starvation, things we've never experienced before, etc.)*. By tabbing memories according to potential for pleasure and pain, our emotions enable our brains to learn from our experiences and to rapidly narrow access to context-specific memory.

Like the reptilian brain, the mammalian brain operates as part of our subconscious so it has no concept of time and it doesn't understand written or spoken language. Which is why the nervous employee can't remember their boss' name when trying to introduce her; and why we mumble like our mouths are sewn shut during a frightening dream. Our mammalian brains can't speak. The language of our mammalian brains is the language of emotions such as fear, sadness, disgust, curiosity, surprise, love, pleasure, embarrassment, and guilt. The reason emotions are also known as feelings is because our emotions are physically present in our brains as neurochemicals that we can feel.

To learn from our experiences our brains must feel our experiences. Feelings of love, anger, pride, sadness, guilt, and shame create powerful changes to our bodily state such as increased heart rate, sweaty palms, cottonmouth, rapid breathing, and blood rushing to our face. As an example, embarrassment is one of the least talked about and most essential of our social emotions. Embarrassment makes us feel bad about our mistakes so that we can learn from them and not repeat them. One of its side effects—blushing—signals to others that we recognize our mistakes and are not cold-hearted or oblivious. Shame, and its related emotion pride can be felt even when no one else knows we screwed up or did something of which we're truly proud.[78] Conscious awareness of our own and others emotions as they are happening is the essence of emotional intelligence.

Where did our emotions come from? The evolution of the human species began about 4 to 6 million years ago.[79] Which means 99% of our brain's evolutionary history was spent living as hunter-gatherers and less than 1% in modern/agrarian societies. Today, when we perceive the world through the lens of our emotional brains we are perceiving it in much the same way as our hunter-gatherer ancestors did when they ran around the forest in loincloths searching for roots and rabbits while trying to evade man-eating predators. It took thousands of years for our emotions to develop and it will take thousands more for them to vary in the slightest.

Our hunter-gatherer emotions aren't irrelevant. They're simply outdated. We will always need our emotions to help us learn, adapt, and interact with the world around us, yet in most cases the emotional response options provided by our unconscious older brains are excessive reactions to minor modern-day aggravations that have nothing to do with our physical survival (e.g. getting our toe stepped on). Herein lies the emotional catch.

When the emotional brain is in control our intuition is only capable of selecting response options that match our current emotions. All response options that fail to match the current emotion are inhibited. Fear focuses our memories on avoidance behaviors and inhibits knowledge of false alarms and past successes. Anger focuses our memories on past confrontations and inhibits knowledge of compassion and calm.

Blind rage, blind ambition, and blind lust, such as I experienced while staring obliviously into the eyes of Eileen, are all byproducts of our emotional brain's capacity to inhibit or to blind our thinking brain from options that enable us to make sense of what's going on around us and sensible choices about what to do next. This creates predictable patterns of behavior and, most often, flawed results.[80]

Caution: Predictable patterns of behaviors can be used against you by competitors. Time teaches that Evolution is a competitive business and predictability is one pattern that ensures a competitor will be out of business real quick. *"Always take a different route home than the one you took to get to your destination." Rogers's Rangers.* To survive, our Homo sapiens ancestors learned they needed to balance the effectiveness of their patterned behaviors with just enough variability to spare them from being predictable[81]. The way our Homo sapiens brain evolved to accomplish this was by developing a neocortex.

*Road rage is a common reptilian brain response
that is activated when one feels threatened*

The neocortex: Homo sapiens means wise human. The neocortex (Latin for "new brain") is the part of our brains that makes us wise, and what biologically distinguishes our species from our closest living and extinct relatives (chimpanzees and Neanderthals). The neocortex controls higher-level processes such as logic, reasoning, creative thinking, math, and language. Critically, the neocortex is the only part of our brains that can understand language and speak, it's the only part of our brain that can think forward in time, and it's the only part of our brain that is able to consciously monitor sensory information. In other words, it's the only part of our brains that is capable of making sense of what's going on around us and sensible choices about what to do next. Say it out loud and you'll see.

> *If any organ of our body should be substantially different from any other species it is the neocortex, the center of extraordinary human cognitive abilities. It is, therefore, surprising how little modern research has been done to elucidate how this human difference emerged.* P. Rakic

Size vs. Speed. Although the neocortex is three times the size of our older unconscious brains, its position on top makes it the last to receive bottom-up sensory information and the slowest to react. First-mover advantage applies in biology. Studies show when our senses sense something such as the sound of a stick snapping behind a bush or the sensation of a loved one accidently stepping on our toe, our reptilian and emotional brains are alerted within twenty milliseconds, while awareness of the neocortex occurs 280 milliseconds (about one-fourth of a second) later.[82]

As a result of this awareness gap, our brain's first instinctive reaction to any type of stimuli is always unconscious, emotional, and without context. We feel fear before we know what we're afraid of. We become angry before we realize what made us mad. And we make choices based on emotional response options that were learned from our distant past (think road rage) instead of the adaptive stimulus of what's going on around us in the context of the moment (a parent driving their child to the hospital). When our emotional brain is engaged it blocks our neocortex's capacity to make sense of what's going on around us. The result is senselessness.

How do we train our thinking brains to break free from the prison of our prehistoric emotions in the context of the moment when we need to make sense the most? *"There were all kinds of things I was afraid of at first, ranging from grizzly bears to 'mean' horses and gun-fighters; but by acting as if I was not afraid I gradually ceased to be afraid."* Theodore Roosevelt

Remember the old saying that thoughts control our actions and behaviors? It's been accepted as fact for centuries until a few years ago when science discovered it actually works the other way around.[83] The next time you're stuck in traffic and you feel stressed out and mad, force a smile onto your face while looking in the rear-view mirror and you'll instantly feel glad. When we put a smile on our face we make ourselves feel happy. Try it right now. Actions control thoughts and emotions. What does this mean for leaders? It means we can change the way we think and the way we feel by physically changing our actions and behaviors and we can do it at any time, in any place, under any circumstances. All we have to do is engage our neocortex.

Engaging our neocortex is essentially a technique where we pay attention to the present. By focusing our senses on the sights, sounds, and physical sensations going on around us in the here and now, we can achieve mental clarity of what's actually happening in our lives. Engaging your neocortex is as easy as counting up to or down from ten while taking a couple long, full, deep breaths.[84] *"When angry, count to ten before you speak. If very angry, a hundred,"* Thomas Jefferson. By engaging our conscious neocortex we instantly disengage our unconscious older brains and vanquish anger, fear, and panic while also alleviating pressure, stress, and anxiety.

Instead of trying to answer her question about the lesson I kept counting seconds, it helped me to stay calm and think.

People like Thomas Jefferson and our ancient ancestors have been engaging their neocortex by breathing and talking to themselves for thousands of years even though they had no knowledge of how or why it works. Conscious awareness of our three-part triune brains enables us to make sense of it. The neocortex is the only part of our brains that can speak, and it's the only part of our brains that can take conscious control of unconscious processes like breathing and smiling. Once engaged, our neocortex puts us in command of our nervous system. You control your mind, not the other way around. Think about it. Emotions dominate human behavior until we start thinking about them.

Think of your neocortex as a muscle. In much the same way you can't just walk into a gym for the first time and bench press 250lbs, the untrained neocortex will not be strong enough to overpower your older/emotional brains unless you exercise it regularly. How do we strengthen our neocortex? The same way we strengthen our arms, chest, back, and leg muscles: Resistance Training.

Every time we **resist** the temptation to act on our emotions (e.g. eating, drinking, smoking, shopping, sex, etc.) we strengthen our neocortex and make it easier to overpower our emotional brain the next time a similar situation occurs. The more resistance we apply, the stronger our neocortex gets. Moment-by-moment, day-by-day, decision-by-decision, the more we engage and empower our neocortex the more powerful it will get. If you want to be who you really are and have a positive influence on the trajectory of your life and the lives of those you lead, you need to focus on strengthening your neocortex. *"True power is sitting back and observing everything with logic,"* Bruce Lee.

A strong neocortex is especially critical in life or death survival situations. Interviews with survivors of both man-made and natural disasters reveal that only ten percent of people are able to stay calm and think in the midst of a survival emergency.[85] In any type of survival  situation we have a choice: we can choose the unconscious, emotion-generated response option, or we can take our time (one-fourth of a second) and put a lid on our emotions by consciously choosing to engage our neocortex.

Why do we sometimes choose the initial unconscious, emotion-based response option—e.g. fear/panic; while other times we choose the follow-on, consciously aware, logic-based response options from our neocortex: stay calm, think? The answer is self-evident. It's our species' greatest evolutionary advantage. **It's Freedom of Choice.**

Freedom of Choice is defined by the capacity to make a choice based on two or more response options. When we have only one option (e.g. run away) we have no choice. When we are consciously aware of two or more options (e.g. stay calm, don't make eye contact, make yourself big, back away slowly, etc.) then we have choice. If our brains are free to choose between two or more response options without an external agent influencing us such as fate, divine will, or physical coercion, then we have freedom of choice.

Freedom of choice is not an abstract concept or consideration. Rather it's an Evolutionary Stable Pattern of human behavior that emerges from the relationship between the three sub-systems of our triune brain. Conscious awareness of two or more response options is only possible when we take our time (about one-fourth of a second) to engage our neocortex. *We can panic or we can stay calm and think.* Time is the fuel that powers the process of free-thinking.

Whether the choices we make are sensible or senseless depends on the context of the moment in which we make them. Taking evasive action to avoid an obstacle on the road, buying or selling stocks, planting and harvesting crops, or the seminal evolutionary choice of conception, are all examples of the sensitivity of the choices we make to the context of the moment in which we make them. **Freedom of choice is about time.**

How do common sense leaders know when the time is right to make a sensible choice? The same way we know when the time is right to cross a busy street. And the same way we know when the time is right to stop talking to a classmate. We know it when we sense it as long as we take time to engage our neocortex and pay attention to what's going on around us. Conscious awareness of our triune brain's capacity to produce and choose between two or more response options is our sense of freedom of choice. **Thank you, Sister.**

CHAPTER 4 SUMMARY OF KEY CONCEPTS

The Triune Brain metaphor describes the three distinct evolutionary stages in the development of the human brain. Our three interconnected brains sit one on top of each other in order of evolutionary development. All three systems interact with each other to influence different aspects of thought and behavior so to truly "know thyself" you have to know about all three.

Reptillian Brain:

- **Evolutionary role:** selfish brain that helps us survive as individuals.
- Oldest part of the brain, deals with basic bodily functions.
- **Responsible for** our Instincts: Survive, Thrive, and Evolve, also described as the 4F's: Fight/Flight, Feed, and Fornicate.
- Wired to detect the unfamiliar as danger and therefore negative emotions.
- To accomplish its purpose it carries out a fixed program of predictable responses to external triggers.
- It does not learn from its mistakes and understands only images not language.
- **Satisfied when** safe from danger and no uncertainty.

Mammalian/Emotional Brain:

- **Evolutionary role:** social brain that enhances the function of our reptilian brain by enabling us to learn from their experiences.
- The way the mammalian brain accomplishes this is by attaching emotions to our memories. All emotions do the same thing in different ways. They encourage us toward things associated with pleasure *(eating, drinking, progress, etc.)* and steer us away from potential pain *(embarrassment, guilt, failure, etc.).*
- Without the emotional brain we would keep doing the same things in a ritualistic way without ever learning from our mistakes.

- **Responsible for** our positive emotions, learning, emotional memory, and spirituality.
- **Satisfied when** feels trust, social bonds, higher status/respect.

Neocortex/Thinking Brain:

- **Evolutionary role:** Predicting brain that provides conscious awareness of two or more response options.
- Newest part of our brain it controls higher level processes such as logic, reasoning, creative thinking, language, math, and integration of sensory information.
- **Responsible for** sensory perception, spatial reasoning, generation of motor commands, conscious thought, intellectual memory.
- Only engages when we pay attention to what's going on around us.
- Considered the seat of consciousness, receives signals of all significant neural activities.
- Access to the global wisdom of our three part brain it enables our freedom of choice to make sense of whats going on around us and sensible choices about what to do next
- Your neocortex is what you consciously think with. If you want to control the direction of your life, you need to focus on strengthening this part of your brain.
- **Satisfied when** learning, anticipating future rewards, connected to a higher purpose, in flow.

CHAPTER 5

Identification Friend or Foe?

How to Make Sensible Choices in Complex Unfamiliar Situations

*"Do you ever pigeonhole other people, experiences, or events?
Is it bad to do so? No—in fact the tendency to categorize
and label is a keystone of human intellect and essential
to any but the most primitive thinker."* Morton Hunt

October 2001, 0245 (local time), 25,000 feet above Afghanistan:
"Hard Right," the pilot screamed over the inter-aircraft communications system (intercom) as the aircraft and my head violently whiplashed left to right. My first thought was "surface to air missile."

I was wearing an MTX Halo[86] parachute and immediately began snapping, tightening, and checking each buckle in the order I learned at jumpmaster school. "Look grab. Look grab, pull, pull, check," I mouthed while lifting my hands and moving my head in the universal pantomime sequence all Halo jumpers go through as part of their pre-jump ritual to rehearse the activation of their main and reserve parachutes.

"All systems are green," the captain updated over the intercom. "That was close guys, we almost collided with the other AC-130. Sounds like they misunderstood their altitude directions but we got them squared away."

It was good to know it wasn't an enemy missile or mechanically related, but the fact we almost ran into another AC-130 gave me pause. Most training exercises and real world operations I had been on over the previous fifteen years had an AC-130 flying overhead at one time or another during the operation. In all those years and all those training events I never recalled having two AC-130's in the air at the same time over the same target. However, this wasn't a training event. This was the opening raid of the war against terrorists and every military service, every unit, and every weapon system in the U.S. inventory was available for duty.

Add in the fact that this was the only show in town, and you have the timeless military planning recipe that calls for as much combat power and as much redundancy as possible. In addition to the two AC-130's there were over 100 other aircraft involved (helicopters, cargo planes, fighter jets, refueling aircraft, command and control aircraft, electronic jamming aircraft, etc.), making this one of the most complicated and intricate plans in modern military history. Plan is a verb, not a noun. Planning is how our brains prepare for the unexpected. I kept my parachute on and buckled just in case.

The mission of the two AC-130's and their crews was to provide fire support and visual over-watch for an air assault raid on a Taliban compound located on the outskirts of the enemy-infested city of Kandahar. I was on board the AC-130 as the Ground forces liaison officer (referred to in the military as the L-N-O). The military defines the duties of the LNO as follows: "A member of one unit attached to another unit in order to ensure unity of purpose and mutual understanding of action." In this case, to assist the aircrew with making sense of what was happening on the ground below.

According to the U.S. Air Force "the AC-130 is a heavily-armed long-endurance aircraft equipped with an array of air-to-ground oriented weapons (105mm howitzer, 25mm Vulcan cannon, and 40mm Bofor's cannon) that are integrated with sophisticated targeting sensors, satellite navigation, and fire control systems. The aircraft is capable of delivering precision firepower or area-saturation fire over a target for extended periods of time at night and in adverse weather. The sensor suite consists of thermal, infrared (IR), and side-looking radars. These sensors allow the gunship to visually or electronically identify targets on the ground in the harshest of weather conditions".[87]

"The helicopters are ten minutes out: oxygen masks on, depressurize the aircraft, open gun doors, the mission is a go," the captain announced over the intercom.

*AC-130 with 105mm howitzer and 25mm cannon
protruding from left side of aircraft.*[88]

A few feet from my seat, hydraulic arms slowly separated symmetrical sheets of steel from the fuselage of the aircraft to expose firing portals through which the barrels of the 105mm and 25mm cannon would now protrude. Like driving down the highway in a convertible going 200 MPH or standing next to a blast furnace, the roar of the wind was ear-splitting and the air too thin to breathe so everyone on board wore fully enclosed aviator helmets with soundproofing insulation, face shields, and oxygen masks through which we talked and breathed.

"Panther, this is Mantis, we are five minutes out." "Mantis" was the commander of the helicopter raid force. "This is Panther, we are on station and see no movement or activity in or around the target." "This is Mantis, roger, thanks, keep me updated, out."

The compound had been under continuous electronic and visual surveillance for the last ninety-six hours. Even though we were confident there were no enemy personnel inside the target we had no way of knowing if there were any nearby. The target sat on the outskirts of Kandahar, which was considered the religious capital of Taliban-controlled Afghanistan. U.S. Intelligence had information that numerous terrorist leaders such as UBL, Zawahiri, and Zarqawi were living in and around Kandahar in the months, weeks, and days prior. Yet, without eyes on the ground, we couldn't confirm or deny whether any of them were there at that time. I guess you could say that the only thing we knew for sure about the area in and around the target was that we didn't know anything for sure. Which is always the best way to approach the unknown.

In front of me were two 13-inch video display terminals. The monitor on my left showed the image from the Infrared (IR) targeting camera, while the monitor on the right showed the image from the Thermal targeting camera. A single joystick allowed me to adjust the direction of the cameras and to zoom in and out. In general, the Infrared image provides better resolution quality, while the Thermal image provides better human detection capability because it works off heat. As an example, if an enemy fighter is hiding behind a wall the IR camera may not detect him but the thermal camera will pick up a glowing red heat signature as his body heat rises up and over the wall like the flames from a fire.

If anyone was hiding in or around this target I was determined to find them. It was my purpose. I used a simple scanning method taught to me by one of our snipers and easily recalled using the military march cadence, "left-right-left." When it comes to guiding principles and mnemonics, universality is everything. I use the same technique whether I'm searching a target for hidden enemies, searching for cars as I cross the street, or searching my house for my phone. I start on the left side, work my way back to the right and methodically repeat until the entire search area is complete. I scanned every inch in and around the target searching for discrepancies such as movement, discordant shapes, and contrasting colors. Then I rechecked to see if anything changed. I detected nothing.

Next to the video screens was my radio control panel. This mission required active monitoring of four different radios: the inter-aircraft communications radio which linked me to the pilot, co-pilot, weapons officer, and crew; two separate satellite radios used by our higher head-quarters for command and control; and perhaps the most important radio for my role as LNO, the fire support radio. On this mission the fire support radio was the only direct link between the two AC-130's and the guys on the ground conducting the raid.

Military doctrine reinforces that the more radios you monitor the more overall situational awareness you have. But nothing in life is free and the price you pay for an increase in overall situational awareness is a decrease in situational specifics. *The human brain is only capable of paying attention to one thing at a time.* When you are talking and/or listening to one radio conversation your brain is incapable of making sense of what's being said on the others. It's a biologic fact: if you're not paying attention to something you cannot comprehend it. Like texting while you're driving; when you're texting you're no longer consciously driving. You are a catastrophe waiting for a contingency.

"The helicopters are one minute out," the Captain relayed over the intercom.

I zoomed out my Infrared camera to provide a panoramic view of the target and surrounding area just in time to see the image of the first MH-47 Helicopter float into the picture. In infrared green it looked more like a giant grasshopper then a helicopter as it braked, flared, and crested over the eight-foot-high rock wall that surrounded the compound. As it hovered in preparation to land, its image gradually faded then com-pletely disappeared from view. The dust and debris kicked up by the two massive turbo-powered rotors created blinding brownout conditions so severe that 99.9% of pilots in the world would have had to abort. But these weren't the 99.9%. These were the 0.1%. Onward they flew.

Brake, flare, hover, touchdown, disgorge, lift, accelerate and climb. While flying in the blind. Like clockwork, each of the helicopters fol-lowed the same routine. Except the last one. Theoretically, you wouldn't want to be the first helicopter to land on an enemy target during a night-time raid. However, if the target is empty and you're dealing with severe brownout conditions you'd much rather be first than last because by the time the last helicopter approaches the target most every untethered dust particle in and around the target has already been blown airborne.

CH-47 Heavy Lift Helicopter preparing to land in Afghanistan.

The blinding brownout conditions meant the pilots were 100% dependent on their instruments, and the crew's eyes, to slowly feel their way forward and down. Speed kills and smooth is fast. In training the pilots take all the time they need. If they don't feel good about landing in brownout conditions they simply pull up, go around, and try it again. In combat, the enemy always has a vote so there's rarely any extra time to take.

To vanquish fear and panic, elite pilots train their brains to focus on the two things they can control—the aircraft and their emotions. In this case, you could actually hear them on the radio as they did both. Speaking in a cool, calm, collected manner is one of the most effective methods of quieting our emotional brains as well as the emotions of everyone else who is listening. Calm like common sense is contagious.

"Look out," one of the crew members yelled over the radio as the tail boom of the final helicopter clipped the eight-foot-high rock wall then violently whiplashed sideways. In what would turn out to be the first of many examples of heroic airmanship that night, the pilot immediately compensated, steadied, and finessed the wounded but still air-worthy aircraft onto the ground for a hard but upright landing. Out from the back burst the bruised and eternally appreciative operators. I breathed a sigh of relief for them as they planted their feet onto the relative safety and security of enemy-occupied ground.

Mantis called in the code word that confirmed the entire assault force had landed and the raid was underway. While the guys on the ground did their job, I stayed 100% focused on doing mine. I increased my sweeping search pattern in longer left-right-left arcs that stretched one to two kilometers around the target. "Nothing seen around target," I updated Mantis using the fire support radio. But before he could respond to confirm that he heard what I said someone screamed: **"Enemy busload of terrorists."** The fire support radio went silent for a second. Then it erupted.

"Last calling station, say again what you said about an enemy bus," "How many terrorists are on the bus?" "Did someone say there was more than one bus?" "Say again names of terrorists on the bus?" "Last calling station can you confirm whether there are one or two buses?"

Radio traffic flows just like highway traffic. When too many people try to get on the highway at the same time it creates a traffic jam that eventually brings all traffic to a standstill. When too many people try to talk on their radios at the same time it creates a frequency jam that brings all radio traffic to a halt. To make matters worse, someone was intermittently holding down the push-to-talk button on their radio handset—a phenomenon known as hot mic-ing that jams the entire network. As a result, the communication flow between the AC-130's and the men on the ground was now 100% gridlocked.

All I could do was listen intently for the radio traffic jam to clear up so I could attempt to reestablish contact with Mantis. Unfortunately, in situations such as this everyone else was doing the same thing.

"The busload of terrorists is heading east," the original caller screamed and once again the radio erupted with calls for additional information and clarification. The sound of the caller's voice and the fact he didn't identify himself made me certain the caller wasn't Mantis, but that didn't mean it wasn't someone else on his team who might be in contact with the enemy.

My priority was the safety and security of the assault force so I rescanned every inch of the only two roads leading into the target. I checked both roads out to five kilometers. I found nothing. *"How could a 'busload of terrorists' appear out of nowhere? And how could I have missed it? Stay calm, think."*

"We have visual on enemy busload of terrorists," announced the Weapons Officer over the intercom as he took control of the targeting cameras and aligned the crosshairs center-sector on top of the slow moving bus.

"Enemy busload of terrorists? This doesn't look or sound right?" As much as I had to take it seriously to ensure the safety of the assault force, it was an almost comical description when said out loud (in this case to myself inside my helmet). Why would a bunch of terrorists hop on a bus at 0300 local time instead of dispersing into the hills or the surrounding sea of urban sprawl situated a few hundred meters south of the target? It didn't make sense.

"Prepare to engage," the weapons officer directed as the weapons operator loaded a 105mm round in preparation to fire.

"Ready to fire," alerted the weapons operator.

"Fire," responded the weapons officer.

Boom began the bombardment. Seven seconds after the concussive boom, I watched on my video screens as the round impacted the ground

AC-130H gunship weapons operators, load a 105mm howitzer while flying a close air support mission in support of special operations ground forces somewhere over Afghanistan.[89]

below. In infrared green the earthen upheaval from the impact looked like a large splash of viscous black ink. The round splashed a hundred or so meters off to the left of the still slow-moving bus. The radio gridlock opened up for a split second and the unidentified caller screamed, "we got 'em now." A split second later it was back to gridlock. With these the opening shots fired by American forces after 9/11, it was hard to deny the feeling that the handcuffs were finally off. Most every soldier, sailor, airmen and marine involved in the initial invasion wanted to do something tangible against the enemy that committed the carnage known as 9/11.

Make no mistake about it, I wanted what we were looking at to really be a busload of terrorists too. After all you don't stumble on juicy targets of opportunity like a busload of terrorists very often. However, after too many to count dry holes and/or inaccurate intelligence tips over the past ten years, most of us in the Unit had developed what Einstein described as an "incorruptible sense of skepticism." In this case it was palpable because what I was hearing on the radio and what I was seeing on the ground didn't add up.

Along with my fellow Unit members, we were deployed in combat zones around the world almost continuously during the previous ten years. Experience only matters if you learn from it. Time and feedback teach that "first reports are almost always inaccurate, incomplete, or both," I reminded myself. Why would a bunch of terrorists load a bus? Did anyone actually see a bunch of terrorists get on this bus? If not, what about this bus makes it an "enemy bus"? There are no machine guns mounted on top of it or any enemy flags painted on the side of it. When dealing with uncertainty it's common sense to question everything. Instead of seeing a juicy target of opportunity all I saw was a question mark.

I continued trying to get through to Mantis to make sure he wasn't trying to get through to me. No luck. The chatter was unrelenting.

"Right one hundred," came the corrective command from the weapons officer.

I kept my eyes focused on the bus and my mind focused on the facts: *"I know what I saw and this bus could not have come from the target. So where did it come from? Maybe it came from somewhere else in the city,"* I rationalized, yet the only place we (the U.S.) had surveillance assets focused was the area around the target. *"Maybe the bus was so well camouflaged that none of us spotted it until the helicopters spooked them?"* Whenever you're two or more suppositions deep you're in over your head. No matter how hard I tried I couldn't make sense of it.

"Ready to fire," announced the weapons operator.

"Fire," the weapons officer instantly responded.

This time the round splashed on the ground two to three hundred meters off to the right of the still slow-moving bus.

"Left one hundred," commanded the weapons officer.

"We got it bracketed," someone screamed excitedly as the bus suddenly skidded to an abrupt and angled stop. Seconds of stillness seemed to stretch into minutes. No one jumped out.

"When you're fleeing in a bus that's being bombarded from above and hasn't been hit, why in the world would you slam on the brakes and turn your hard to hit moving target into a sitting duck? What if they ran out of gas or a piece of shrapnel took out the tires? Both are plausible, but neither makes sense of why the terrorists would stay on the bus? What would I do? I'd get off that bus as quickly as possible and run for cover, which there was plenty of on the boulder encrusted hills that surrounded the road. No one got off the bus.

"Ready to fire," the weapons operator responded.

"Fire," the weapons officer commanded.

This time I felt the Boom of the 105mm howitzer reverberate in my stomach and it didn't feel good. From the very first day an operator begins their career at the Unit they're taught that positive identification of the enemy is a non-negotiable prerequisite for any type of kinetic engagement. "Shoot first, ask questions later" only applies to photography. In training, if you inadvertently shot an unarmed or friendly paper target with training ammunition you were admonished on the spot. If it became a pattern over time you were thrown out of the Unit. Killing is easy. Anyone can do it because it only takes one finger—your trigger finger—and you don't need to think about it. Target discrimination is difficult. It takes knowledge, hundreds of hours of practice, and the ability to pay attention to what's going on around you. It takes a thinking brain.

This time, the rounds landed 200 meters behind the bus.

Still no sign of human movement in or around the bus.

"That's strange," the pilot slipped over the intercom. "Strange, indeed," I murmured to myself. To be continued.

REFLECTIONS/LESSON LEARNED
How do our brains make sense of what we perceive?

Perception is the process of distilling sensory information into context-specific knowledge of patterns that make sense to our brains. The biologic way our brains are hardwired to perceive the world is explained by the complimentary principles of contrast and coherence. Contrast occurs when our nervous system perceives a discrepancy between what we know/expect to see (*e.g.* "*no enemy activity around the target*") and the adaptive stimulus of what's going on around us in the context of the moment (e.g. "*Enemy busload of terrorists? This doesn't look or sound right?*"). When our brains perceive a discrepancy we instinctively expend energy to make it cohere[90]. Why is that? What does that mean? How do we make sense of it?

The human eye can detect candlelight in
pitch-blackness up to 50 km away.[91]

Our nervous system is designed to detect contrast in stimulation rather than constancies. Your ability to read the previous sentence is based on the contrast between the dark ink and the white page, if they were both white your brain wouldn't pay attention because your eyes wouldn't perceive contrast on the page.

Likewise, when some of the words in this sent_nce are mi_sing letters our brains unconsciously pay attention to the discrepancy between what we perceive (unusual word patterns) and what we know (spelling patterns for common words) and then instinctively expend energy to make the discrepancy cohere. Your pattern recognizing neurons are doing it for every stroke of every letter you read. Unconsciously contrasting what you see on this page with everything you know—you know a lot—and then effortlessly filling in the blanks based on your deeply hardwired kno_ledge of w_rd patterns. Nicely done.

The term **cognitive consistency** is used to label our biologic need for a consistent, coherent world where things fit together and make sense. When someone screamed "*busload of terrorists,*" what I heard over the radio didn't cohere with what I saw on the ground or what I expected to see based on past experiences. When we find ourselves paying attention to something random and/or have a bad feeling about a situation and we're not sure why, it's likely because our unconscious brain is trying to alert us to a discrepancy. Don't dismiss it, pay attention to it.

It is sheer myth to believe that we need merely observe the circumstances of a situation in order to understand them. **Patterns do not speak for themselves.**[92] Only our neocortex can give them voice by paying attention to and thinking about them. How do we pressure test the patterns we perceive to see if they actually make sense? We use one of our ancient ancestors' most innovative sense-making adaptations: **We say it out loud so we can see.**

The arc of human evolution skyrocketed when our species learned to speak. Saying what we're thinking out loud to ourselves and to others is an evolutionary capacity that enables us to put any situation in context of the moment to see if what we're thinking actually makes sense.

> *"Enemy busload of terrorists?" As much as I had to*
> *take it seriously to ensure the safety of the assault force,*
> *it was an almost comical description when said out*
> *loud (in this case to myself inside my helmet).*

Giving voice to what a person is seeing can change their perception of it. Why is seeing and hearing knowledge critical in learning to adapt to it? We can't fully illuminate our thoughts and ideas unless we translate them to something tangible. Saying what we see, hear, smell, think, or feel out loud makes our thoughts physical. The reason we can record our voices is because sound waves are physically present as compressed air molecules. Although invisible to the naked eye, we can feel air molecules as the wind in our face and as the rock-solid support they provide to the tires on our cars and bikes. By making our thoughts physical we enable additional senses (our own and those around us) to collaborate and pressure test the sense we make.

> *"Why would a bunch of terrorists hop on a bus at 0300 instead of*
> *dispersing into the hills or the surrounding sea of urban sprawl?"*

It's not reality unless it's shared. The brain can only think of one thing at a time, yet our other senses and the senses of the people around us enable us to override this sensory blind spot. When separate elements are seen, heard, and/or felt together we discover patterns and relationships we may have missed when we thought about them one-dimensionally. By enabling our brains to actually hear, see, and feel what we're experiencing, we engage more (sensory) brainpower in analyzing and solving the problem and so gain added insights.[93] The more senses we involve the more sense our individual and collective brains can make.

> *How could a "busload of terrorists" appear out of nowhere?*
> *And how could I have missed it? Stay calm, think.*

What's the secret defense against impulsiveness, as well as psychological paralysis, in life or death situations? Talk to yourself and to those around you. Say what you're thinking and feeling out loud. Remember that your brain is designed to help you survive. A growing body of research has shown that labeling an emotion or describing our feelings with words (*"no need to panic"*) can help to downregulate the affect and change the way we react to similar situations in the future.[94] In their book, *Words Can Change Your Brain*, authors Andrew Newberg, M.D. and Mark Robert Waldman write: "a single word or phrase has the power to influence the expression of genes that regulate physical and emotional stress." *Stay calm, think.*

Freedom of speech is the verbal manifestation of freedom of choice. We choose to speak. Saying what we're thinking and feeling out loud to ourselves and others is how we pressure test what we perceive. It's how we share knowledge. And it's how we build a structurally sound foundation of knowledge to better prepare us for whatever the future throws our way. Say it out loud and you'll see.

> *Instead of technology rendering the need to say*
> *it out loud obsolete it's made it absolute.*

Part II: Twenty-four hours earlier I met with the Captain of the AC-130 and his crew for a pre-mission briefing inside the aircraft while it sat on the blistering hot asphalt tarmac of our desert island staging base. Standard operating procedure for all aircrews before departing on any type of flying mission is to conduct a comprehensive overview of the mission, the purpose, and all relevant operating procedures.

The AC-130 was no stranger to me. My entire military career was threaded by the presence of and coordination with this jack-of-all-missions fire support platform. In addition to coordinating with AC-130's during hundreds of training events I had controlled the AC-130 during ground combat operations in 1989 and 1998, and I had attended and graduated from the U.S. Air Force Air-Ground Operations School in Hurlburt Field, Florida.

When I arrived, the crew were scattered around the inside of the aircraft as they waited for the Captain to begin the briefing. "Right on time," announced the Captain as I climbed into the aircraft from the passenger door located on the starboard (right) side of the craft. After introducing me to the rest of the crew the Captain began his portion of the briefing.

"Our mission tonight is to provide fire support for an air-assault raid on a Taliban-controlled compound located in the outskirts of Kandahar." While he talked he passed out copies of the mission timeline and spoke briefly about the storied history of the AC-130 to include real-world examples of the heroic contributions of its crews. He added a somber reminder. "Despite all of the technological advances it is still a relatively slow-moving aircraft that is susceptible to anti-aircraft fire which has resulted in at least eight AC-130's lost during combat operations since the Vietnam War.

"The weapons and the technology are only as effective as we make them," the Captain continued. "Chaos on the ground combined with chaos in the air, combined with individual issues around comfort and convenience can all combine to kick our butts at any time during the flight. To be successful we have to work together as a team, and the only way we can work together while dispersed around the aircraft is by communicating with each other and sharing information. It starts and ends right here in the cockpit where we verbally narrate and repeat everything we say whether we're talking amongst ourselves or whether we're communicating with each of you. Remember to think about what you are going to say first, then speak clearly and concisely and repeat what you hear to make sure it's what the other person meant."

AC-130 Cockpit crew on the way back from a mission in Afghanistan[95]

The technique used by military air crews to clarify, simplify, and dis-
ambiguate spoken communications over all two-way communication
devices is known as voice procedure. Although most commonly used by
aircrews, the origins of voice procedure comes from the sea where the
safe navigation and survival of all sea faring vessels depended on clear
and concise communication between the helmsman and the officer on
the bridge.

Disambiguation is a critical function of voice procedure. Due to any
number of variables, such as radio static, a chaotic/loud environment,
or the similarity in the sounds of words and numbers, a critical piece
of information can easily be misheard or misunderstood. For instance,
when an air traffic controller tells a pilot to fly at *eleven* thousand feet it
can easily be misunderstood as *seven* thousand feet where, unbeknownst
to the pilot, other aircraft are flying. To reduce ambiguity, all key and
essential information such as the speed and altitude of the aircraft is
always said out loud, spelled phonetically, then repeated (e.g. "Seven, I
spell: Sierra, Echo, Victor, Echo, November, Seven"). As an additional
safety measure the person receiving the communication always repeats
the command, comment, or question.

"Speak clearly and repeat what you hear, okay, guys?" the Captain summarized. "Yes, Sir," the crew responded with credible conviction as they stood up, gathered their stuff, and headed off to their individual workstations to conduct pre-flight checks of their equipment. The Captain motioned for me to follow him outside. Which I did.

"Hey, Sir," he began, "I just want to tell you how glad I am to have someone from the ground tactical unit on board to help me and the crew better understand the mission and what the guys on the target need us to do to support them. None of us have ever supported a real-world raid with friendly forces running around the target so please take everything we just discussed regarding communications to the extreme. You'll be working with the weapons officer in the back of the aircraft but he can get real busy with the gun crews so if you have a question or comment about anything feel free to talk directly to me." He then pointed toward the horizon and said, "the latest weather report says a low pressure system is moving into the target area tonight along with heavy cloud cover, heavy winds, and heavy turbulence which means there's a big storm on the way. It might get a bit choppy back there tonight so stay buckled in and try not to eat a big meal before take-off."

I was totally impressed by the young Captain. Even though he was the most junior person on the aircraft that night (a typical Captain in the Air Force has between three to eight years of service), he had something that many leaders with many more years of experience never "get." He was consciously aware of how much he didn't know. To compensate as a leader he did everything he could to ensure everyone around him understood how essential it was to share information and knowledge.

"Boom, Boom," went the 105mm howitzer as two more rounds blasted out the barrel and blazed earthward at just a smidge under the speed of sound. The rounds exploded on the road a hundred or so meters behind the still stationary bus.

"Add one hundred," was the corrective call from the weapons officer to the crew who rapidly reloaded their now red-hot weapons.

A few seconds after the rounds impacted, a body flew out the right front door of the bus followed immediately by a single-file stampede of human figures that flowed over and around the motionless body on the ground. I counted them as they came out: *two, four, six, ten, twelve, sixteen.* They kept coming. Suddenly the body recovered and stood up. Instead of joining the stampede that was fleeing the bus, the body appeared to be doing everything it could to impede it. To no avail. The fleeing passengers continued to rush right past.

After trying unsuccessfully for what must have been the tenth time to get through to Mantis on the radio, I called our higher headquarters and asked them to relay my questions about the bus, and to let Mantis know what we were doing and why he wasn't hearing from me.

"The platoon of terrorists are fleeing the bus," the original caller screamed over the fire support radio. If saliva could travel with sound waves I'd have been wiping spittle from my ear. The caller's tone was panic-urgent.

"Roger," replied the weapons officer, "we have visual on enemy personnel fleeing the bus."

"That's not how a bunch of terrorists exit a bus that's being bombarded," I injected over the inter-aircraft communications radio. My words announced my entry into the conversation for the first time that night.

"They are walking down the middle of the road not running away," I added while adjusting the IR camera to max zoom. The images weren't much sharper but they were bigger and this allowed me to focus on their shapes, sizes, and behaviors for clues.

"They're staying together not star-bursting or splitting up," I updated a few seconds later.

Once an incident. Twice a coincidence. Three times a pattern. The more I said out loud and described what was happening the more I felt like I was beginning to see.

"Who else would be out at this time of night, Panther?" the weapons officer asked with a hint of frustration.

"Not sure," I replied over the intercom without taking my eyes off my video screens, "but it is Eid[96] so there could be some kind of religious tradition...like our version of Midnight Mass on Christmas," I added. *Metaphor is how we learn about one kind of thing in terms of another.*

At the Unit our intelligence analyst's primary purpose was to make us (the operators) "intelligent." The way they accomplished it was by priming our minds with context-specific knowledge of the people, place, customs, and culture of the country we were deploying to. They were very good at what they did. Although I didn't know enough about Eid to know whether it included something akin to Christian Midnight Mass,

I did know enough to comprehend its cultural significance, and, critically, its potential to influence both the Afghan people's and the enemy's
patterns of activity and behavior.

"Never heard of it," the weapons officer responded.

He might as well have said "snap out of it," because that was the
moment I realized that when it came to understanding what was happening on the ground below, my fellow Air Force crew members weren't
seeing the world through the same context lens as I was. Up until a
month earlier (September 11th, 2001), Afghanistan was likely one of
the most obscure and least understood countries on the planet. Yet we
had been studying it for potential contingency operations since 1998.
The more context-specific knowledge we learn and confirm over time
the sturdier the foundation of knowledge upon which we stand and
the more confident we are in the strength and surety of what we know.
Knowledge of patterns is power, it's also empowering.

"Ready to fire," announced the weapons loader.

"The humans that fled the bus are still staying on the road and
they're still staying together," I injected.

"Fire," commanded the weapons officer.

The rounds landed in almost the exact same spot as those previous. The aircraft's ability to fire its weapons accurately was likely affected
by the heavy winds and turbulence we were experiencing. "I need to
recheck the data on that gun," the weapons officer announced as he
began scouring the reference books spread open in front of him.

"Captain, this is Panther, we have approximately twenty-six, that's
two-six, humans walking down the middle of the road not running…
they are staying together not star-bursting or running for cover behind
the surrounding rocks and trees," I emphasized. *Words matter. When we
think of and refer to people as humans we are far more likely to treat them
humanely.*

"Roger that, Panther," the Captain responded, "I checked with the
pilot on the other AC-130 and he told me the LNO riding in his aircraft
confirmed the target as a 'busload of terrorists.'"

"Did you say the LNO on the other aircraft?" I interrupted. "How
can an enemy target on the ground be confirmed by someone six thousand feet in the air?" A split second after the words left my mouth I
answered my own question. *"It can't."*

"Right one hundred?" the weapons officer ordered in a tone of voice that sounded more like a question than a command.

"Weapons Officer, this is the Captain, stand-by...Panther, can you confirm or deny whether or not the humans on the road are armed combatants?"

Hunching over my monitor with the IR camera on max zoom I strained my eyes and began narrating what I saw: "The humans on the road are still walking, not running...they are still staying together, not star-bursting...they aren't carrying anything on their backs and their hands are holding...standby while I check all of their hands...their hands are holding...other hands...the humans on the road are holding hands with each other, they're noncombatants not enemy."

"Ready to fire," announced the weapons operator.

"Cease fire," the Captain and I countermanded.

"This is the Captain, all stations stand down, I repeat stand down. The LNO is reporting that the humans running down the middle of the road are noncombatants not enemy. We'll replay the videotapes and talk about it tomorrow after we get back, right now we're heading back to the target to cover the exfiltration of the assault force."

For the first time since the helicopters landed, the fire support radio went silent. I was finally able to get through to Mantis. He told me that the target was secure. No enemy had been found on or around the target. And there were no significant injuries to friendly personnel. He also told me that from the moment he landed to the moment of this call he was unable to talk to me or the other AC-130 and had no idea what happened to us. To say that he was pissed off would be an understatement.

We stayed in the air another six hours that night. It was a long tense six hours.[97] There was plenty of second-guessing going on back at HQ. "What if the terrorists were wearing burkas[98] to disguise themselves as women? What if the terrorists were using the woman and children as human shields?" Did we save a bunch of innocent civilians or did we allow some of the world's most wanted terrorists to escape and live to fight another day? No one, including me, knew for sure who was or wasn't on that bus. All I knew for sure was that I did the right thing.

I knew I was going to have to explain the logic of why I called a cease-fire so to help pass time on the long turbulent flight back to base I wrote all my thoughts down in my notebook. Here's what I wrote:

The purpose for which we were up in the air tonight was to provide reconnaissance and fire support for the men on the ground during the raid. An anonymous radio call reported a "busload of terrorists." First reports are almost always either inaccurate, incomplete, or both. There was nothing about that bus that made it "enemy" (e.g. no machine gun turret on top, no flag or external markings, etc.), the only thing that made it suspicious is that it was driving around in the middle of the night which could be related to a major religious holiday. "Shoot first, ask questions later," only applies to photography. Positive identification of the enemy is a prerequisite before firing in any type of engagement. The humans on the bus were walking down the middle of the road not running. They were staying together not star-bursting into the surrounding hills. They weren't holding weapons they were holding hands. Never harm non-combatants.

Whether you are looking at it from a purely altruistic perspective (never harm non-combatants), or from a purely actuarial perspective (don't waste ammo and time chasing a suspected enemy when you may need it later for a confirmed enemy), shooting at any target that you cannot positively identify as an enemy threat simply does not make sense.

Once we were out of enemy airspace the Captain called his counterpart on the other AC-130 and confirmed that it was their LNO, not the men on the ground, who called in "the busload of terrorists" target. "He's a Navy fighter pilot," the Captain added.[99]

"Holy shit, what are they doing putting a Navy pilot on board an Air Force aircraft as a subject matter expert on an Army special operations raid?" the weapons officer asked in disbelief. If the Staff Officer who came up with the idea had said those words out loud before they approved it they likely would have seen how little sense it made and saved themselves from making a near-catastrophic mistake.

"When we say it out loud we make it physical and we can see."

After landing at the crack of dawn, the crew and I immediately headed back to the Tactical Operations Center to watch replays from the gun camera videotapes and hopefully confirm or deny who was really on the bus. It didn't take long. All the large humans had veils/burkas on their heads/bodies, and all the small humans did not (little boys don't wear head gear and little girls don't wear burkas until approximately puberty). Critically, there were no weapons or objects of any kind on any of their bodies or in their hands. "Definitely non-combatants, not enemy," the intelligence analyst confirmed. By reviewing the other AC-130's tapes we were also able to confirm that the bus was over five kilometers away from our target when it was first spotted and misidentified.

Perhaps the biggest insight had to do with the first body thrown off the bus. It was a man. By watching in slow motion we could tell he was doing everything he could to keep the women and children on the bus. Taliban custom forbids a woman from talking back to a man. *The conflicts that cause our brains the most friction are conflicts between what we're ordered/told to do and what the reality of the situation going on around us reveals we should do.*

In the context of the chaotic moment as bombs were blowing up all around them, the woman on the bus had to make a choice. They could either obey the orders from "the man" and stay in their seats as the bombs crept closer to obliterating them, or they could free themselves from the shackles of a senseless man-made-up custom by paying attention to what the situation going on around them was telling them to do instead: *grab their children, get off the bus, and get away as quickly as possible.*

The woman chose the Common Sense Way. Freedom of Choice and Freedom of Speech to make sense of what was going around them and sensible choices based on the purpose and people they were given the privilege to lead. *"Let's do this."*

As it would turn out, they made one of the best survival choices of their lives. By choosing to get off and get away from the bus they provided powerful sensory evidence to our infrared enhanced eyes that enabled us to make sense of what we were seeing and ultimately make sensible choices about what to do next: *"cease fire."* "The choices we make in the context of the moment are the catalysts for Natural Selection."

REFLECTIONS/LESSON LEARNED
How to make sensible choices
in complex unfamiliar situations.

When it comes to making sense of the world around us and sensible choices about what to do next, no system is infallible. It is both a biologic and mathematic fact that our brain's first emotional response to any situation is more likely to be wrong then right. The common sense way changes the game by rewiring the brain with a system of checks and balances against senselessness.

There's no substitute for a prepared mind. In life or death survival situations all we got is what we got. It turns out we got a lot:

The brain makes sensible choices about what to do next by comparing and contrasting sensory inputs from the patterns of life as they're going on around us in the context of the moment, to our foundational knowledge of patterns stored as combinatory codes in the galactic caverns of our memory. From this neural process the logic of why we do what we do and choose what we choose emerges: *"Cease Fire."*

What's going on around us + What we know = Why
we do what we do and choose what we choose.

Note: This is not a real math problem. It's a metaphor for what's actually happening in our brains. Conscious awareness of the process enables us to call on it when needed and to build on it for better choice-making in the future.

The logic of why replaces orders, commands, and provides checks and balances against senseless chains of command. In the pages that follow you'll learn:

1) Where the logic of why comes from.
2) How to ensure the logic of why makes sense.
3) Three benefits of putting the logic of why into practice:
   a) Priming
   b) Persuasion
   c) Checks and Balances against Senselessness

Where does the logic of why come from? The logic of why we do what we do and choose what we choose emerges over time from the relationship of its parts: 1) The patterns of life in the context of the moment + 2) foundational knowledge of patterns = 3) logic of Why

1) The adaptive stimulus of the patterns of life as they're going on around us in the context of the moment:

> *No activity in or around the target; "Busload of terrorists"*
> *called in by an unidentified caller; No information on where*
> *the bus came from; Nothing about the bus makes it enemy;*
> *They're walking on the road not running; They're staying*
> *together not star-bursting; They're holding hands not weapons.*

(+)

2) Our brain's foundational knowledge of patterns stored as combinatory codes in the galactic caverns of our memory. In aggregate everything we've ever learned and who we are:

> *Our mission is to provide fire support to the ground force;*
> *First reports are almost always inaccurate, incomplete, or*
> *both; Positive ID of target as "enemy" is prerequisite before*
> *engaging; Religious holiday; "Never harm non-combatants";*
> *"Do unto others as you'd want them to do unto you."*

(=)

3) The logic of why we do what we do and choose what we choose:

> *"This doesn't look or sound right," "They're non-*
> *combatants, not enemy," "Cease fire."*

Life is complex. It's never just about one thing. Instead it's always about a whole bunch of things. The logic of why emerges over time from the relationship of its parts 1 + 2 = 3. To make sense it has to add up. *"What I heard on the radio and what I saw on the ground didn't add up."*

We can't make sense of anything unless we pay attention to it. The biology of our brains explains it. To pay attention to what's going on around us our neocortex needs a purpose. The logic of why provides our neocortex with the logic of purpose. When striving to understand the choices we make, it's not the choice itself (yes, no, buy, sell, etc.), it's the logic of why we used to make the choice that explains, communicates, and validates whether the choice makes sense or is senseless.

Ancient Greek thinkers developed the concept of logic to describe the process of trying to make sense. They believed that logic and its rules were part of the fabric of the universe. What the Greeks, nor anyone else until the last few decades, had any way to understand is that logic is a verb not a noun. Logic is a neural process by which our neocortex loops together context-specific knowledge of patterns to reveal patterns and relationships that make sense of our experiences (*e.g. dark clouds, heavy winds, pressure drop = big storm is on the way*).

In life or death situations like "identification: friend or foe" how do we ensure the logic of why actually makes sense?

1) First we say it out loud and/or write it down. As discussed in Part I, by saying our thoughts and feelings out loud and/or writing them down we make them physical. The key is to articulate to yourself and others both what you're thinking as well as what you're feeling.[100]

> *"Enemy busload of terrorists? This doesn't look or sound right?"*
> *As much as I had to take it seriously to ensure the safety of*
> *the assault force it was an almost comical description when*
> *said out loud (in this case to myself inside my helmet).*

By saying it out loud and making it physical we enable our brains to reflect on what we're thinking and expose thoughts & emotions that don't make sense—*"enemy busload of terrorists"*—while enlightening our thinking around those that do—*"why would a bunch of terrorists hop on a bus?"* The more senses we involve the more sense our neocortex can make.

2) The second way we make sure the logic of why can support the weight and gravity of the choices we make on it is to ensure it's based on knowledge of three or more context-specific patterns (aka facts we can see, hear, smell, taste, feel with our senses):

"The humans on the road are still walking not running, they are staying together not star-bursting, they aren't carrying anything on their backs and their hands are holding...standby while I check all of their hands...their hands are holding other hands."

Once an incident, twice a coincidence, three times a pattern. Three or more context-specific patterns form the basis or foundation of knowledge upon which the logic of why stands: *"They're noncombatants, not enemy."*

The Rule of three is a universal guiding principle that helps substantiate good reuse. Over time, with feedback, a pattern can be thought of as a foundational pattern if it has been applied to a real world solution at least three times. *"Positive ID of a target as enemy is prerequisite before engaging."* This is where timeless guiding principles come from. Asking "three whys" can help you dive a little deeper and see if you should continue moving forward or if you need to start over from scratch. What's the big deal about three?

Nature loves threes. The most structurally sound self-supporting pattern in nature is the tripod. If what we say or do doesn't have at least three legs to stand on it's probably not standing on solid ground. The reason we can't pivot off falsehoods or lies is because they can't support the weight and gravity of the choices we make on them. To get your point across in a speech or a professional paper you have to provide three supporting facts or assertions; first of all, second of all, and...

Thirdly, we ensure the logic of why speaks the language of our triune brains. The logic of why doesn't tell us what to do or how to choose, it tells our triune brains why something does or doesn't make biologic sense. Motivation is defined as a process that initiates, guides, and maintains purpose-oriented behaviors. Motivation is what causes us to act. In the case of our triune brains our purpose is expressed as a series of goals established by the pleasure and fear centers of our unconscious emotional brain.[101]

All aspects of our nervous system including our senses are calibrated by our emotional brain to detect things that could help us or alert us to things that could bring us harm. To speak the common language of our triune brains the logic of why must cohere the emotion-based goals of our old brain with the reality revealing logic of our neocortex. After all, they are in pursuit of the same thing.

Although our thoughts and emotions directly influence each other through interconnected neural pathways it seems at times like they speak different languages. Trying to describe our feelings with words is like trying to decipher a code or a foreign language. The key to deciphering a code or understanding a foreign language is to find the common ground upon which they stand. The common ground and common language upon which both our emotion and logic-based brains stand is our biologic purpose: to survive, thrive, and evolve. To make sense to our triune brains, the logic of why we do what we do and choose what we choose must cohere with our biologic purpose:

> It will keep you safe and secure (survive), your friends
> and family will respect you (thrive), and it will make your
> community a better place to live in the future (evolve).

When there is coherence within and between our emotion and logic-based brains they interact constructively to expand awareness and permit optimal psychological and physiological functioning.

Three benefits of putting the logic of why into practice

1) **Priming:** Leaders lay the foundation for successful choice-making by priming their people's minds with a foundation of context-specific knowledge of patterns. In aggregate, the logic of why something does or doesn't make sense: *"our purpose is to provide fire-support"to the ground forces," "positive ID of target as enemy is a prerequisite," "never harm non-combatants," "do unto others as you'd want them to do unto you,"* etc.

Priming is an unconscious form of human memory whereby exposure to one stimulus (e.g. a word, guiding principle, or image) influences the way the brain responds to a subsequent stimulus. To see how it works prime your brain by reading the first word in each set below and then filling in the blanks with the missing letter for the words that follow.

Hot So_ p   2) Clean So_ p

You likely chose "u" to make the first word Soup, and "a" to make the second word Soap. What we choose depends on the context lens through which we view it. There's no substitute for the prepared mind. Survival success isn't just about the knowledge we have, it's about our ability to access/call-on that knowledge in the context of the moment when we need it the most.

By priming our minds with context-specific patterns just before carrying out a related action or task we alert specific sections of our brains to get ready, to be prepared, and to expect the possibility of some new or related information that will need immediate matching:

- Combat Leaders prime their teams before every mission: "pay attention to what's going on around you," "keep your head up and eyes open," "don't be in a hurry to die," "positive ID of the target as enemy is prerequisite before engaging," etc.

- Parents prime their children before they walk out the door: "look both ways before you cross the street," "never talk to strangers," "if you get lost stay calm and stay where you are," etc.

- Firefighters prime each other on their way to a wildland fire: "always stay in the black (already burned areas)," "keep the fire in front of you and the wind at your back," "maintain visual contact with the man to your left and right," etc.

Top of mind is why we prime

2) Persuasion: Persuasion is the centerpiece of all social and business activity. If you want to persuade yourself or someone else to do something for or with you, you have to speak the language of our triune brains by saying out loud the logic of why it does or doesn't make sense.

In the context of the chaotic moment outside Kandahar, as bombs were bursting all around them, one or more women likely chose to speak up: "if we don't get off this bus right now we're all going to die" (survive), "we shouldn't listen to what 'the man' is saying because the man doesn't care about us" (thrive), "now let's grab our children, get off this bus, and get away" (evolve).

If you are trying to persuade someone of the validity of an idea you have to explain the logic of why it makes more sense than the status quo or other competing ideas. The person who can formulate and communicate the sturdiest logic of why almost always wins.[102]

- If you want a job, you have to explain the logic of why it makes sense to hire you: your experience, proven track record of success, the benefit you'll bring to the hiring manager and the organization, etc.

- If you want to persuade customers to use/buy your company's products or services you have to explain the logic of why it makes sense to them: it makes them look and feel better, it's safer, cooler, higher quality, sleeker design, longer lasting, has a money back guarantee, etc.

- If you want your teammates to go along with a new way of operating or a reorganization you have to explain the logic of why it does or doesn't make sense to them: "it's based on your feedback," "it will improve productivity and profits," "and if it doesn't work we'll keep changing until it does," etc.

The logic of why is the time-tested common language of our triune brains. Great coaches, commanders, CEO's and parents intuitively understand its *persuasive power.*

3) Checks and Balances against senselessness: The logic of why provides a built in system of checks and balances that help expose misguided commands, orders, and choices before they see the light of senselessness.

- Saying the logic of why out loud is one of the most effective safeguards against senselessness. When a leader issues an order, command, or decision directive, they must say out loud the logic of why the order, command, or decision makes sense to the person/people who receive it.

- If a leader issues an order, command, or directive that doesn't make sense ("let's chase after that bus") then subordinates are encouraged to ask, "how does 'chasing after the bus' cohere with our purpose and adapt to what's going on around us?"

- Leaders who care about their people say out loud the logic of why their orders, plans, and directives do or don't make sense. It's also what good parents do. Think about how you talk to your people and how your boss talks to you. When leaders don't explain the logic of why (e.g. "because I said so," "just do it," or they relay their orders through subordinates and emails) it's either because they never learned how to lead the Common Sense Way or because they don't care about their people.

Ironically, the biggest benefactor of implementing the logic of why standard may be the leaders themselves. When leaders say the logic of why out loud you will be amazed at how many orders, directives, and choices will never see the light of senselessness. If I had asked out loud "what's the logic of why we are chasing this bus?" It would have only taken a couple of seconds of thinking out loud to reveal: 1) we were no longer providing fire support for the ground forces (our purpose), 2) we never confirmed the identification of the caller, 3) there was nothing about the bus that made it an enemy bus or a threat to us.

Technology hasn't made saying the logic of why
out loud obsolete, it's made it absolute.

CHAPTER 5 SUMMARY OF KEY CONCEPTS

- Our nervous system is designed to detect contrast in stimulation rather than to detect constancies.
- The term **cognitive consistency** is used to label our biologic need for a consistent, coherent world where things fit together and make sense.
- **Patterns do not speak for themselves.** Only our neocortex can give them voice by paying attention to and thinking about them.
- **The arc of human evolution skyrocketed when humans learned to speak.**
- **Saying what we're thinking out loud** to ourselves and to others is an evolutionary capacity that enables us to put any situation in context of the moment to see if what we're thinking actually makes sense.
- **It's not reality unless it's shared.** The more senses we involve the more sense our individual and collective brains can make.

- **To make sense of any situation** in life whether simple or complex **our neocortex needs a purpose.**

- **The logic of why provides our neocortex with the logic of purpose,** it informs why we do what we do and why we choose what we choose.

- What's going on around us + What we know = The logic of why we do what we do and choose what we choose.

- Three ways to pressure test the logic of why:
  - ► **Say it out loud** or write it down so our other senses and those of the people around us can see.
  - ► **Ensure it's based on three or more context-specific patterns** that we can see, hear, smell, taste, touch and make sense of.
  - ► **Ensure it coheres with our biologic purpose (survive, thrive, evolve),** and adapts to what's going on around us otherwise it can't and won't ever make biologic sense.

- Three benefits of putting the logic of why into practice:
  - ► **Priming:** Leaders lay the foundation for successful choice-making by priming their brains with a common foundation of context-specific knowledge and principles. In aggregate, the logic of why something does or doesn't make sense. Top of mind is why you prime.
  - ► **Persuasion:** If you want to persuade yourself or someone else to do something for or with you, you have to speak the language of our triune brains by saying out loud the logic of why it does or doesn't make sense. Firstly, secondly, thirdly….
  - ► **Checks and Balances against senselessness:** The logic of why provides a built in system of checks and balances that help expose misguided commands, orders, and choices before they see the light of senselessness. Instead of technology rendering the need to say it out loud obsolete it's made it absolute.

CHAPTER 6

Freedom of Choice to Learn

How to Go With the FLOW

"The art of Command is the ability to improvise," SLA Marshall.
There are hunters and there are the hunted. Be a hunter.

How would you organize if you had no guidance for how to organize? When I first got on the ground in Afghanistan during the winter of 2001–2002 we had no orders, no plans, and no on-the-ground chains of command. The rapid defeat and retreat of the Taliban and their foreign-fighter allies had overrun the Pentagon's time-phased plan while our ongoing pursuit of the enemy had outrun the electronic tentacles of our out of country chains of command.

Since the character of the war yet to come was still unknown the various special mission units on the ground were free to self-organize and operate in ways that did not necessarily reflect their usual doctrinal or departmental divisions. Instead of following plans from the past that fly in the face of facts and forfeit our freedom to affect the future we did the same thing explorers, inventors, and entrepreneurs have done throughout the ages when faced with similar circumstances. We used common sense and developed the situation.[103]

"A-F-O" teams, as we called them, were frequently formed and reformed around a mix of my colleagues from the Unit, as well as Green Berets, Air Force CCT, Navy SEALs, Afghan Freedom Fighters, and Intelligence personnel from Other Government Agencies. A-F-O stood

143

for Advanced Force Operations. More of a verb than a noun, before Afghanistan AFO described what small special operations teams were supposed to do in preparation for potential future missions and follow-on forces.

"Get some men out into the frontier to figure out what's going on, find the enemy then kill or capture them," the Commanding General of all U.S. forces in Afghanistan told me in early January when he flew in to Bagram Air Base (See map). More than anything else AFO was a learning organization. If your purpose is to learn then it makes sense to lead and organize your teams to accomplish that purpose. To find and destroy a fleeing enemy you have to learn where they're located first. When the environment you're focused on consists of 645,000 sq. miles of unfamiliar mountains, rural hamlets, and diverse populations of people, it takes time and context-specific experience to learn.

Although AFO started out with only about forty-five men on the ground, these were forty-five of the most highly trained and experienced operators from some of the world's most elite units. There were no templates or SOPs driving the composition and/or location of the

"Successful Commanders make plans to fit the circumstances but do not try to create circumstances to fit plans," Patton.

teams. Instead of trying to predict the future we focused our energies on learning from, adapting to, and interacting with the present so we could influence the future as it unfolded in front of us. DTS.

To stay on the path of the fleeing enemy, AFO had to be nimble which meant picking up and moving to new locations whenever the enemy situation dictated. One of the side effects of AFO's nomadic always on the move lifestyle was that the teams were almost always short on food, fresh water, batteries, and basic comfort items, such as soap, toilet paper, and extra clothes. The teams were isolated from each other and hundreds of miles away from the nearest resupply and reinforcements. Yet I never heard a single one of them complain about any of those things.

This was what we trained our entire professional lives to do. Our purpose made sense and we had the operational freedom to accomplish it. When you have both you have everything you need. Never underestimate the power and potential of a small group of highly trained and motivated individuals who are free to accomplish their purpose and couldn't care less about getting credit for it.

We were five: me, a fellow Unit member, a special operations mechanic, a military contractor who worked for an Other Government Agency, and our Afghan-American cultural advisor. On this day we were driving through the sign-less streets of Kandahar on our way to

Kandahar Province, Afghanistan[104]

link up with some of our AFO teammates who were setting up a new base of operations located in a former Taliban leader's residence on the north side of town. We planned to check out the sight of the bus bombardment on our way back.

The vehicle we were driving in was a white Toyota Land Cruiser with off-road package, specially modified suspension, and low-vis satellite antenna for always-on connectivity. While Toyota SUVs and pickups were one of the most common vehicles seen around Afghanistan they still turned heads and drew attention in cities such as Kandahar where vehicle ownership was limited to those who worked directly for the Taliban and/or the wealthy.

As mentioned in the previous chapter, Kandahar was the Taliban capital from 1996 to December of 2001. During that period it was also home to a virtual who's who of the world's most wanted terrorists including Mullah Omar, Osama Bin Laden, Abu Zarqawi, and all of their most trusted subordinates, staffs, and family members. The swiftness of the Taliban's downfall and retreat was physically apparent by their abandoned homes, headquarters, and ransacked offices. What wasn't so apparent was how the people of Kandahar felt about it.

The sky was dark and cloudy, the temperature was in the low 40's, and a light drizzle floated in the air. Although unusually blustery for Kandahar (it's normally sunny and temperate), the rainy weather was what most every Afghan had been wishing and waiting for during the previous four years of drought. It had rained heavily the night before

Afghans driving a Toyota Land Cruiser

and we were told by one of our sources that the citizens of Kandahar were dancing in the streets to celebrate. The clouds parted and it stopped raining a few minutes after we entered the city.

Up ahead, two bodies bedecked in blue burkas walked solemnly down the right side of the street. Dave (the driver) slowed the vehicle ever so slightly so we could inspect. Just a few weeks earlier we were the ones trying on burkas as potential disguises for infiltrating Taliban controlled cities and towns. We watched their svelte figures warily.

If an Afghan woman left her house every inch of her body had to be covered with a burka, a long, loose-fitting garment usually blue in color that covers a woman's entire body from head to feet. A dark mesh strip enables the woman to see where she's going without anyone seeing who she is. Taliban law banned women from going to school, reading books, speaking out loud, getting a job, or accessing healthcare. Before the Soviet Union invaded in the late 70's women made up over 50% of Afghanistan's teachers and healthcare workers. After Taliban law was implemented (around 1996) women became prisoners in their own homes and were essentially made invisible in public life. Violators were flogged, beaten, or stoned to death.

"Those are definitely woman, no doubt," Dave (the driver) mumbled. Seconds after the words left his mouth the woman in the blue

Photo of Two Women wearing Burkas

burka closest to the road stopped and lifted up her facial veil to flash what looked to me like an appreciative and proud smile. Like a bunch of tourists seeing some sort of sacred sight for the first time, we were acutely aware of both the significance and sensitivity of what we were witnessing. I smiled back and tried not to stare.

She wasn't anything like I might have imagined if I had ever imagined what an Afghan woman wearing a burka actually looked like before that moment. "Happy," "hard-living," and "naturally pretty" was how the guys in the back seat would later describe her. By choosing to defy Taliban law and show us her smiling face she showed us who she really was—a person—and she showed us how she felt about being free. Saying it out loud enabled us to see.

"Activity, five o'clock," alerted Hammer who was sitting behind me in the back right seat. A tall, wiry Texan in his late 30's, Hammer was a sniper/reconnaissance expert who was best known for being both a great shooter and a great stalker (he could sneak up on anything). He and I had served together in Bosnia during multiple capture operations. He was always dialed in, always calm, and like a lot of the senior operators at the Unit, always logical. I probably wouldn't have agreed to drive through Kandahar that day if he wasn't with us. **Bravery has a lot to do with the company you keep.**

From my position in the front passenger seat, I watched through my side-view mirror as a bearded old man dressed in a dish-dash and turban bolted across the street behind our vehicle while waving his arms high above his head and screaming something in Pashtu.[105]

"What is he saying, Ali?" I asked our Afghan-American cultural advisor who was sitting in the middle of the back seat. A fit-looking fifty-something with a close-cropped carpet of thick, salt-and-pepper hair, Ali was on an extended sabbatical from his job as a Wall Street stockbroker. A few days after 9/11 he volunteered his services by calling a friend in the federal government and telling him he wanted to "pay back his new country by volunteering to help out his old one." Ali was our eyes, ears, and voice, and one of the unsung heroes of those early weeks and months in Afghanistan.

Ali leaned forward to respond to my question, but before he could tell me what the old guy was saying he screamed "look out" while pointing straight ahead at a massive Jinga truck that was barreling down the middle of the road on a head-on collision course with our vehicle. My head whiplashed left then back right as Dave executed a picture-perfect defensive driving maneuver. Zigging the steering wheel an inch to the right at the last second to avoid the Jinga truck and then immediately zagging it an inch back to the left to avoid over-correcting and going off the road into a drainage trench.

"Holy shit that was close," someone in the backseat said. "Good job, Dave," someone else added.

BOOM.

"Fuck," times five we shouted as a loud explosion under the front of the vehicle shocked the awe out of all of us. The vehicle was wobbling but still road-worthy and moving forward.

"Guns up," Hammer narrated calmly from the back seat as each of us swung our weapons out our already opened windows. All senses scanning in search of enemy signs.

"Front left tire is gone, we're riding on the rim" Dave updated while pulling off the road into a grove of dead-looking fruit trees.

"Can't tell the extent of damage until I get the wheel off and look under the vehicle," Dave whispered loudly while reaching under his seat for the lug wrench.

"Sounds good, Dave, the rest of us will pull security," I announced.

"Okay, guys, let's set up a security perimeter around the vehicle." "Clock sectors stay the same, stay close to the vehicle and maintain visual contact with each other," Hammer added.

"Let's do a radio check on AFO command frequency before we move out," I whispered loudly over my shoulder as I slinked out the right front door of the vehicle slow and low. "And watch out for mines," I added over the radio as I planted each of my feet with the precision of a paranoid tightrope walker. The street was empty. The two women in burkas and the old man were gone. So too was our brief foray into normalcy.

Disguises, deception, and diversions was the way we described the tools of the ambush trade. We spent a significant amount of our deployment time over the past five years designing and detecting ambushes. The burka women, the old man screaming, and the near head-on collision with a speeding Jinga truck, this one seemed to have all three.

When your survival is on the line it's far better to take the extra time and effort to learn whether the unusual sound in the bushes is a predator than to dismiss it as a random rustle of leaves. *Freedom of choice is about time. Don't be in a hurry to die. Take time to pay attention to what you're experiencing.* This is how we trained our brains to survive in combat zones. It's not paranoia it's common sense.

Silence serenaded the situation. The baritone thumping of a heavy machine-gun broke it. "Contact," Hammer announced over the radio. "Possible enemy machine gun fire two o'clock," he added. Unaware of it at the time, his initial description would heavily influence both our decision-making and our destiny.

"Get down and get cover," were the last wizened words I heard from Dave as he scurried toward the trunk of nearby tree. I called our higher headquarters on the satellite radio to give them a situation report (sit-rep), "We're taking possible enemy machine gun fire vicinity grid one-two-three-four-five-six[106]…our vehicle is currently disabled, request surveillance and reconnaissance aircraft as soon as possible, over."

"Roger," responded the radio operator at HQ, "we have an unarmed Predator (pilotless drone) inbound to your location at this time, estimated time of arrival is three minutes, keep us updated on the vehicle." "Roger, Panther out."

AFO Safe-house, Eastern outskirts of Kandahar: Earlier that day we gathered together for our pre-mission prep brief in the back yard of one of our safe-houses located a couple of kilometers east of Kandahar.

Predator/Pilotless Drone Flying over Afghanistan

Surrounded on three sides by desert, it was a medium-sized (roughly 2,500 square feet), white, single story, adobe-style home with a massive backyard and a seven-foot-high stone wall that enclosed the entire compound.

The first priority of all leaders whether it's the first day on the job or the first day of coming together as a team is to loop their people together with a **common sense of shared purpose.** That's how we ended up in Kandahar that day. We were driving around the country to get all of our AFO teams looped together on the same sheet of music with regards to our purpose and how we should accomplish it.

Besides being from different branches of the government and different units in the military, every AFO team had a different environment they had to adapt to (e.g. different ethnic and tribal affiliations of the people, different terrain and weather, and most importantly different enemy situations). *How would you organize if no one told you how to organize?* When you organize to learn you learn how to organize. The way we learned to organize was to stay small and build learning-feedback loops not hierarchical ladders (build loops not ladders).

All living systems learn based on feedback from their environments. Organizations that share the knowledge they learn (e.g. about the people, places, and the purpose they are trying to achieve) are more adaptable and successful than those organizations where knowledge is stove-piped up and down the hierarchical chain of command. Learned knowledge of patterns provides our brains with common options, and common options provide us with freedom to choose between them based on the adaptive stimulus of what's going on around each of us (e.g. different terrain, weather, tribal affiliations, and different enemy).

We are one and we are one of many. Sharing the knowledge and options we learned over time enabled all five teams to evolve to higher levels of organizational behavior. Combat experience only matters if we learn from it. To operate in the five different areas of the country (see map) where we believed we had the best chance of finding the enemy and accomplishing our purpose we learned it made sense to stay small, stay decentralized, and stay looped together.

It's easy to understand why leaders of large hierarchical organizations such as the military are skeptical of decentralization. Even though decentralization enables individual teams in an organization like AFO

In January-February of 2002 we had AFO teams in five locations:
Kandahar x 2, Orgun, Khowst, and Gardez.

to learn from, adapt to, and interact with a much larger environment, decentralization also makes it more difficult for large hierarchical organizations to coordinate and control their teams efforts. Why is that? The reason isn't because of some inherent flaw with decentralization as a principle, instead the flaw is found in the way large hierarchical organizations are taught to lead and organize decentralized teams.

When decentralized teams are commanded and controlled by centralized hierarchies the knowledge learned by the teams is sent up their dotted-line ladders for stowage in the collective memory (neural and electronic) of their commanders and staff at each different level of the hierarchy. When the teams need to take action on the same or related knowledge the hierarchical decision-making process requires approval from the same collective memory. *"Tell me again who this guy is?" "Can you put your request onto a power point presentation and run it by us on tomorrows VTC?"*[107] *"The Commander needs to approve this and he's sleeping right now, can you call back when he wakes up?"*

In combat opportunity doesn't knock often. When it does it usually runs away as fast as possible so you have to be ready to give immediate chase. If you want to be nimble you have to be quick. As we'd learn over and over in the years that followed, the amount of time it takes to get permission from a VTC-obsessed hierarchy is more than enough time to allow opportunity to slip away, over and over, again and again. *The strength and power of the chain resides in the brains it constrains. When the success or failure of the mission and the survival of the men are hanging in the balance, it makes sense to unleash the power of your brains.*

To truly unleash the power of our decentralized brains, leaders must realize that the collective intelligence an organization needs to succeed is contained everywhere within it. Intelligence has no hierarchy. The knowledge an operator on the ground in Afghanistan needs and the knowledge their Commanding General at Army Headquarters in Tampa, Florida needs can't be segregated. But it can be combined. Centralization is not the answer. **Aggregation is.**

"A decentralized system can only produce genuinely intelligent results if there's a means of aggregating the information of everyone in the system. Without such a means, there's no reason to think that decentralization will produce a better, smarter result." John Surowicki author "Wisdom of the Crowds"

To aggregate the knowledge each of the teams were learning and make it available to all the other teams across the country and across time we borrowed a technique that one of our senior operators, code-named Iron-head, came up with on a previous mission in the Balkans. To ensure continuity of knowledge amongst geographically decentralized teams, many of who were rotating in and out of country every 90 days, Iron-head created a document he called the depository of knowledge. The bedrock of the document was our purpose as outlined by the United Nations and NATO: to locate and capture persons indicted for war crimes. It also included our Unit guiding principles and all the key context-specific knowledge we had learned about the people, the history, the terrain, and the specific war criminals we were focused on capturing at the time.

We implemented the same process for AFO. As mentioned in my first book, instead of calling it the depository of knowledge we called it our foundational logic. We memorialized our foundational logic on

Enemy Sentry in Mountains near Shahi Khot, Afghanistan[108]

a single sheet of paper and marked it "need to share" as required reading for every member of AFO whenever they arrived in country and/ or whenever we conducted mission briefings. To keep our foundational logic updated with the fire-hose of new knowledge we were learning on the Afghan frontier each day, we added the AFO situation report.

The AFO situation report began as a secure communication process we used each night to aggregate and share raw intelligence amongst our five teams. If a team had nothing to report they reported nothing. We didn't have to ride herd over the teams to get them to share information. The process was self-perpetuating. It immediately proved beneficial as a way to rapidly connect the raw intelligence dots that each team was learning from their Afghan sources and from their experiences each day. *"Patterns emerge from the relationship of their parts, patterns combine to make sense, and patterns repeat."*

Our job at AFO Headquarters was to aggregate the knowledge they learned into a summary document—the AFO Sit-rep—which we then sent back out to each of our teams and to every other military unit in Afghanistan (including our Special Operations allies from other NATO countries). We later learned it was the first thing the Commanding General back in Tampa, Florida would read each morning when he arrived at work. Learning-Feedback loops get stronger as they get longer.

To lay the foundation for successful choice making, common sense leaders don't tell their people what to do or how to choose. Instead they prime their people's minds by saying out loud and sharing their common purpose along with all the context-specific knowledge of patterns and principles they've learned to accomplish it. In aggregate: the foundational logic of why they do what they do and choose what they choose.

"Okay, guys, this is our pre-mission prep brief," I explained to the team who were sitting on, and standing around, our Toyota Land Cruiser which was parked in the wall-enclosed backyard of our safehouse. "Since most of us have never worked together and none of us have ever driven around Afghanistan in an SUV together, I'm going to go over a few things to make sure we're all on the same sheet of music regarding our purpose and then I'll turn it over to Hammer who will go over our drive today and how we're going to accomplish it.

"Although we're all from different organizations and units we're all here for the same overall purpose: To 'deny enemy (Al Qaeda) sanctuary in Afghanistan.' To accomplish our overall purpose the Commanding General tasked AFO to: 'Get some men out into the frontier to figure out what's going on, find the enemy then kill or capture them.'[109]

"Which brings us back to today. The purpose of our mission today is to drive to and coordinate with the AFO team located at our newest safe house on the north side of Kandahar. Although some of us have landed on it and some of us have flown over it, none of us have ever driven to it so it's unchartered terrain for all of us. Other than a few Special Forces guys, no westerners have driven through Kandahar since the late 70's so our Intelligence analysts have asked us to pay close attention to the people, the terrain, the infrastructure, and the mine-fields.

"As important as it is to understand what our purpose is it's also important to understand what it's not. We aren't actively patrolling or looking to get into a fire-fight which is why we're driving in a low-vis Toyota Land Cruiser instead of an armored Humvee. Most of the people in Kandahar have never seen westerners before so the way we interact with them today could heavily influence the way they think about our teams who will be living and operating here in the future. We have to maintain a low profile but that doesn't mean low-class. Remember to be respectful, be polite, and be adaptive. We can never win in Afghanistan if we lose the hearts and minds.[110]

"If there are no questions I'm going to turn it over to Hammer who'll go over our drive through Kandahar today."

"Thanks, Panther," Hammer responded as he began his portion of the briefing.

"This is a forty-mile drive today and even though our intent is to stay low-vis and not draw any unwanted attention to ourselves there's always the possibility that we could inadvertently drive into the shit. The best way to prevent driving into an enemy ambush or I-E-D (Improvised Explosive Device) is to detect it and avoid it before it happens. Keep your heads up and eyes open at all times. If you've ever seen a house cat looking and listening for mice in a field it's a good image to think about whenever you need to focus your senses and pay extra-close attention to what's going on around you. If we all stay alert, we all stay alive," Hammer emphasized.

Hammer taught me the pay attention like a cat technique many years earlier while he and I were searching for a war criminal who often used disguises to elude capture. I've used the technique ever since to listen better, to write better, to learn better, and to choose better. No one told Hammer to share the pay attention like a cat technique with the team that day. Everything he told them he told them because he cared. *The value of what we give or what we get from any human interaction depends on the knowledge our brains learn from it.*

"Wherever you sit in the vehicle determines your clock direction of responsibility with twelve o'clock always in the middle of the front windshield," Hammer continued. "Panther is sitting in the front passenger seat so he has responsibility for covering the ten o'clock to two o'clock sector, I'm sitting behind Panther in back right seat so I have two o'clock to six o'clock sector, Rich, you'll be sitting in the back left seat so your sector of responsibility is six o'clock to ten o'clock. Ali, since you're sitting in the back middle seat, you're free to focus on whatever you and Panther think is most important. You guys probably noticed I skipped Dave (the driver)."

Hammer paused while he placed his hand on Dave's shoulder. Dave was a Special Operations mechanic. Born and raised in Michigan he was about six feet tall with receding blonde hair, a thick grizzled beard, and a quiet accommodating demeanor. Dave grew up building and racing stock cars which made him both a great mechanic and one of our best combat drivers. "Dave is the driver," Hammer emphasized. "The reason Dave doesn't pull security is because the driver only has one job. He drives. As the driver he holds all of our lives in his hands. Which is why you'll never see Dave take his two hands off the steering wheel. If the enemy starts shooting at us Dave won't be shooting back and that's where the rest of us come in.

"Panther mentioned earlier that none of us have ever worked or driven around in an SUV together but even if we had we'd still go over 'actions on enemy contact' which is a time-tested Army 'battle drill' that's as useful today as it was when they came up with it after Vietnam. It's also easy to remember with three simple steps: Deploy, Suppress, and Report." Here's how he explained it:

"**Deploy:** If we drive into an ambush our first priority is to immediately drive out of the ambush. If our vehicle can't get out of the kill zone then get out of the vehicle and **Get Down** preferably behind or under cover.

"**Suppress:** If the enemy fire is effective and we can identify where it's coming from then we'll use whatever firepower is appropriate to suppress it. Time is of the essence when it comes to suppressing effective enemy fire, so remember that unarmored windows like ours are both see-through and shoot-through. If the windows are up and you need to get a quick shot off then treat the windows like they're not even there. Whether inside the vehicle or out don't shoot unless you have something to shoot at otherwise you're just telling the enemy where you are and wasting ammunition.

"**Report:** Communication of information is our life-blood in any type of contingency. To stay alive we have to keep the communication flowing. So while one of us gets on the radio and sends a situation report back to higher headquarters the rest of us should be communicating everything we see and hear to everyone else around us. Remember to stay calm and think about what you are saying. If something doesn't look or sound right to you, or you have a different take on what someone else is seeing, you have to speak up."

After Hammer finished discussing "actions on enemy contact," Dave (the driver) began his portion of the briefing by going over our primary and alternate routes which he had highlighted on an acetated 1:50,000 Russian map. Dave began by pointing out that we were "driving around in a country that had no road maintenance, no signs, no painted lines, no lights, no laws, and no cops to enforce the no laws." Yet as we'd all seen over the previous weeks, and as Hammer and I experienced in the early days of Bosnia, when every other part of a society is broken down, for some reason driving still works. Why is that?

Every operator goes through defensive driving school upon entry into the Unit and one of the foundational principles the instructors drill into every student's head regarding driving is: "When in doubt, go with the flow." Whether you find yourself in a country where you're unsure of the traffic laws, or a country where there are no traffic laws, use common sense and go with the flow. How do we go with the flow while driving?

Simply pay attention to what's going on around you and drive in the same general direction and speed as the other vehicles while maintaining a safe comfortable distance from the vehicles in front of and to the sides of you. If you need to pass, merge, change lanes, or turn, communicate the same way the people around you do (e.g. blinkers, horn, hand and arm signals, or flashing headlights, etc.). And finally, follow the Golden Rule: Do unto others as you'd want them to do unto you. Reciprocity is the currency of human interaction. You get what you give in life so make sure you treat your fellow drivers the same way you'd want them to treat you, with courtesy and respect. *When in doubt go with the flow.*

On every mission in every country we worked in during the 90's (e.g. Lebanon, Panama, Colombia, Somalia, Bosnia, etc.), driving played a significant role in both our survival and our success. For too many of my fellow Unit members to count, the dangers of driving had also taken a significant physical toll. The dangers of driving stay with us whether we're driving to learn about a target, driving to follow a target, or driving home to see our families. Driving is a mission critical survival skill that should be prioritized accordingly. (Note: During the U.S. Military's first two years in Afghanistan (2001–2003), more soldiers were killed while driving vehicles back in the U.S. than were killed by enemy fire in combat.)

Dave concluded his portion of the briefing by doing a walk-through talk-through of the entire vehicle during which he went over how to operate all controls, latches, and special equipment. He also made sure everyone knew what contingency supplies we were carrying in the back: an advanced trauma first aid kit, a full-size spare, two jacks, four extra quarts of oil, five gallons of gas, five gallons of water, two rolls of duct tape, 5,000 rounds of 5.56 ammo, and a tool kit.

After Dave finished he turned it back over to me so I could "say a few words about the Rules of Engagement (ROE)."[111] The official R-O-E Annex during those first few weeks and months in Afghanistan was six pages long but could be summed up in two words: Reciprocal R-O-E.

"Reciprocal R-O-E means we're authorized to respond to any threat based on discrimination and proportionality. We discriminate whether it's a friend or foe, threat or not, risk vs. gain, and we respond proportionally. We don't shoot at anything we can't positively ID as enemy, we don't chase after a kid who throws a rock at us, and we don't wave at a terrorist that shoots at us. Understand what's going on around you and respond with discrimination and proportionally," I emphasized.

"How do we know who's enemy and who's not?" Rich, the military contractor who worked for an Other Government Agency, interrupted and then added, "So far they all look the same to me." With the AC-130 incident still top of mind here's how I responded: "when the shit hits the fan you can count on three constants: chaos, complexity, and confusion. Whether you live or whether you die depends on your ability to make sense of what you're experiencing so take a deep breath, stay calm, and remind yourself that: first reports are almost always inaccurate, incomplete, or both; positive identification of any target as 'enemy' is a prerequisite before engaging; never harm non-combatants; do unto others as you'd want them to do unto you; and finally say it out loud so you can see. You may be the only one who does or doesn't see the enemy so speak up."

"Okay, guys, that wraps up our pre-mission prep brief," Hammer announced. "Let's grab our radios and do a final commo check, then lock and load our weapons and get ready to roll out of here in ten minutes."

Back to the Ambush: Figuring out what action you should take when under fire depends on the location and effectiveness of the fire you are receiving. Determining the exact location of machine gun fire in a city is difficult due to the urban terrain induced echo. After the first couple of minutes we could tell the direction of fire (southeast) and the rate of fire (around 500 rounds per minute), however, even though we could hear the bullets whizzing overhead there was no sonic crack which meant the bullets were flying at least 25–50 feet above us. Whether wishful thinking or experience based skepticism it just didn't add up.

The street we were on was a hard-packed dirt road. Small, one and two-story box-shaped homes with six to eight foot high walls around them lined the road on both sides. There was no vegetation, no birds or animals, and thanks to the machine gun fire, no human activity.

My radio cracked to life so I pressed my headset close to my ear to hear what our higher HQ was saying. "The Predator has positive ID of the target at grid coordinates one-two-three-four-five-six-seven-eight,[112] approximately four to five enemy personnel on top of a building firing a large caliber weapon." The target description was based on what the fire support and intelligence officers were seeing as they watched the Predator's live video down-link from their desert island command center located over 300 miles away.

Hammer and I plotted the target grid coordinates on our 1:50,000 maps. Hammer plotted quicker and shared his thoughts over the radio: "the location of the machine gun is one and a half kilometers (1,500 meters) away…there's no way they can see us, which means they're either trying to get us to shoot back so we give our position away, or they're shooting at someone else."

"Let's give 'em a taste of their own medicine," Rich, the military contractor, yelled out. "I'm going to lob a few forty millimeter rounds in the general direction to see if that has any effect on them."

"Don't waste your ammo," Hammer yelled back.

"I got plenty of ammo to waste," Rich responded as he flipped open the leaf sight on his M203 grenade launcher in preparation to fire.

"Hold your fire," Hammer reiterated over the radio as Rich shook his head in frustration. Just then Dave (the driver) gave an update over the radio: "looks like the blow-out was caused by a defective rim not a spike strip or I-E-D…we should be ready to go in two minutes."

"Roger, the rest of us will be standing by," I replied.

I looked across the street and saw Ali our Afghan-American advisor talking to a young boy with a dirty face and tattered clothes. The boy was standing in the doorway of a house that was located a few feet from the tree Ali was kneeling behind. Ali waved at me when he saw I was looking at him then sprinted to the back of our vehicle where Hammer was kneeling, so he was close enough to tell both of us what he learned.

"I asked that boy if the old man who ran across the street screaming was Taliban and he said, 'No, the rain last night prevent the old man
from crossing the river where he normally does so he had to go the long
way, and that made him late for the Jinga bus he takes to Pakistan every
week.'"

"We have two F-16's on station with two each 500-pound laser
guided bombs," the fire support officer back at HQ announced on the
radio.

"Both aircraft have laser lock on target at this time and are ready to
engage on your command," he added with urgency.

"This is Panther, tell the aircraft to Standby," I responded with equal
urgency. "Roger, they'll be standing by when you're ready," the fire support officer replied.

I locked eyes with Hammer and mouthed the question "What's your
recommendation?" He shook his head horizontal and responded over
the radio to ensure everyone could hear: "the two women in burkas were
just walking down the street and happy to see us, the old man was chasing a bus that almost ran us off the road, the flat tire was a blowout, the
machine gun fire is ineffective, and we're in a city packed with civilians,
if we apply the Rules of Engagement we discussed back at the safe-house
there's no way we can approve the drop." *Patterns combine to make sense.*

"Roger," I responded followed by two clicks of the radio handset.

Dave turned the vehicle around and gave the thumbs up signal to
let everyone know the vehicle was good to go and ready for exfil. While
the rest of the team took a knee around the vehicle, I called our higher
HQ and told them: *"We cannot positively ID the target as enemy so the
F-16's are 'not cleared,' I say again 'not cleared' to engage the target."* I then
requested the aircraft "stay on station" for another fifteen minutes while
we drove the rest of the way through the city to our safe-house. With
those final words I sprinted to the vehicle and hopped in the front passenger seat as we sped away.

While the machine gun continued firing, we turned our attention
toward navigating Kandahar's sign-less maze of similar looking walls,
houses, and streets. As mentioned earlier, in 2001–2002 there were no
street signs, no GPS mapping software for the area, and no local guides to
show us the way. We had to navigate through Kandahar the old fashioned
way: with topographic maps, wrist compasses, and by going excruciatingly

slow. The only one who spoke during the drive was Dave as he narrated the route of travel (which he had memorized before we left).

For the rest of us, it was all senses scanning back and forth across our clock sectors. Every seemingly insignificant detail was now potentially significant. *"If you've ever seen a house cat looking and listening for mice in a field it's a good image to think about whenever you need to focus your senses and pay extra-close attention to what's going on around you. If we all stay alert we all stay alive."* Hammer's advice had primed our minds and prepared us well.

Once we arrived at the Kandahar safe-house we breathed a collective sigh of relief. Yet instead of high-fiving each other we immediately began trying to put all the pieces together so we could figure out what had just happened. I called Jimmy (my deputy commander) and gave him an update on everything we discussed. "Are you going to put this in the AFO Situation Report tonight?" Jimmy asked. It was a great suggestion. Most of the information in this story including the Rules of Engagement is from the account we put together for the AFO Situation Report that night and then shared with all other forces in Afghanistan.

A few nights later Jimmy's hunch paid off. One of our Special Forces/ Green Beret colleagues called us on the secure satellite-phone and told us that he and his team read the AFO sit-rep and realized that the guys shooting the machine gun were the Afghans they were training from the newly formed Kandahar militia.

An Afghan soldier firing a machine-gun from a roof-top in Kandahar

"They went up on the roof of their barracks to conduct target practice on a pile of rocks out in the dessert," he explained. "We've warned them numerous times about shooting from the roof for just this reason but I think they finally learned their lesson, because after we told the Afghans what happened they told us they actually waved at the F-16's as the aircraft flew overhead."

It's difficult to describe with words how I felt while he was telling me about the Kandahar militia members except to say it was pretty much the same way I felt when I saw the videotapes of the women and children getting off the bus, and the same way anyone feels when they realize they came within a finger pull or radio response of a major catastrophe. *To learn from our experiences we must feel the experiences. Sharing knowledge we learn from our experiences over time enables evolutionary learning.* After thanking my Special Forces friend for the feedback, he asked me if it was okay if he "translated the Rules of Engagement we used so he could share it with the Afghans they were training?" "Of course," I told him, "it's not classified it's common sense," and "feel free to pass it on."

When the logic of why we do what we do and choose what we choose makes sense over time a positive learning-feedback loop emerges and the logic of why becomes foundational logic of why (FLOW). **Once internalized all you have to do is pay attention to what's going on around you and go with the FLOW.**

The Enemy of Friendly Fire is Common Sense.

REFLECTIONS/LESSONS LEARNED
Freedom of Choice to make sense of what's going on around us and sensible choices about what to do next.

Successful leaders and organizations have the demonstrated ability to recognize patterns and translate them into action usually before their competition can react. This is because they've either consciously or unconsciously internalized the concept of Foundational Logic of Why (FLOW).

Afghanistan is where I first learned the decision-making and problem-solving power of FLOW. The AC-130 incident taught us the importance of staying centered on our purpose as well as sharing all the key context-specific patterns and principles we'd learned over the years to accomplish it.

We shared the same FLOW we learned while flying the AC-130 mission with our fellow team members on the ground where it worked equally well while driving around Kandahar. Although we continued to use and refine the concept of FLOW it took another ten years before I learned the biologic underpinnings of why and how it works.

In the pages that follow you'll learn:

1) What FLOW is and the biologic basis upon which it stands.

2) How FLOW is related to LOW (Logic of Why).

3) The three primary benefits of putting FLOW into practice:
   a) Power of Purpose
   b) Building Best Teams
   c) Evolutionary Learning

1) What is Foundational Logic of Why?

Foundation is the basis on which a thing stands and/or is supported.

Logic is a neural process that describes the way our neocortex learns, organizes, and retrieves context-specific knowledge of patterns to reveal patterns and relationships that make sense of the world. To make *logical* sense of any pattern our neocortex needs a purpose.

Why refers to the cause, reason, or purpose for which something is done.[113]

Foundational Logic of Why (FLOW) is a metaphor for the biologic way our thinking brains learn, organize, and retrieve knowledge of patterns to accomplish any purpose. When said out loud and shared, **FLOW provides our brains with a common sense of shared purpose and direction for accomplishing it.**

FLOW for Kandahar Mission:

Our purpose today is to drive across Kandahar to coordinate with the AFO team located in our newest safe-house on the north side of town; Stay alert and stay alive, Deploy, Suppress,

*Report; Positive ID of a target as enemy is a prerequisite before
engaging, Never harm non-combatants; Do unto others as we'd
want them to do unto ourselves; Say it out loud so you can see.*

To lay the foundation for successful choice-making common sense
leaders don't tell their people what to do or how to choose, instead they
prime their people's minds by saying out loud and sharing their common purpose along with all the context-specific knowledge of patterns
and principles they've learned over time to accomplish it. In aggregate,
the Foundational Logic of Why they do what they do and choose what
they choose.

What is the biologic basis upon which FLOW stands? Our brains
learn, organize, and retrieve knowledge by using what cognitive science refers to as concept clusters.[114] Take a few seconds to think about
everything you know about any of the following concepts: Leadership?
Driving? Ambushes? No matter what your background you will notice
that your brain stores massive clusters of knowledge related to any concept you think about.

To put our thinking into context and focus our thoughts, our neocortex needs a purpose (e.g. leading teams in combat, driving on the
highway, reacting to an ambush, etc.). Once focused with a purpose, our
neocortex instinctively begins aggregating all the context-specific patterns and principles we've learned over a lifetime to accomplish it (e.g.
"take care of your people," "when in doubt go with the flow," "deploy,
suppress, report," etc.). All our brains need is time to think.

We have FLOW for everything we do and everything we choose in
life though we're rarely consciously aware of it. One reason FLOW is
so common yet so rarely said out loud or written down is that most of
the time our FLOW only exists as a bunch of interconnected thoughts,
ideas, and life experiences inside our heads. *Time is the fuel that powers
the process of free thinking.*

To reveal your own, take a minute to sit down with pen and paper
(secure devices) and think about any complex decision, problem, opportunity, or activity you're dealing with (e.g. professional, personal relationships, family, religion, politics, health, etc.) and ask yourself what's
my purpose and what are the key patterns and principles I've learned

to accomplish it? From there your brain begins sorting through all the context-specific patterns and relationships you've ever learned. Stay calm, think. Then sit back and allow your intuition to do what it does best.

Intuition is an exquisitely simple sense-making algorithm that uses a yes/no process of elimination to logically search and retrieve the best match answers from our brain's massive neural knowledge base.[115] Intuition is holistic. It evaluates your total knowledge to arrive at everything you know about any thing. In essence your theory about any thing.

There's no substitute for a prepared mind. FLOW doesn't tell our brains what to do or how to choose. Instead FLOW primes our brains with a common sense of shared purpose and direction upon which we are free to choose based on the adaptive stimulus of what's going on around us. What follows is the comprehensive FLOW we put on paper for the first time after the Kandahar mission:[116]

AFO FLOW for Kandahar Mission (Jan 2002)	
Purpose:	**Lessons and Guiding Principles:**
• **U. S. Military:** Deny enemy sanctuary in Afghanistan • **AFO:** Get some men out on the frontier to figure out what's going on then find the enemy and kill or capture them • **AFO Team:** Drive across Kandahar to coordinate with the Special Forces team located in our newest safe-house on the north side of town	• Pay attention to what's going on around you, Blend in anywhere, The only failure is a failure to try (Learn, Adapt, Interact) • When in Doubt Develop the Situation • Audacity, Audacity, Audacity • Always Listen to the Guys on the Ground • Get Down, Suppress, Report • Whether we live or whether we die depends on our ability to make sense of what we're experiencing so take a deep breath, stay calm, and remind yourself that: • First reports are almost always inaccurate, incomplete, or both • Positive identification of a target as enemy is prerequisite before engaging • Never harm non-combatants, Do onto others as you'd want them to do onto you • Say it out loud so you can see

FLOW replaces strategy, plans, and decision-making dependence on disconnected chains of command. **Once internalized all our brains have to do is pay attention to what's going on around us and then go with the FLOW:**

> *"The two women in burkas were just walking down the street and happy to see us, the old man was chasing a bus that almost ran us off the road, the flat tire was a blowout, the machine gun fire is ineffective, and we're in a city packed with civilians."*

When leaders say out loud and share FLOW for a particular decision/endeavor they create individual conscious awareness and collective shared reality amongst their teams:

> *"If we apply the Rules of Engagement we discussed back at the safe-house, there's no way we can approve the drop. Hold your fire."*

The choices we make in the context of the moment are rarely fire and forget activities. They almost always lead to branch and sequel choices that have the potential to be even more significant than the original. FLOW provides context-specific coherence and consistency to all future branches and sequels of the choice:

> *"We cannot positively ID the target as enemy so the F-16's are 'not cleared,' I say again 'not cleared' to engage the target."*

Conscious awareness of FLOW empowers decentralized teams like AFO with the freedom to make coherent-adaptive choices across time and space (geographic separation) with maximum speed before the competition has a chance to call back to their Headquarters and ask for permission. In this way FLOW enables unity of purpose and flexibility for decentralized operations by geographically dispersed agents and teams.

Our common purpose and direction (FLOW) +
the adaptive stimulus of what's going on around
us in the context of the moment = the logic of
why we make a coherent-adaptive choice

To update: a coherent-adaptive choice is a choice that coheres with our FLOW (see Kandahar FLOW above) and adapts to the patterns of life as they're going on around us in the context of the moment: *"flat tire, and under ineffective and unidentified fire in Kandahar."* A coherent-adaptive choice is a sensible choice "Hold your fire." *(To make sense it has to add up)*

The only individuals and organizations that can make coherent-adaptive choices in a rapid and consistent manner are those that have internalized a robust foundation of logic of whys.

2) What's the relationship between Foundational Logic of Why and Logic of Why? FLOW and LOW are part of the same thinking process. Like freedom of choice, the key relationship between FLOW and LOW is time. Time is the fuel that powers the process of free-thinking. The logic of why informs why we do what we do and why we choose what we choose in the snapshot of time we know as the context of the momen":

The woman in the blue burka closest to the road
stopped and lifted up her facial veil to flash what
looked to me like an appreciative and proud smile.

When the logic of why we do what we do and choose what we choose makes sense over time a positive learning-feedback loop emerges and the logic of why becomes foundational logic of why (FLOW).

"Over time, with feedback, we confirmed
the Afghan people weren't the enemy."
LOW + Time + Feedback (+/-) = FLOW

Like character and culture our individual FLOW is an autobiography of all the context-specific knowledge of patterns and principles we've learned over a lifetime to accomplish any purpose. To understand the character or culture that influences a person(s) to do what they do and choose what they choose we understand the foundational logic of why (FLOW) upon which the person/people stands.

> *"By choosing to defy Taliban law and show us her smiling face, she showed us who she really was—a person—and she showed us how she felt about being free. Saying it out loud enabled us to see."*
> *FLOW + Time + Feedback (+/–) = Character/Culture*

3) **What are the three primary benefits of putting FLOW into practice?**

A) **The Power of Purpose:** What we do and what we choose is informed by the purpose, or context lens, through which we view it. To maximize the potential and performance of any type of team—combat, corporate, country, or sports—they must have a common sense of shared purpose (CSSP) and direction for accomplishing it.

Whether it's the first day getting together with a new team, or the first day dealing with a new problem or opportunity, it is the responsibility of all leaders to loop their people together with a common sense of shared purpose and direction for accomplishing it.

> *"That's how we ended up in Kandahar that day. We were driving around the country to get all of our AFO teams looped together on the same sheet of music with regards to our purpose and direction for accomplishing it."*

FLOW x 2(+) = Common sense of shared purpose and direction

All human teams are looped together by a common sense of shared purpose, most often informally and or unconsciously. I am one and I am one of many. We exist both as individuals and as members of numerous groups/teams at the same time (family, friends, professional, political, spiritual, sports, etc.). The bond that links and holds all groups/teams together is their common sense of shared purpose. It's the invisible "why" and "how" that bonds countries, companies, and communities; parents, patriots, and political parties; families, friends, and freedom fighters. FLOW provides the common ground of common purpose and direction upon which all high-performing teams stand.

FLOW = Common Sense of Shared Purpose
= High-Performing Team

Like gravity, it's difficult to fully comprehend the bonding power of FLOW until it goes away. When our FLOW is forgotten, falls apart, and/or fades away, so too does the team. Think of what happens to work friends after they stop working together; think of what happens to sports teammates after they change teams; think of what happens to neighbors after one of them moves out of the neighborhood; and think of what happens to couples after they stop loving each other. The bonding power of FLOW isn't philosophic or psychologic. It's biologic.

~~*FLOW = Common Sense of Shared Purpose*~~
~~*= High-Performing Team*~~

Conscious awareness of the bonding power of FLOW enables common sense leaders to form and reform high performing teams for any purpose, at anytime, anywhere, for any situation.

B) **High-performing teams:** Even though most of us had never worked together before and weren't from the same unit, or government

AFO and Afghan allies fighting for a common purpose—
Freedom—Afghanistan, March 2002.

agency, or in some cases from the same country, AFO was still a close-knit high-performing team. The biology of our brains explains it. When two or more brains share a common sense of purpose and are free to self-organize they instinctively collaborate, communicate, and reciprocate to accomplish it. Think of finding food, fighting fires, fending off floods; think of friendships and families.

Collaboration is working together to produce, achieve, or accomplish a common purpose. The evolution of all life on earth is the increase of biological collaboration. From proteins and cells, to tissues and organs, to plants and animals, to families and communities, to ecosystems and planets, life is biologic collaboration at every scale. Before there was evolution or our species, there was collaboration between our cells to ensure their survival and extend that survival into the future via reproduction.[117] The catalyst for biologic collaboration is our common sense of shared purpose: to survive, thrive, and evolve.

> *"We either hang together or we hang separately."* Ben Franklin, 1776

The primary means of surviving and evolving toward higher levels of order, differentiation, and progress is the **communication** of knowledge. The evolution of the human species skyrocketed when we humans learned to speak. Learned knowledge of patterns provides our brains with options and options provide us with freedom to choose between them based on the adaptive stimulus of what's going on around us. To ensure we accomplish our collective purpose we must keep the communication of knowledge flowing between team members.

Common Sense of Purpose + Freedom of Choice =
Collaborate, Communicate, Reciprocate[118]

Reciprocity is the self-governing pattern of behavior upon which trust and building best teams is based. We speak or behave in certain ways and others respond based on what we said or did. This is how children learn values, and emotional intelligence. Treat your friends poorly and you won't have friends for long, make your friends laugh and confident and they will make you popular. Leadership is no different. Take care of your people and they will take care of you. Treat your people like crap, and they will crap all over you.[119]

The common denominator pattern of every high-performing team in human history is their capacity to collaborate, communicate, and reciprocate. Think of the best work teams, best sports teams, best first responder teams, and the best family teams. It's an evolutionary stable strategy that's baked into our DNA. How can we prove it?

Isn't it amazing that almost anyone, regardless of age, intellect, or experience, can learn to drive a two-ton vehicle harmoniously on heavily trafficked highways full of humans? How do we pull off something so seemingly complex and so dauntingly dangerous (46k U.S. deaths per year)? Highways full of humans operate off the same FLOW as swarms of birds and schools of fish: to survive, thrive, and evolve, we instinctively collaborate by communicating and reciprocating.

Collaborate, Communicate, Reciprocate, Driving is Common Sense

We begin collaborating with other drivers as soon as we merge into traffic by paying attention to what's going on around us and following the common operating principles known as the rules of the road. We drive in the same general direction and speed as the vehicles around us, while maintaining a safe, comfortable distance from the vehicles to our front and sides. To continue collaborating we communicate and reciprocate.

If we need to pass, merge, change lanes, or turn, we communicate our intention the same way the people around us do (e.g. blinkers, honk horn, hand and arm signals, or flashing headlights, etc.). Collaborating by communicating knowledge and intent will get things moving in the right direction but to sustain a collaborative relationships over time there must be some sort of governing system. Reciprocity is the currency of human interactions and the evolutionary stable pattern of human behavior upon which trust and building best teams depends.

To reciprocate while driving we follow the Golden Rule: Do unto others as we'd want others to do unto ourselves. We slow down and speed up based on what the cars in front and around us are doing, we allow others to merge in and out of traffic and on and off the highway in expectation that others will do the same for us in the future. When another driver flashes their lights to warn us of a speed trap up ahead we instinctively return the favor by warning others after we pass. To survive, thrive, and evolve while driving we humans follow the same common sense principle as the most successful teams in human history, we Collaborate by Communicating and Reciprocating. Once internalized all we have to do is pay attention to what's going on around us and go with the FLOW.

C) **Organizational/Evolutionary Learning:** Most large hierarchical organizations have learning disabilities. They can't learn from the choices they made in the past because there's no physical record (said out loud or written down) to memorialize why they made the choices. The lack of process has a hierarchical purpose. Learning from and memorializing what happened in the past (positive and negative) could theoretically expose the senselessness of the hierarchical decision-making process itself, as well as the choices made by the leaders who are incentivized to keep it aloft. When things don't go well or not as planned the hierarchy would rather forget about it then be held accountable. Which explains why most large hierarchical organizations and their leaders make decisions and solve problems like amnesiacs.

History matters. We live life forward and understand it backwards because history reveals patterns and patterns reveal what's likely to happen in the future. Although the past and future may seem like separate worlds they are indelibly linked inside our brains. Knowledge of the past (aka memory) is how we create knowledge of the future, called forethought. Brain injured patients who cannot remember their pasts are unable to imagine the future; like large hierarchical organizations they can't think forward and progress because they have no knowledge of what happened in the past to pivot on.

In the weeks, months, and years that followed, the FLOW we learned from the AC-130 and Kandahar missions had a profound influence on every aspect of our thinking and decision-making. The lessons we learned and the knowledge we accumulated changed the way we made decisions and solved problems. We learned to adapt. It also made us realize something else. Our long-term success or failure in Afghanistan and Iraq would depend on our capacity to capture what we learned along the way and pass it on to those that followed. Sharing and memorializing knowledge we learn from our experiences over time enables evolutionary learning.

FLOW + Time + Feedback = History/Evolution

CHAPTER VI SUMMARY OF KEY CONCEPTS

- When the logic of why we do what we do and choose what we choose makes sense over time a positive learning-feedback loop emerges and the logic of why becomes foundational logic of why (FLOW).
- LOW + Time + Feedback = FLOW
- The purpose of FLOW is to provide our brains with a common sense of shared purpose and direction upon which we can accomplish it.
- To find our individual FLOW we simply ask ourselves a question: What's my purpose and what have I learned to accomplish it? Make sure you have a pen and paper handy so you can write down everything that flows out.
- To find our collective FLOW, we call an agenda-less meeting.
- It is the task of a leader to connect/unite their people with purpose.
- FLOW provides a common foundation of logic upon which decentralized teams and individual operators/agents are free to make sense of what's going on around them and sensible choices about what to do next.
- Once internalized all our brains have to do is pay attention to what's going on around them and go with the FLOW.
- **Three benefits of putting FLOW into practice:**
  - ▶ **The Power of Purpose:** FLOW is the invisible glue that holds all human teams together. What we do and what we choose is informed by the purpose, or context lens, through which we view it. To maximize the potential and performance of any type of team—combat, corporate, country, or sports—they must have a common sense of shared purpose (CSSP) and direction for accomplishing it.
  - ▶ **High-performing teams:** No matter where we come from or how different our backgrounds or how differently we see the world, when two or more brains share a common sense of

purpose and are free to self-organize they instinctively collaborate, communicate, and reciprocate to accomplish it. *Think
of finding food, fighting fires, fending off floods, think of families,
and AFO.*

► **Organizational/Evolutionary Learning:** Sharing and memorializing knowledge we learn from our experiences over time
enables evolutionary learning.

FLOW + Time + Feedback = History/Evolution

CHAPTER 7

Climate Change

How to Create a Healthy Leadership Climate

Ft. Lewis Washington, South Rainer Training Area, 0300, November, Late 1980's: After five hours there was no longer any doubt about it, we were lost. It was supposed to be a five-kilometer (three-mile) tactical movement. Over the past five hours the platoon likely logged three times that distance. When it comes to humping heavy loads across thickly forested and hilly terrain every step of extra distance is doubly frustrating.

Although the temperature was in the mid-40's, the wet Washington air and the ice cold winds born over the glacial fed waters of Puget Sound made the mid-40's feel like freezing. As long as you keep moving at a steady pace you can work up enough body heat to fend off the freeze. You have to keep moving.

The last update from the Platoon Leader was passed back through the column three hours earlier: "the patrol base is a hundred meters up ahead." That was the last thing we heard from the Platoon Leader. Five hundred meters later the Platoon Leader had pretty much lost face. One thousand meters later (by my pace-count) the men began moving like molasses at a speed appropriately called painfully slow.

All forests are difficult to move through at night. Old growth forests like South Rainier distinguish themselves due to three unique features: the darkness, the dampness, and the deadfall. All three are progenies of the same family tree.

The forests of Western Washington are dominated by giant conifers, such as Sitka spruce, western red cedar, and Douglas firs. Covered by moss and rising to towering heights of 250 feet and higher, the tops of the trees create a cathedral-like canopy that blocks almost all the ambient light. Even when wearing night vision goggles it was hard to see your hand in front of your face. Which makes seeing your map almost impossible.

Rain falls frequently in South Rainer with total precipitation averaging between four and six feet each year. The result is a lush green canopy of shrubs, large leafy fauna, plants called epiphytes that grow on top of other plants, as well as nurse logs which are downed or dead trees that support new plant life. Every inch of the forest floor is either covered or coated in green. (See Photo) "Jungle" is the most common word people use when they first experience South Rainier, which makes sense of why the U.S. Army used it in the 1960's and 70's to train and prepare new recruits for deployment to Vietnam.[120]

The final feature that makes movement in these forests both difficult and dangerous is deadfall. Deadfall is a tangled mass of fallen trees and branches. Randomly strewn across the forest floor and usually camouflaged by green undergrowth, deadfall not only slows you down it also takes a brutal toll on the shins. The bruises and abrasions got so bad at times that some Rangers wore soccer shin pads so they could avoid any new injuries and allow the old ones to heal. As an added bonus, the bruises and abrasions are almost always followed by a fall.

As a result it was standard operating procedure to treat deadfall the same way as other hazards such as water obstacles, steep drop-offs, or poison plants. When the first person in the formation encountered deadfall on the trail it was expected that they'd pass a detailed description back through the column as a warning for those that followed. Reflecting both the seriousness of the hazards and the genuine concern for the well-being of their fellow Rangers, the descriptions were often quite detailed and in retrospect quite humorous: "Deadfall, twelve inches off the ground at ninety-degree angle to the trail, multiple branches with sharp edges." Helping the guy behind you helps him avoid getting hurt and helps the entire platoon to move quicker and quieter. It also feels good.

Where are we? If you're moving tactically and there's not enough light to see your map the best way to keep track of where you are is by using your watch, your pace count, and your compass. Over the last two hours the platoon had walked a total of 1,500 meters during which we made a series of four ninety-degree left turns each about 500 meters apart. Four ninety-degree turns in the same direction and same distance equals a square. You didn't need a math degree to understand what was happening. We were walking in circles. Still no word or explanation from the Platoon Leader.

"What is he doing up there? He has to know he's lost. Why the 'F' hasn't he updated the rest of the platoon?" I mumbled to myself. Cold, wet, tired, frustrated, and pissed off. The timeless Ranger recipe for a drone-fest.[121] Onward we trudged.

As the Company Executive Officer (XO), I wasn't actually a member of the 2nd Platoon. The XO's primary job is to assist the Company

Commander in mission planning and execution. In peacetime the Company XO is more accurately described as the company operations officer responsible for coordinating all training and logistics such as food, ammo, vehicles, and aircraft, etc.

The Company XO is technically second in command of the Company so for contingency purposes on any type of tactical movement the Company Commander and the XO always split up (e.g. ride in separate vehicles, fly in separate aircraft, or walk with separate platoons, etc.). On this night, I was moving with 2nd Platoon while the Company Commander was moving with the 1st Platoon. I guess you could call it "tactically tagging along."

The mission of the 2nd Platoon was to conduct a tactical movement to a location specified by the Company Commander where they were to set up a patrol base[122] and bed down for the night in preparation for a new mission that they would receive in the morning. This was the first time I had the opportunity to move tactically with the 2nd Platoon. The Platoon Leader was relatively new so I didn't have any firsthand knowledge about his leadership experience.

A Platoon Leader's job is to command the platoon but it's the Platoon Sergeant and the squad leaders who control it. The Platoon Sergeant of the 2nd Platoon was a combat vet and one of the most senior members of the battalion. The squad leaders were all top notch. And the rest of the platoon, like the rest of the company, was stacked with some of the finest soldiers and Sergeants in the Army. Which made the senselessness of our current situation even harder to fathom.

Clearly they were having problems with their navigation. So why didn't I do something about it? During the first three hours of the movement I was trying to do unto them as I'd want any observer or higher-ranking person to do unto me. Stay out of their decision-making loop and let them operate like they would have to operate on a real world mission. If they make mistakes or encounter problems they should be allowed to work together as a team to learn how to fix them. That's how we learn to lead. Having said that, there is no way I would have waited this long and allowed the platoon to get this lost, if not for the fact that there was a significant barrier between the Platoon Leader and me.

I was moving in the back of the forty-man column while the Platoon Leader and Platoon Sergeant were both moving near the front. Using the military standard of five-meter intervals between men multiplied by forty men meant that the platoon column—which contracts and expands like an accordion as it moves through, around, and over restrictive terrain—was between 200 and 400 meters long. Getting from the back of the column to the front of the column while moving in darkness and densely forested terrain not only takes a lot of time but also creates a lot of commotion and confusion which combine to make it tactically unsound.

I had a radio on my back but to make contact with another radio in this type of terrain required both radios to have their twenty-foot long whip antennas attached and extended. Thanks to the jungle-like undergrowth the only way to get the antenna up and extended was to do so while stationary. We had only stopped one time in the last five hours and when we did I managed to get the antenna attached and extended but was unable to make contact with the Platoon Leader before the column started moving again. I'm not sure what I would have said to him or how I could have helped him on the radio anyway. What I really needed to do was to talk to him face-to-face with map in hand.

Should I stay or should I go? Instead of doing something about it I chose to do nothing and suck up the pain.

Then it started to rain.

Followed a few seconds later by a human wave of hand and arm movements passed back through the column to signal a halt. *"About F-ing time."* It felt good to finally take a knee. Like the thunder following lightning a few seconds later, I heard the faint rumble of "the word" as it was passed from Ranger to Ranger, from the front of the column to the rear, from the man in front to the man behind.

The Ranger in front of me was my link to the rest of the platoon and the only other person I had talked to over the last five hours. When he approached I heard a strange sound. I figured out what it was as soon as he started to talk. "Sir, ch ch ch ch, word just got passed back from the Platoon Leader that we're almost there so he wants everyone to don their Gore-Tex rain gear underneath their uniforms, ch ch, ch, ch."

It took me a few seconds for my brain to cut through the chatter and comprehend what he just said. "Did you say 'underneath our uniforms,' Corporal?" I replied as my teeth began to chatter too. "Yes, Sir, it's a platoon S-O-P, the Platoon Leader says that wearing Gore-Tex over our uniforms makes too much noise as it rubs together while we walk. He says wearing it underneath our uniforms helps muffle the noise and prevents the enemy from hearing us before we hear them."

"Un-freaking believable," was what I wanted to say but I kept my thoughts to myself as the Corporal hurried back to his rucksack to start stripping down and bundling up.

As much as I wanted to charge forward through the column and challenge the Platoon Leader on the senselessness of his order, my chattering teeth reminded me that I had another priority. "There's no way I'm stripping down to my skivvies in the freezing rain to put my Gore-Tex on underneath my uniform. It doesn't make sense. I'll just wear my Gore-Tex top and bottoms over my uniform like they're meant to be worn." I quickly pulled my Gore-Tex jacket out of my rucksack and had one arm in the sleeve when I thought about the Corporal and the other Rangers in front of me. "If they have to wear their Gore-Tex underneath their uniform how can I, with good conscience, walk behind them with mine on the outside?"

Then it started to pour.

Yet instead of putting my Gore-Tex jacket on as quickly as possible, I just stood there frozen in thought. Caught between making sense and senselessness my mind was impaled on the horns of an ethical dilemma. The sound of the Corporal's voice and a lot of commotion up ahead snapped me out of it. I flipped down my night vision goggles to see what I could see just in time to witness what appeared to be some sort of ancient tribal dance ritual. I was droning I knew. Of course it wasn't a dance ritual. It was the four guys in front of me trying to take their pants off without taking their boots off first. It didn't work well when we were little kids and it doesn't get any easier as your feet and boots get bigger. After dropping their pants, they each began hopping around on one foot while pulling and prying to get the non-hopping pant leg free from the boot. This was Exhibit A for why putting your Gore-Tex on under your uniform doesn't make tactical sense. Then one guy tipped over. Like bowling pins, when he tipped he took out the guy next to him who also tipped over and took out the other two. This was the first time I sensed the seriousness of our situation.

Then something unexpected happened. They started laughing. Hysterically. And I laughed with them. At miserable movements like this one, laughing at falls isn't considered rude or impolite. The wipeouts and the laughs that follow provide some of the only highlights from otherwise frustrating and forgettable long nights in the bush. It didn't last long. Once those that fell realized how much wetter and colder they were the laughter faded and anger and frustration returned to prominence.

The mud groveling fall was both Exhibit B and a timely lesson for me. After giving a hand to the four guys groveling on the ground I no longer had any doubt about what the right thing was to do so I told them, "you guys need to put your Gore-Tex on over our uniforms as per Company and Battalion S-O-P." Then I added, "this is a safety issue and if anyone asks you can tell them the XO told you to do it."

Unfortunately, it turned out to be a lesson only half-learned. In my rush to put my Gore-Tex on as quickly as possible I bone-headedly attempted to step into my Gore-Tex bottoms without taking my boots off first. Balancing on one leg I threaded my left boot through the left Gore-Tex pant leg and started to pull. These were the earliest versions of Gore-Tex rain suits so they didn't come equipped with zippers or snaps that allowed you to loosen the bottom of the pant leg first. The only way to get them over my boot was to pull harder. Which I did. Then I tipped over and fell face first onto the spongy moss that covered the forest floor. Then something not so unexpected happened. Howls of laughter erupted from my four fellow fallers. And once again I laughed too.

Laying on the forest floor sopping wet and freezing cold with one boot stuck inside my Gore-Tex pant leg made me realize how senseless my choices were leading up to that moment. *"Get your shit together,"* I scolded myself. My timing was impeccable.

"Has anyone seen the XO?" someone whispered loudly. His tone was angry urgent. "XO, are you back here?" I scrambled to pull myself up and wipe the mud off my face but it was too late. "XO? Is that you?" I took a deep breath and stood up, "Yes, it's me," I replied with all the self-deprecation I could muster. It was Sergeant X, a squad leader at the time, probably twenty-four years old and already known as one of the finest and fittest warriors in the Battalion. Although he never worked directly for me, he and I had conducted a couple of long-range reconnaissance missions together and he was one of the NCO's I had the good fortune of working with repeatedly throughout my time in the 2d Ranger Battalion.

"Please don't tell me you were putting your Gore-Tex on under your clothes too?" I didn't answer. "I'd make fun of you, Sir, but I tried to do the same thing until I heard a strange noise in the woods behind me. I thought it was a critter sneaking up on me and then I realized it was one of my guy's teeth. He was so wet-cold he could barely talk and that's when I realized this is starting to turn into a serious safety issue.

"I tried calling the Platoon Leader and Platoon Sergeant on the radio but wasn't able to make contact so I figured I'd walk back here and talk to you about it. While making my way through the platoon column I discovered the entire platoon is dangerously cold, tired, frustrated, and red-hot pissed off. Which is why everybody—including you, Sir—are starting to do some really stupid shit."

Sgt X's feedback hit me like a punch in the face. It also ended my senseless debate. I shook my head as reality sunk in, *"I waited way too long. Yes, I'm just tactically tagging along with the platoon tonight but that doesn't mean I'm no longer a leader. As second in command of the company these guys are my guys too."* All the reasons I had come up with to stay in the back of the column now seemed like a self-centered rationalization to do nothing: "Too hard to put up my long whip antenna," "too much time and too difficult to make my way through the column," what I should have been asking myself was, "what would I want a leader in my position to do if I was one of the Rangers walking circles in the freezing rain?" *"Thanks for slapping me out of it, Sgt X,"* I thought to myself.

"Do you know where we are?" I asked Sgt X with a hint of embarrassment. "I do now, Sir. I foolishly stopped following along after the first hour because I couldn't see my map without turning on a light."[123] He explained, "I also figured there was no way we could possibly get lost on a movement this short (5 km/3.1 miles). After an hour of zigzagging and no word on what was going on I realized I needed to figure out where we were. Luckily, I was watching my compass and keeping a pace count so I had one of my guys throw a poncho over my head while I used a finger light to figure it out. How about you, Sir?"

"I lost track of my pace count during the last ninety-degree turn. I was trying to subtract the distance we walked after the previous turn but I was so pissed off I couldn't do the math. Can you show me where you think we are on the map?"

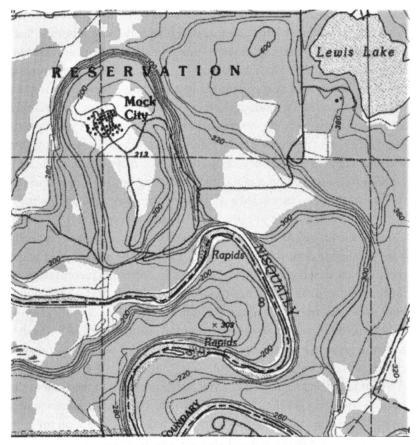

Nisqually River Floodplain, Ft. Lewis, Wa.

"Roger that, Sir," he responded as we huddled together to form a light-blocking human cone around his acetated map which he illuminated with a tiny, finger light while using a blade of grass as a pointer. "As you know, Sir, the most prominent terrain feature around here is the Nisqually River (See Map). If you walk a hundred meters up the column you'll come to an incredibly steep drop-off which as you can see on the map is clearly defined where all these contour intervals come together. Those bunched up contour intervals signify the edge of the Nisqually River floodplain," he explained while tracing the floodplain as it meandered along both sides of the river.

The next challenge was figuring out our general location on the Nisqually River floodplain. "We moved a long way tonight but the fastest a platoon this size can move in this type of terrain is around two kilometers per hour," Sgt X explained. "So even if we had been moving in a straight line at max speed for the past five hours there is no way we could have moved far enough to have wandered outside the training area otherwise we would have crossed one of the fire roads that define its boundaries," he emphasized as he traced the outline of the training area with the blade of grass. "As you can see on the map, the only place it's possible to cross the floodplain without crossing any fire roads is inside this area right here," he circled a spot on the map the size of a thumbnail.

"This is where we're at right now, Sir, which is good news because it means the fire road is less than 200 meters north of us. We've actually been paralleling it for the last half hour. To get to the patrol base and get these guys warmed up as quickly as possible, I strongly recommend we move directly north to the fire road and then handrail[124] it for about a kilometer until the fire road turns south. Our patrol base destination is only three hundred meters from that point. As impressed as I was that he knew where we were I was even more impressed with the process of elimination he used to figure it out.

"Good job, Sgt X, now I need you to follow me up to the head of the column so we can get the Platoon Leader and Platoon Sergeant squared away." "Roger that Sir, if it's okay with you I want to go check on my guys first and I'll jump in behind you when you pass."

"Sounds good," I told him as he hurried back to his squad up ahead. For the first time in many hours I no longer felt angry, frustrated, cold, and tired. Part of it was knowing where we were and that we weren't that far away from where we needed to go. Mostly it was my renewed sense of purpose, and a platoon full of Rangers who were counting on me to accomplish it.

As mentioned earlier, the main reason that moving through a forty-man column at night in difficult terrain is considered tactically unsound is because it's almost impossible to do so without creating a lot of commotion and noise. With the column now halted it was going to be even more difficult because most of the men were either sitting on their rucksacks or taking a knee next to a tree. Which meant that their exact locations would be almost impossible for me to see. The only way to prevent accidently stepping or falling on them was to alert each and every one of them as I was coming through.

"XO coming through," I whispered as I waded into the column.

"Who?"

"XO."

"'Exxo?' Are you new?"

"XO coming through, right side of trail."

"Ow."

"Sorry about that."

"Hey man, that's my leg."

"I couldn't see it, XO coming through."

"What the fuck?"

"Sorry about that."

"Who the hell are you?"

"The XO, who are you?"

"Smith."

"XO coming through."

"Watch out for the two hundred foot drop-off up ahead."

"Thanks man, XO sliding down."

"Who goes there?"

"It's me, the XO, coming through."

"You got any extra MRE crackers."

"No, have you seen the Platoon Leader?"

"Where?"

"He's losing it, Sir," Sgt X announced as he merged in behind me. "The Platoon Leader is straight ahead."

"XO, what brings you up front?" the Platoon Leader asked nonchalantly, while sitting on the ground and staring at his map with a poncho over his head.

I took a deep breath, *"stay calm, he's new and maybe he really has no clue."* I began by describing the seriousness of the situation going on behind us. "Of greatest concern," I emphasized, "is that most of Platoon is now dangerously wet-cold." He didn't say anything so I asked him, "How can you possibly think it makes sense to strip down into your skivvies for any reason during a tactical movement, much less a tactical movement in a rain-storm?"

"We actually came up with the idea together," the Platoon Leader responded indignantly. "Who's we?" I replied. The Platoon Sergeant cleared his throat to let me know he was standing a few feet off to my right.

"What seems to be your problem with it? Sir," the Platoon Sergeant asked with a hint of condescension. The Platoon Sergeant's unexpected involvement and apparent support not only surprised me, it also made any more discussion concerning the Gore-Tex underwear a dead-end waste to debate. He was both a senior Platoon Sergeant and a combat vet while I was a Lieutenant who hadn't seen combat yet. He could fall back on things like "mental toughness," "discipline," and "experience," while all I could fall back on was that the men and I were freezing our asses off. Compounding my disadvantage was the fact I was starting to shiver uncontrollably. Which was a timely reminder that what mattered most at that moment was making sure the Platoon Leader and Platoon Sergeant knew where we were and how to get the platoon to the patrol base as quickly as possible.

I took a knee to talk directly to the Platoon Leader. "We can talk more about your Gore-Tex underpants SOP in the after-action review tomorrow morning, right now we need to get to the patrol base and get these guys warmed up as quickly as possible. Do you have any idea where we are right now?" I asked loudly enough so both of them could hear the question. They responded with thundering silence. "I think I got it figured out. Sir," Sgt X piped in as he stepped into the light. "Is that Sgt X? Hop under my poncho, Sgt X, and let's compare notes," replied the Platoon Leader.

While Sgt X oriented the Platoon Leader and Platoon Sergeant with his map, I did what I always did when I got wet-cold. I dropped to the ground and started knocking out perfect form push-ups. The motivation for attempting perfect form is that they are the hardest to perform and quickest to warm you up.

A few seconds after I finished fifty, the Platoon Leader announced to everyone in ear range: "Okay, we're all set, we're going to head toward the road and then handrail it the rest of the way to the patrol base." Then he told the Platoon Sergeant to pass back to the rest of the platoon that we'd start moving again in five minutes. With that warning, Sgt X and I realized we had to hurry back through the column to grab our rucksacks before the men started moving. I asked him to lead the way this time, which he did.

"Sgt X coming through."

"Oh geez, not again."

"Sgt X coming through."

"Huh?"

"Wake the F up, Ranger."

"You're standing on my hand."

"Sorry about that."

Even though we had only spent a few minutes with the Platoon Leader and Platoon Sergeant it was immediately apparent that the mood of the men had changed from bad to worse. A few seconds after a brutal climb out from the bottom of the 300-foot Nisqually River floodplain, Sgt X raised his closed fist directly in front of my face. The closed fist is the military hand and arm signal for "freeze." As in "become a statue" of whatever position your body is in when you see it. After a couple of seconds of looking and listening he whispered, "There's something moving out there." We both stayed stock still with eyes and ears pointed outward into the forest. And then I heard it too. Something was definitely walking around out there.

The eye is attracted to contrast, so motion stands out. A human figure was walking through the woods about fifty meters from us. The outline of a helmet and weapon confirmed he was a Ranger. *"Maybe he's out there taking a piss,"* I thought until I heard him start mumbling something. "Is he talking to someone?" I whispered. Sgt X didn't waste any more time wondering. "Hey, Ranger, this is Sgt X, are you okay?" No response. Then the mumbling got louder. "Let's go check it out, Sir," Sgt X said as we both began walking directly toward him, cautiously at first.

"Maybe he lost something," Sgt X commented as he turned on his red lens flashlight so we could see. "Are you okay, Ranger?" Sgt X asked as we arrived. Still no response. Then the Ranger turned his back on us and broke his silence:

"Popcorn, popcorn, who wants popcorn, get your popcorn while the butter's hot," he screamed at the top of his lungs.

Neither of us needed any more clues. Every Ranger is trained to detect and treat the symptoms of hypothermia. Intense shivering occurs first, followed by unsteadiness in balance or gait, slurred speech, lack of interest, confusion, irritability, and, sometimes, in cases such as this one, hallucinations. Once the symptoms of hypothermia set, in body temperature plummets rapidly. When body temperature goes below eighty-two degrees the victim can collapse in a coma and die.

"Medic," Sgt X alerted at the top of his lungs while both of us switched to white lens flashlights. "This is a real world emergency, everyone go to white lights," I added as we waved our flashlights up and down to help the medic locate us. Within a few seconds the platoon medic came crashing through the brush and went right to work.

"I'll take one of those popcorns, Ranger," the medic told him in conversational calm. "I just need to get you warmed up first, if that's okay with you?" There was no response from the popcorn salesman so the medic nodded to me to assist him as we gently sat the Ranger down against the moss-covered trunk of a nearby fir tree. The medic continued talking in the same calming tone while his surgical scissors made quick work of the sopping wet uniform. As quickly as the uniform came off, Sgt X began wrapping the Ranger in a warming cocoon of double down-filled sleeping bags.

While the medic continued to stabilize the patient, Sgt X organized the stretcher team and I set up my radio to call our Company Commander (Captain Gildner) and let him know we had a medical emergency.

"His body temp is ninety-one degrees so I think we got him in time, Sir," the medic updated, "now we need to get him out of this rain and back to the rear as quickly as possible or his body temperature could drop again real quick."[1]

"Captain Gildner and the Battalion Ambulance are waiting for us on the fire road," I explained to Sgt X and the stretcher team.

Even though it was only 200 meters to the road it was 200 meters of dark, damp, deadfall, which made carrying a 200 lb. patient on a stretcher just as potentially risky as the hypothermia we were treating him for. We almost dumped him twice in the first fifty meters. Cocooned inside two sleeping bags that were zipped up to his face we didn't need a thermometer to tell that he was starting to warm up: "I'm not liking this," "you

---

1 Mild hypothermia = body temperature of 95°F to 90°F or 35°C to 32°C (shivering, chattering teeth, confusion).
Moderate hypothermia = body temperature of 90°F to 82°F or 32°C to 28°C.
Severe hypothermia = body temperature below 82°F or 28°C.

guys are scaring the shit out of me," "Doc, please get me the 'F' off this stretcher and let me walk on my own." As much as we wanted to grant him his wish the medic reminded us that "he wasn't out of the woods yet," a witty play on words that made everyone laugh and also realize it was the hard right so we continued to gut it out.

When we got to the road my company commander Captain Gildner was waiting with the ambulance and a couple of senior medics. Hypothermia was, and still is, a big deal in the military in general and the Rangers specifically. A few years earlier, two Ranger students died of hypothermia and the incident lived on as both a guiding principle and a lesson for all Army leaders: "Hypothermia isn't caused by soldiers and bad weather, it's caused by leaders and bad choices. Hypothermia is preventable."

The mantra was repeated so often and was so intuitively ingrained that in the rare instances such as this one, where it actually happened, the leaders involved instantly understood the seriousness and potentially career-ending ramifications if they were at fault. A comprehensive report of this incident would have to be completed immediately and sent as a high priority message for distribution all the way up the Army chain of command.

After the ambulance departed I thought it was just me and Captain Gildner until I noticed somebody else standing alone in the shadows a couple of hundred meters down the road. His body shape and bearing told me it could only be one person, the Battalion Commander Lieutenant Colonel (LTC) John J. Maher.

"Okay, Pete, tell me what happened," Captain Gildner began. I told him about the three-kilometer movement that took us five hours, and that nobody knew what was going on because we didn't get any updates after the first hour. Then I told him about the freezing rain and the order to "don Gore-Tex underneath our uniforms," and about the guys falling down while they tried to take off their pants, and that I stupidly fell down too. Then I told him about Sergeant X finding me, and what he told me about his guys' chattering teeth, and how he figured out where we were and squared away the Platoon Leader.

Even though it was too dark for me to see his face, I could tell Captain Gildner was beside himself with anger. Whenever he got really mad he'd start walking around in little circles while he talked. "This is un-freaking believable, Pete," he lamented as he logged his first lap, "what happened when you went to talk to him about the freaking Gore-Tex underwear?" I told him about my conversation with the Platoon Leader and Platoon Sergeant, and that Sergeant X had already figured out where we were, so instead of wasting more time trying to talk sense into them we focused the conversation on getting them back on track.

When I got to the part about me and Sergeant X heading back to grab our rucksacks before the platoon started moving he stopped me. "So instead of calling me on the radio you were on your way to get back in line and continue following along like some sort of mindless lemming for the rest of the night?" Before I could say "Yes, Sir" and acknowledge my now painfully apparent F-up, he continued, "for all you know, Pete, they might have changed their minds and decided to head down to the Nisqually River to conduct a poncho-raft river crossing." Hilarious in hindsight but he didn't laugh so I didn't either.

"I know you were probably trying to be respectful and let the platoon work things out on its own, but this is a good example of a situation where your responsibility as a leader overrides your responsibility to let somebody learn. There's no punishment for bouncing what you're seeing or hearing off someone else which is the main reason you're humping that twenty-pound brick (the radio) around on your back. If you had called me I would have told you this is the third time he's done this in the last six months and then I would have told you to take over the platoon on the spot.

"When were you planning on telling me about this, Pete?"

"I didn't want to bother you in the middle of the night, Sir, so I figured I'd tell you about it tomorrow morning," I admitted, once again fully aware of how stupid it now sounded. He took a deep breath.

"What's my job, Pete?"

"To command the company?"

"Nope, that's my job description. My job is the same as yours; it's to take care of the men in this company.[2] Taking care of the men isn't some

---

2 I was very fortunate throughout the early part of my career to work for so many amazing leaders. The military at its best is a sprawling leadership academy. After a couple years of attendance, you have seen and heard about the importance of taking care of your people and doing the right thing so many times, over and over, that it sticks with you for life.

touchy-feely thing that means we coddle them—that's not the purpose they came here to accomplish. Taking care of the men means making good choices that set the conditions for them to succeed. That's how we create a healthy leadership climate."

Leadership climate was a topic that leaders in our Battalion talked about a lot. Yet it wasn't Captain Gildner's words that taught me, and the rest of the leaders in the company, how important it was, it was his actions and his choices.

He told us to "think of a leadership climate the way we think of an actual climate; you can see and feel the effects of the climate all around you." When a leadership climate is healthy it sets the conditions for everyone and everything under it to grow, progress, and succeed. Everyone wants to live under a healthy leadership climate so when they find one they like and trust they put down roots and work together as a team to make it better for the future. But when the leadership climate is unhealthy, individual growth is stunted, the people who live under it are miserable, instead of focusing on the mission and how to make things better all they think about is going somewhere else or getting out.

Even as I stood there in the middle of the road shivering like a sorry sack of dog excrement, I knew he was teaching me an important lesson. I already knew and appreciated him as the best Company Commander in the Battalion; over time, and across many other leadership experiences, I would come to realize he was a key part of the best command climate I ever had the opportunity to be part of. And that's where the other guy on the road that night came in.

After Captain Gildner finished talking he told me, "The Battalion Commander wants to have a word with you, he's been standing out here for three hours waiting for the platoon to arrive so he may not be in the best of moods."

As I hurried down the road to meet with him I glanced at my watch, it was 0430. This was a Company training exercise on a Tuesday night so why would the Battalion Commander stay out here this late and in this weather? Even though I recognized there was still a possibility I might get kicked out of Ranger Battalion for what happened I felt no trepidation as I approached him. I didn't fear my Battalion Commander. I respected him. There's a big difference between being reprimanded by someone you trust and respect, and someone you don't. Trust and

Respect aren't earned in a single transaction; instead they are built over time by the aggregate of all of our actions and choices. In all the time I worked for him he was always logical, always fair, and everything I ever remember him telling me made sense. So whatever he decided, I had no doubt I'd respect his decision.

Born and raised in Georgia, he was 6'4 inches tall and spoke with a slow Southern drawl and a deep calming voice that he used to impart his signature wit, and homespun wisdom whenever he talked.

He began by telling me I was lucky to have a Company Commander who allowed me to learn, and then reiterated that letting your people learn has limits. "A good rule of thumb that has always worked for me is anytime the men are senselessly suffering it's time to intercede." He went on to tell me that although he was ultimately responsible for the leadership climate in the Battalion, he couldn't create or maintain a healthy leadership climate without his subordinate leaders at every level.

"I have a responsibility to understand how my subordinate leaders interact with their people. That relationship is the glue that holds every great combat team together. I wasn't planning on watching Captain Gildner and you interact tonight, but what I saw reinforced what I already knew, that you guys make a great combat team. I was hoping to watch the Platoon Leader and Platoon Sergeant set up their patrol base and, who knows, maybe they might have set up the best patrol base I'd ever seen and I would have walked away thinking I saw a combat-ready platoon. I wouldn't have had any way of knowing about the five-hour treasure hunt they lead their men on before they got here, nor would I have known that the reason the men all looked overweight was because they were wearing their Gore-Tex rain suits as underwear." Once again I wanted to laugh, but he kept talking so I kept silent.

"That's why I depend on leaders at all levels like Captain Gildner, Sergeant X, and you. I can't monitor the command climate where you're at because I don't live there. A leadership team has to work together by always sharing what they see." He then told me to think of myself as one of his climate monitoring stations. "If you see a tornado touch down you have a responsibility to share that information so the rest of the leadership team can take action and make sure none of our people get hurt by it. By not reporting the tornado you're allowing it to destroy the next town in its path and the next one after that. Leaders are most often thought of individually, yet the real power of leaders is collective. Every leader contributes to the creation of a healthy leadership climate and every leader is responsible for maintaining it."

He summed up everything he told me with his signature homespun Southern wisdom: "The only way a leader can see his own asshole is to have someone he trusts tell him what it looks like." This time I laughed out loud and he did too. Then he told me to "remember what happened out here tonight," to learn from it, and to "make sure it never happens again." "Roger that, Sir," I responded with gratitude, relief, and newly learned appreciation for the importance of a healthy leadership climate. "I'll never allow it to happen again, Sir, you have my word."

REFLECTIONS/LESSONS LEARNED
How to Create a Healthy Leadership Climate

Life lessons take time to learn. Only while writing about and reflecting on this period of my life did I comprehend both the immediate and long-term impact of great leaders and great leadership climates:

- **What's the purpose of all leaders?** To take care of their people.
- **How do leaders take care of the people they lead?** By creating and maintaining a healthy leadership climate that allows their people to accomplish their common purpose.
- **What patterns are pervasive in a healthy leadership climate?**
- A common sense of shared purpose and direction amongst all members on all missions all of the time (conscious awareness of FLOW).
- Collaboration across boundaries is common and encouraged.
- Communication is free flowing and omni-directional.
- Reciprocity is the currency of all interactions and the foundational governing principle upon which trust and building best teams is based ("you get what you give").
- Leaders say out loud the logic of why all orders, plans, or directives do or don't make sense.
- The logic of why is always present and/or always available on request.

- A common sense amongst all members of what does and doesn't make sense.

- Freedom of choice to do the right thing on the spot without permission.

- Freedom of speech to speak up, out, or with all leaders.

- Standard Operating Procedures make sense to those that have to follow them.

- There is no favoritism or cliques. Competence, courage, and common sense are prized and prioritized.

- There are no barriers and no restrictions against attacking sense-lessness and bureaucratic aberrations in the system.[125]

- Healthy leadership climates often contain an element of good humor. Team members can laugh about what they are doing and share a good laugh with their leaders.

- The foundation of a healthy leadership climate is leadership in general and senior leadership in particular.

The immediate impact of a healthy leadership climate is exemplified by the common sense leaders it attracts. The long-term impact emerges from the choices those common sense leaders make, the behaviors they model, and the knowledge they pass on to those who are fortunate enough to work with, and for, them.

FLOW+ Time + Feedback = Culture

As mentioned, healthy leadership climates start at the top, in this case with our Ranger Battalion Commander, Lieutenant Colonel John J Maher. What follows is a small sample of the timeless leadership knowledge and principles both he and two of his key subordinate leaders taught to me:

- **Battalion Commander, Lieutenant Colonel John J. Maher:**
  - ▶ "The best form of welfare for our troops when we're not deployed is getting them home in time to eat dinner with their families."
  - ▶ "Unless we are preparing for a mission, the only car I should see in the parking lot past six pm is mine. If you're watching and

waiting for my car to leave you're violating two of our standards because you're telling your people that hanging around for no reason is okay, and you're preventing your people from making it home in time to eat dinner with their families."

► "Friendship is one of the most misunderstood and underappreciated aspects of leadership. Some say you can't be friends with your people, I say have you ever had a friend that you didn't trust and respect? So how can you create a leadership environment based on trust and respect if you don't treat your people the same way you treat your friends? Always remember, friends don't let friends drive drunk, and when a friend does drive drunk real friends take them to task for it."

► "How a leader communicates on the radio is in many cases more important then what the leader communicates. Always take a deep breath before you talk and speak calmly no matter what's going on around you." Tone of voice carries far more weight with our brains than our words (the brain takes 10% of message meaning from words and 90% from the tone of voice and body language used to deliver the words). Your tone of voice is what is queuing your people. Airline pilots and flight attendants are taught this in their version of basic training. "If your people hear you panicking or getting angry on the radio they are more likely to panic and get angry themselves." Actions control thoughts. Take action and control your emotional thoughts by speaking calmly. **When we act calm we calm the way we act.**

Command Sergeant Major Leon-Guerro: As the Battalion Commander's right-hand man, Sergeant Major L-G as we called him, was a muscle-bound Guamanian whose booming voice, powerful handshake, and gap-toothed smile were always a welcome addition to any situation he walked up on. The most foundational lesson he taught us was the guiding principle "don't be in a hurry to die." He was constantly priming our minds with its all-purpose importance. Here's how he explained it to me:

► "Impulsiveness is one of the biggest killers on the battlefield. Warriors are aggressive by nature but acting without thinking instead of understanding the situation first could be the last mistake you ever make. It's what happened at LZ X-ray."[126] One of the biggest and most famous battles of the Vietnam War began when a Platoon Leader—who had been in the Army less than a year—spotted a single North Vietnamese soldier standing on the edge of the jungle clearing as his helicopter was about to land. The instant the helicopter touched down the Platoon Leader jumped out and bolted after the enemy soldier without telling the rest of his platoon where he was going or why. All twenty-nine members of the platoon followed their leader—as they are trained to do—running after him into the jungle until they couldn't run anymore. When the Platoon Leader finally paused to catch his breath, he and his men discovered they were surrounded. The battle of LZ X-ray was actually the battle to rescue the wayward platoon and their impulsive Platoon Leader. Twenty-six hours later, nine men including the Platoon Leader were dead. Thirteen others were severely injured. Only seven were able to walk out of the jungle unscathed.

► Before SGM Leon-Guerro taught me about the perils of impulsiveness I was that Platoon Leader. Fortunately for me (and my men) I spent my first four years in the military waging war against pretend enemies who fired blanks instead of bullets. By taking the time to teach me and my fellow Rangers about the fine line between aggressiveness and impulsiveness, SGM Leon-Guerro changed the way I thought, acted, and lead for the rest of my career. Whether I was thinking of running to the sounds of unknown guns, or running off a helicopter on a dark landing zone, or running into an un-cleared building, conscious awareness of the guiding principle, **"Don't be in a hurry to die"** and the logic of why it makes sense—**"impulsiveness leads people to their deaths"**—saved my own life and the lives of those around me too many times to count. For fellow first responders especially, prime your people's minds before any type of mission by saying it out loud and repeating it.

Battalion XO, Major Bill Leszczynski: Major Leszczynski was a deep thinking, super dedicated and disciplined student of maneuver warfare. Whether we were talking about the pluses and minuses of leaving a stay-behind ambush in the jungles of Panama, or the latest breakthroughs in sports nutrition and human performance, he always seemed to have an insightful anecdote or germane fact to add to the discussion as if it had been sitting on the tip of his tongue from the first moment we started talking.

- ▶ He carried a pocket notebook with him wherever he went and was constantly pausing in the middle of conversations to write down thoughts and insight as soon as they popped up or into his head.
- ▶ I bought my first pocket notebook in 1988 and would go on to write down most everything I learned while carrying it with me for the rest of my military career. I still carry one wherever I go to this day (this paragraph came from one of those notebooks).

Finally, many of my peers in the Ranger Battalion who were Lieutenants and Captains at that time went on to lead some of the most successful missions and units during combat operations in both Afghanistan and Iraq. Many of us have stayed friends throughout our military careers and are still friends today.

The lessons I learned from these leaders and the leadership climate they created became permanently etched inside my brain. Over time, and with feedback, they formed the bedrock FLOW upon which I led and organized for the rest of my life.

Great leadership and great leadership climates go hand in hand. So too do great organizational cultures and great organizational success. Common sense leadership is learned. Pass it on. **It's the Common Sense Way.**

*Captain Gray Gildner in front, I'm standing
behind him over his right shoulder.*

CHAPTER 8

Asteroid the Way

The Way vs. the Common Sense Way

To learn a new idea our brains need a discrepancy to latch onto. If we don't recognize there's a discrepancy between what we know and what we experience then there is little or no motivation to pay attention and learn about it. The biologic way to trigger a discrepancy is by posing a situation, problem, or opportunity that excites, engages, and/or contrasts with something that matters to our brains. It is through discrepancies that the world announces itself to us.[127]

I spent a long time thinking about how to finish this book. What words could I arrange as a source of metaphor to incite the appropriately high level of importance, and life or death sense of urgency, commensurate with changing the way we the people currently think and speak about leading and organizing? And then it hit me.

As I write, and you read this sentence, there's an asteroid barreling through space on a bull's eye collision course with our planet and its orbit. It's happened before and it will happen again, it's a mathematical certainty.

Human knowledge and technological awareness of the Universe are on a collision course with the asteroid. We'll either detect and deflect the asteroid or we may not know what hit us. One of the defining features of a potential asteroid strike that differentiates it from all other natural disasters such as earthquakes, tsunamis, and volcanoes, is that mankind has both the knowledge and the technology to prevent it.

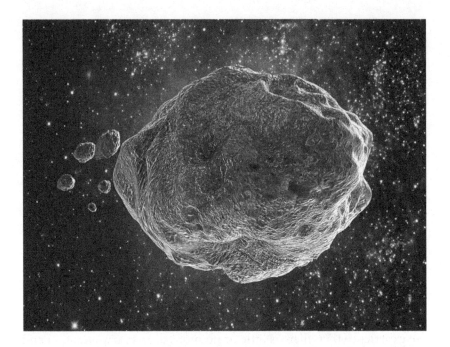

The survival of our planet and our species will depend on the choices our leaders make before and/or after it hits. The future is not preordained. It's unfolding right here, right now, right in front of us. Like touching a rolling ball, when we choose to interact with any situation in life we change its future trajectory (DTS). We have a say in our own destiny. **How will we, the freedom loving people of the planet choose to lead and organize ourselves to ensure we survive, thrive, and evolve in the future?**

This chapter uses the imminent asteroid scenario as a thought experiment to help us find the answer. A thought experiment is an experiment carried out in the realm of the imagination rather than in a laboratory. It is a technique that has played a key role in a great number of scientific discoveries such as the Theory of Relativity by Albert Einstein.

Thought experiments are designed to test ideas, theories, and scenarios in order to examine and learn about their potential consequences. By thinking about the way we lead and organize ourselves in the context of our own survival we can better understand whether the current way makes sense or whether it's senseless.

The Way versus the Common Sense Way	
Which Way Would You Choose?	
(Hint) The answer is Common Sense	
The Way	**The Common Sense Way**
• Process oriented	• Purpose oriented
• Do what you're told to do	• Do what makes sense
• Stay in your lane	• Learn to adapt to patterns
• Follow plans from the past	• Freedom to make sensible choices
• Orders, Commands	• Logic of Why it makes sense
• Strategy, Plans, Disconnected Chain-of-Command	• Foundational Logic of Why (FLOW)
• Wait to be told	• Develop the Situation/Go with the FLOW
• Organizational Structure	• Organize to learn
• Get along or get out	• Collaborate, Communicate, Reciprocate
• Teach them how to follow the process	• Teach them how to think
• Stay anchored to the chain	• Build learning-feedback loops not ladders
• Need to know	• Shared Reality
• Stoic/Not fun	• Humor/Creativity

Thinking about the unthinkable is how we figure things out.

NEWS FLASH: "We interrupt your reading to bring you an important national security bulletin: A consortium of international scientists and space agencies have just confirmed the discovery of a large asteroid barreling through space on a bull's-eye collision course with our planet and its orbit. The asteroid is listed as #52768 by NASA's Center for Near Earth Object Studies (CNEOS) in California and is estimated to measure 2.5 miles across. Estimated time to impact is four years. That's all we know for now. Stay tuned for more updates."

After hearing the News Flash most of us would likely drop whatever it is we were doing and make contact with our loved ones and/or our friends and colleagues to see if they heard what we heard and whether or not they heard anything different.

How do our brains make sensible choices in complex unfamiliar situations?

The Way: As our questions continue to accumulate we'd likely turn to the internet or cell network so we can access information and updates and talk to each other about what we heard or read, etc.

(Versus)

The Common Sense Way: To make decisions and solve complex problems there's no substitute for a prepared mind. Human Intelligence is a pattern recognition process designed to make sense of real world problems and make sensible choices about what to do next. Stay calm, think.

1. The brain makes sensible choices about what to do next by comparing and contrasting sensory inputs from the patterns of life as they're going on around us in the context of the moment: *News Flash.*

2. To our foundational knowledge of patterns stored in the galactic caverns of our memory: *Everything we know about anything.*

3. From this neural process the logic of why we do what we do and choose what we choose emerges: *We need to learn more about asteroid patterns.*

What's going on around us (+) What we know = The logic
of why we do what we do and choose what we choose

The longer we think about and reflect on our decision-making and problem-solving equation the more we realize it doesn't add up. *We don't know enough about asteroid patterns.* When our brains sense a discrepancy between what we know/expect to experience—*another normal day*—and the reality of the situation going on around us—*an asteroid on a collision course with our planet*—they instinctively expend energy to make the discrepancy cohere by learning from, adapting to, and interacting with what's going on around us. It's common sense to develop the situation.

Learned knowledge of patterns provides our brains with options,
and options provide us with freedom to choose between them
based on the adaptive stimulus of what's going on around us.

What follows is a brief summary of some foundational asteroid patterns such as the history and science of asteroids, as well as some of the current options, ideas, and technologies for deflecting them.

Patterns of History: It's not a question of if; it's only a question of when. Our planet and moon have been bombarded by space rocks for the past four billion years and will continue to get pounded for billions of years to come into the future. Impact craters, such as the one pictured near Winslow, Arizona and the craters that pockmark the moon's surface, offer our eyes irrefutable sensory evidence that makes sense of this pattern.

The evolution of every living thing on our planet is indelibly linked to the history of asteroid strikes. Sixty-six million years ago a massive asteroid (10 km/6.2 miles wide) blasted through outer space at over 40,000 mph and slammed into the Gulf of Mexico with a force of impact equivalent to 7,000 nuclear bombs.

Known by geologists as the K/T extinction event the concussive after-shock from the collision initiated a cataclysmic string of natural disasters that swept across the planet as earthquakes, tsunamis, fires, famine, drought, and disease. The temperature of Earth's atmosphere rose above 300 degrees for at least a few hours after impact, causing

Barringer Crater, is a meteorite impact crater located
approximately 18 miles west of Winslow Arizona

almost all vegetation to burst into flames and instantly incinerating almost every living thing that wasn't either underground, underwater, or in some other type of hardened shelter.

Greater than 75% of all species were exterminated. Almost all dinosaurs including T-Rex and Triceratops were wiped out. Their 400-million-year run at the top of the food chain was terminated. The planet was in ruins.

Yet before the dust and debris had completely settled, out from the ground crept and crawled bugs. Lots of them. Right behind the bugs, perhaps in pursuit of them, crawled a mouse-like creature no bigger than a child's shoe. We don't know exactly what their surface features looked like on the outside (see artist's depiction below) but we know enough about what their DNA looked like on the inside to give them a name. We call them our cousins. The universal common ancestor of all mammals alive on earth today (aka the heroes of human evolution).

How'd they do it? Our mouse-like ancestors, and their DNA, survived the asteroid apocalypse the same way they survived the

400-million-year domination of the dinosaurs. By employing a time-tested survival principle still worth saying out loud to ourselves and our loved ones today: **Get Down.** Preferably behind or underneath cover. The laws of nature (gravity, physics, mass and energy) govern the behavior of all projectiles. Knowledge of the laws of nature provides our brains with options to protect. Whether you're being bombarded by projectiles from nature (asteroid, tornado, hurricane, etc.), or from human nature (e.g. bombs, bullets, rocks, etc.), the time-tested survival principle that will help you stay alive and prevent you from getting hit is to **Get Down** (e.g. duck, crouch, take a knee, hit the deck, etc.). It's common sense.

The largest asteroid to collide with earth in modern human history was estimated to be 50 to 100 meters wide (approximately 1/40th the size of the asteroid in this scenario) when it exploded above the Tunguska River in Siberia on June 30th, 1908. One thousand times more powerful than the atomic bomb dropped on Hiroshima, its shock waves rolled across the frozen frontier of Siberia flattening 80 million trees spread over 2,150 square kilometers (830 sq. mi) of uninhabited tundra. By comparison, New York City is 790 square kilometers (305 sq. miles) and is inhabited by 8,491,089 humans*.

Patterns of Nature and Patterns of Human Nature: Warning that an asteroid collision is one of the biggest threats to humanity in the coming centuries, an international group of astronauts, scientists, and concerned citizens met in 2015, and again in 2020, to call for a rapid

expansion of efforts to detect asteroids capable of causing widespread destruction to life on earth.

"NASA has done a good job of finding the very largest objects, the ones that would wipe out the human race," said Ed Lu, an astronaut who flew three trips to the International Space Station. "It's the smaller ones that they haven't found that could destroy an entire country, our food sources, or the global economy for a couple of hundred years, that are the biggest problem," Lu explains.[128] As of 2021, only around one-third of the space rocks with potential to cause massive damage to earth have been detected.[129]

To accurately predict whether an asteroid has our planet in its cross-hairs we need a precise understanding of its trajectory. Key to calculating an asteroid's trajectory is a pattern of nature known by the name of the human who discovered it: the Yarkovsky effect. Ivan Yarkovsky (1844–1902) was a Russian civil engineer who worked on scientific problems in his spare time. Writing in a pamphlet around the year 1900, Yarkovsky noted that the daily heating of a rotating object in space would cause it to experience a force that, while tiny, could over time change the orbit and future trajectory of the object.

Random collisions with other space rocks, as well as the melting and/or breaking away of massive chunks of ice and debris, can also incrementally change an asteroid's shape, weight, and trajectory. "There is no doubt that the Yarkovsky effect could easily throw a wrench into our current and future predictions," said Michael Drake, director of the Lunar and Planetary Laboratory at the University of Arizona.

We have to find it first. In theory, as long as we are able to detect an earth-bound asteroid early enough, we should have the knowledge and technology to come up with a solution to nudge or deflect its trajectory and ensure it barrels by without bashing into us.

Once the asteroid is detected, international space agencies across the globe (e.g. NASA, ESA, RFSA, CNSA, JAXA, etc.), along with their corporate defense contractor partners (e.g. JPL Labs, Space X, Boeing, Northrup Grumman, etc.), will work to determine the answers to the following asteroid impact questions:

- When and where is the asteroid most likely to impact the planet?
- What is the potential damage the asteroid will cause if it explodes above or on the ground?[130]
- When could an impactor spacecraft be launched in order to intercept the asteroid?
- What is the maximum size of an asteroid that can be deflected with a single launch?
- How much velocity change is required to make the asteroid miss the Earth?
- In which direction will the asteroid be deflected most easily?

Note: Many of the answers to these questions will be based on probabilities (e.g. a 10% probability the asteroid with hit earth, and 5% probability it will impact on land, etc.). These probabilities will change over time as data is accumulated.

There are many ideas on how to deflect an asteroid. Some of them sound as simple as they do silly, such as planting solar sails onto the asteroid's surface, or plastering it with black or white paint to use the power of the sun's thermal energy to push it off track. The solution that most international experts (as well as NASA) believe makes the most sense is to send a spaceship to either crash into the asteroid or to shoot something at it, such as a laser or a nuclear weapon. The purpose of all these options is the same: to alter the asteroid's future trajectory. There is no guarantee that any one option will work. No one has ever deflected an asteroid before.

Current estimate for the design, manufacture, and preparation of a customized spaceship is three to seven years. As of 2021, no known planetary defense hardware (special spaceships, missiles, lasers, or other technologies) have been approved, developed, or built, which doesn't leave a lot of wiggle room for an asteroid ETA of four years or faster.

The Test: Now that we've primed our minds with a solid foundation of context-specific patterns and principles let's ask ourselves some context-specific questions designed to pressure test the way we currently choose to lead and organize ourselves to respond.

The Questions: How long did our leaders know about the asteroid before they told us? Are they telling us everything they know? Will they keep us updated with all the facts, and nothing but the facts, as the facts continue to emerge? Or will they compartmentalize knowledge under the guise of physical security, technology secrecy, and need to know? Trust can't be bought or borrowed it must be built over time via the choices leaders make and the actions they take for the purpose and the people they have the privilege to lead.

Do we believe the science? How about the scientists extolling the science? What about their predictions regarding when and where the asteroid will hit and how much damage it will cause? Are they explaining the logic of why their predictions and prognostications make sense?

How do we separate the science from the political scientists and the politics they align themselves with? If groups of international scientists are willing to sacrifice scientific objectivity at the altar of ideology with "climate data," "virus data," and "election data," how will we, the people, be able to trust what they say about when, where, and how an asteroid may crash into us?

Will we default to the current way and defer to the highest-ranking scientist in charge at the time? Or will we use common sense and tap into the wisdom of the crowd to ensure we don't get bamboozled by the so-called experts whose only real expertise is bureaucracy?

If political scientists, political leaders, and "we, the people," disagree on the science of where, when, and whether the asteroid will hit, are our current leaders capable of finding common ground and consensus?

What continent is the asteroid most likely to crash into? Is evacuating a continent an option? What if there's a 50% chance it will hit a continent? What about 25%? If people from one continent need to evacuate to other continents, who will make the call? When will they make the call? Will we, the people, of either continent have a say in the call? What if the people who are being told to evacuate don't think it makes sense to evacuate? Will we, the people, be free to choose? Or will political leaders make the decision for us under the guise of their self-anointed Emergency Powers? Do you trust they'll make the right decision?

Who (what country, organization, individual) is going to calculate the optimal time and location for intercepting the asteroid? How much time would that leave to build and launch a space ship? How do we choose the location for the project, the subject matter experts, the individual leaders, and the corporations that will give us the best shot at success? Will our political and corporate leaders select the best people and build the best teams based on competence, communication, credibility, and common sense? Or will they make their choices based on political affiliation, profit, and personal preferences? *To select the best people and build the best teams always use common sense.*

How will we organize? Will space-faring nations (e.g. U.S., Russia, India, Japan, China, Europe, etc.) collaborate, communicate, and reciprocate to accomplish our common purpose (to save our species and planet by deflecting the asteroid)? Or will the space-faring nations work in silos, compartmentalize the knowledge they learn, and compete against each other. *When we organize to learn we learn how to organize. Build loops not ladders. Collaboration by communicating and reciprocating is the common sense way to build the best teams to accomplish any purpose.*

What if the solution that makes the most sense involves using nuclear weapons? Do we trust other countries to launch a nuclear weapon into space? Do they trust us? What if one space-faring nation goes rogue and launches a hastily designed and untested nuclear-armed impactor ship against the wishes of the other space-faring nations? What if the impactor ship successfully smashes into and deflects the main body of the asteroid but redirects a boulder the size of a nine-story building on a bulls-eye collision course with New York City? Could an asteroid start a nuclear war?

Would we send up another hastily designed nuclear-armed impactor ship and risk the same thing happening again? Or would world leaders decide it's too dangerous to the environment so New York City will have to be sacrificed, its nine million residents will have to evacuate their homes and businesses and move to temporary refugee centers in neighboring states?[131]

Using current examples of national and international decision-making and problem solving on complex issues such as virus containment, immigration, international trade, drug trafficking, and terrorism, it's easy to imagine how tensions will arise and how difficult it may be to sustain calm, fact-based discussions that lead to logic-based greater good solutions. **How will National and International leaders make these types of complex life-changing choices?**

The Way we currently choose to make these types of life-changing choices is to select or elect our leaders, empower them with status, rank, and/or title (e.g. President, Prime Minister, Governor, Mayor, CEO, Commander, Chief, Sir, Ma'am, etc.), and enable them with near omnipotent choice-making authority over the people, places, and purpose for which they were selected or elected to lead. Once selected or elected, the way enables leaders to say or do whatever they want, as long as it's within their own interpretation of law and as long as we the people allow it.

(Versus)

The Common Sense Way is to institutionalize FLOW. FLOW provides a common sense of purpose and direction upon which our brains are free to pivot based on the adaptive stimulus of what's going on around us. To institutionalize FLOW in a situation such as the imminent asteroid contingency, common sense leaders must: 1) Find it, 2) Share it, and 3) Constantly update it.

1) **Find it:** The common sense way to find our collective purpose is to call an agenda-less meeting and talk it out. **Anything our brains can do alone they can do better together. We need each other.** Simply bring people together around a rock, tree, campfire, or table, and ask the question: what's our purpose and what do we need to do to accomplish it? Then sit back and allow the knowledge to flow. Putting our heads together enables us to build upon, pressure test, and branch out from the knowledge we know.

In situations where we may not know how to frame our purpose specifically, we can always frame it biologically: *To survive, thrive, evolve.* Our biologic FLOW forms the bedrock foundation of every decision we make and every problem solving effort we undertake. **To put our biologic FLOW into practice we say it out loud and share it:**

> *To survive, thrive, and evolve we must prevent*
> *the asteroid from striking the planet.*

Once focused with a common sense of purpose our brains instinctively begin aggregating all the driving factor patterns we've learned over a lifetime to accomplish it. Even the most complex of problems or opportunities have an identifiable or underlying pattern to them. Driving factors are the key patterns and relationships that influence whether or not you accomplish your purpose (e.g. the Yarkovsky effect, the laws of physics, weather patterns, human behavior patterns, patterns of history, etc.). If you understand your purpose then you'll recognize the diving factor patterns when you see, hear, feel, and experience them. Stay calm, think.

What follows are examples of some driving factor patterns and principles that might emerge from an asteroid related agenda-less meeting:

Driving Factor Patterns:

Answers from NASA's Asteroid Impact Questions (e.g. current data on when and where the asteroid is most likely to impact the planet, current damage estimates for both air and ground bursts); timeline for deflection efforts with milestones for building and launching a spacecraft; the history and science of asteroids; The Yarkowsky Effect; lessons learned from the international group of astronauts, scientists, and concerned citizens who met in 2015 and 2020, etc.

Driving Factor Principles:

Common sense is the common ground and common language that connects us all. We are one. To make decisions and solve problems use common sense and develop the situation. To select the best people and build the best teams always use common sense. When we always do what's in the best interests of the people we always do what's in the best interests of our purpose. Collaborate, Communicate, Reciprocate. etc.

2) **Share it:** To lay the foundation for successful choice-making common sense leaders don't tell their people what to do or how to choose, instead they prime their people's minds by saying out loud and sharing their common purpose along with all the driving factor patterns and principles they've learned over time to accomplish it. Once internalized all our brains have to do is pay attention to what's going on around us and then go with the FLOW:

Our common purpose and direction (FLOW) + the adaptive stimulus of what's going on around us (updated asteroid impact facts)= the logic of why we do what we do and choose what we choose (Develop the Situation to deflect the asteroid)

When striving to understand the choices we make it's not the choice itself (yes, no, buy, sell, etc.), it's the logic of why we used to make the choice that explains, communicates, and validates whether the choice makes sense or is senseless. To ensure the choices we make and actions we take make sense, the logic of why standard provides leaders with three built-in checks and balances to safeguard against senselessness:

A) Say the logic of why out loud and/or write it down to make it physical so our other senses and those of the people around us can pressure test it and see if it makes sense. *The more senses we involve the more sense we can make.*

B) Ensure the logic of why consists of three or more context-specific patterns and/or time-tested principles that we can see, hear, smell, taste, touch, feel and make sense of. *First of all, secondly, and third....If it doesn't have three legs to stand on it's probably not standing on solid ground.*

C) Ensure the logic of why coheres with our common purpose *(our FLOW)*, and adapts to what's going on around us in the context of the moment *(updated asteroid patterns)*. A coherent-adaptive choice is a sensible choice *(Develop the Situation to deflect the asteroid)*.

Note: In situations where time is of the essence the logic of why can be as simple as "I got a gut feeling about this." Context is everything, so if the leader telling you they have a gut feeling is trusted and the situation warrants, you may say "good enough" and go along. The key is that you now understand that the logic of why you are doing what you are doing is based solely on your leader's gut feeling. If an incoherent pattern pops up that dispels the gut feeling you can self-correct and try another way or go back to the drawing board and come up with a new way. Freedom of choice to change our minds is common sense.

3) **Constantly Update it:** Over time, with feedback, our brains learn whether or not the choices we made are sensible or senseless. Our potential to survive, thrive, and evolve in the future will depend on our ability to capture what we learned along the way and pass it on to those that follow. When the logic of why we do what we do and choose what we choose makes sense over time a positive learning-feedback loop emerges and the logic of why becomes part of our (FLOW).

Logic of Why + Time + Feedback (+/–) = Updated FLOW

Sharing and memorializing the knowledge we learn from our experiences over time enables evolutionary learning.

Updated FLOW + Time + Feedback = Character/Culture/History

As we go through the remaining questions imagine the difference it would make if we held ourselves, our political leaders, our scientists, and the mainstream media accountable to the **logic of why standard** and its built-in system of checks and balances against senselessness. If a political leader doesn't say out loud and/or write down the logic of why a new law, emergency order, tax, or regulation makes sense, then there is no law, order, tax, or regulation. When our brains understand the logic of why a choice was made in the past we can recognize when it's failing to achieve its purpose in the future. Instead of hoping we the people forget what they said and did in the past we can hold our leaders accountable and ensure they do the right thing to make the choice cohere.

Back to the Asteroid: On the personal front, every choice you make from this day forward will be influenced by the level of trust you have in the leaders above you (e.g. CEO, Mayor, Police Chief, Governor, President, etc.). New job? New house? New school? Start or end a relationship? Bring a child into the world? Does it make sense to buy, make, or acquire anything other than sustainment supplies (e.g. food, water, underground shelter, etc.)? Does it make sense to keep working every day? Does it make sense to leave your money in stocks and electron-only accessed banks? How long will you wait until you begin taking your money out? Money talks, cash is king, gold rules the world.

As the months tick by, most every person, place, and organization on the planet will be focused on the asteroid. What option will give us the best chance at deflecting it? How much time is needed to prepare various options for deflecting it? How much time would that leave until impact day? Should we stay or should we go? Everyone will have a strong opinion because everyone's survival will be on the line. Staying well informed will require a constant flow of unbiased, verifiable, fact-based information. With the survival of our families, friends, and our species on the line how will we, the people, know who and what to believe?

The mainstream media[132] will beg us to trust them as our primary source for asteroid-related information and updates. However, if the best indicator of future behavior and performance are our behaviors and performance from the past, is trusting the mainstream media as a reliable source for survival-related information even an option?

We now have physical evidence, in the form of recently unclassified documents, that almost everything the mainstream media told us about "Russian Collusion," The Mueller Investigation, Spying on American citizens, Ukraine corruption, and the coronavirus was wrong or knowingly false. Victor Davis Hanson (Historian, Hoover Institute, Stanford University, 2020)

Can we go around the mainstream media and get all of our information from the internet? Recent patterns of behaviors by Big Tech[133] such as: coordinating echo chambers of political propaganda by using search engine manipulation, content censoring, and shadow-banning; falsifying political polls in order to manipulate the people whose choices are influenced by them; and brazenly bragging (in undercover videos) about how they manipulate content based on the politics of their customers, reveals Big Tech's Orwellian capacity and intent to drown out or deny access to information they don't agree with while promoting that which supports their political agenda and views.[134]

The common denominator pattern that connects Big Tech and the mainstream media (hereafter referred to as the corporate media) is political partisanship. Studies assessing news content and coverage by the corporate media between 2017 and 2020 reveal a 95% negative content and coverage rating of the political leader and political party they despise, and a 96% positive content and coverage rating for the political party they support.[135] *Patterns emerge from the relationship of their parts, patterns combine to make sense, and patterns repeat.*

Back to the Asteroid: Will the corporate media objectively report all the facts and nothing but the facts as they occur? What if the corporate media's favored political party and political leader are running the country during the asteroid contingency and making a series of disastrous choices that are slowly but surely dooming the entire planet to destruction? Will the corporate media cast a blind eye and a technological cover over the facts in order to protect their favored political leaders?

What if the political party and political leader that the corporate media despises are running the country during the asteroid crisis? Will they treat them fairly and objectively? Or will the corporate media apply their 95% negative spin to any and all choices the political leader they despise makes even if those choices are clearly in the best interests of we, the people, and the planet?

It was very interesting because it wasn't the way any candidate had ever been covered in my lifetime and certainly not by institutions like CNN and The New York Times, which I had followed all my life and who I had watched and read religiously. And I started to see this thing happening that, oh, the press is involved in an election and not reporting on it, they're part of the story and they want to determine its outcome. And it became, as it went on...maddening. Frightening... Bret Easton Ellis

To better understand the way the corporate media could influence our decision-making and problem-solving as we search for solutions to a life or death contingency such as an imminent asteroid, it's beneficial to understand the way the corporate media influenced our decision-making and problem solving during other life or death contingencies that occurred in the recent past.

"Accurately understanding and sharing lessons from the past is an essential step for gaining insight into and preparing for the future."

The bright, shining benefit of the 2020–2021 worldwide virus pandemic was that it enabled us to observe patterns of behaviors that we never could have imagined if we hadn't seen, heard, felt, and experienced them with our own senses. What follows is a brief summary of how the corporate media influenced our decision-making and problem solving as we searched for solutions to the life or death virus contingency:

- On March 19th, 2020, as the Corona/Wuhan/COVID 19 Virus was just beginning to circle the globe, the President of the United States mentioned Hydroxychloroquine during his daily press conference, here's what he said: *"Nothing will stand in our way as we pursue any avenue to find what best works against this horrible virus. Now, a drug called chloroquine or hydroxychloroquine, this is a common malaria drug. It is also a drug used for strong arthritis. But it is known as a malaria drug, and...the nice part is, it's been around for a long time... And it's shown very encouraging—very, very encouraging early results.*

- Hydroxychloroquine (HCQ) was approved by the Food and Drug Administration for the prevention and treatment of malaria in 1955.[136] According to *The World Health Report 1999:* "prior to the introduction of HCQ, the world sustained around two million deaths each year from malaria."

- Since the early 1960's all military personnel who served in or near high malaria threat areas have had to take HCQ tablets.[137] Having spent significant portions of my military career in the jungles of Panama, Honduras, Guyana, and Colombia, I estimate I have taken over 50 HCQ tablets to protect against malaria.

- HCQ is on the World Health Organization's (WHO) List of Essential Medicines.[138] In 2017, it was the 128th most commonly prescribed medication in the United States with more than five million prescriptions.[139] Over three million HCQ tablets are taken every day by rheumatoid arthritis and lupus patients.

- In 2005, the National Institutes of Health (NIH) published a study in *Virology Journal* that identified chloroquine (an earlier version of HCQ) as a "potent inhibitor" of the SARS virus.[140] The researchers stated authoritatively: "Chloroquine can effectively reduce the establishment of infection and spread of the SARS virus," which is 79% genetically similar to the COVID-19 virus and ten times deadlier.

All of the above information was available on the 19th of March 2020, yet instead of going to the CDC's website and/or talking with practicing virologists who had successfully treated thousands of patients with HCQ, the corporate media chose to ignore the facts and go with an echo chamber of negative commentary instead:

"The President's Embrace of Unproven Drugs to Treat Coronavirus Defies Science." (NYT, March 20th, 2020)

"Thus far, there is little scientific evidence that chloroquine, or its closely-related analogue hydroxychloroquine, are effective in treating COVID-19." (@CNN) March 30th, 2020)

"HCQ is dangerous," "It will KILL you," "It has concerning side effects," "It's akin to taking 'camel urine.'" (Various Political Pundits)

Was/is HCQ safe? What follows is the actual FDA approved safety profile for HCQ as listed on the Center for Disease Control (CDC) website the day the President mentioned it (Mar. 19, 2020):

"Hydroxychloroquine can be prescribed to adults and children of all ages. It can also be safely taken by pregnant women and nursing mothers."[141]

Ironically, HCQ is one of the safest prescription medications ever approved by the FDA. By comparison, aspirin is not considered safe for young children or pregnant woman or nursing mothers.[142]

Was/is HCQ effective for the prevention and/or treatment of the Coronavirus? Dr. Vladimir Zelenko, a New York based family medicine physician did the clinical legwork in support of what became known as the Zelenko protocol which uses a three-ingredient cocktail of hydroxychloroquine, azithromycin, and zinc. The effectiveness of the Zelenko protocol on virus patients was both dramatic and statistically significant. Yet the Zelenko protocol was dismissed as "anecdotal" by senior leadership at the Center of Disease Control (CDC), criticized by political scientists, and completely ignored by the corporate media.[143]

"I don't care what 'they' say anymore, I would rather speak directly to the American people and tell them I have some very good news for [them]. We have an answer to the terrible infection, we have a very effective way of treating it. In the high-risk groups there is a 99.3% survival [rate] and an 84% reduction in hospitalizations. There is also a 100% survival rate in low-risk patients when [our] treatment is started in the first five days [of the onset of] an infection."[144] *Dr. Zelenko, 2020.*

A peer-reviewed retrospective study conducted by Henry Ford Health Systems in Detroit on July 2nd, 2020 confirmed Dr. Zelenko's results by showing that "HCQ cuts the death rate in half when it is administered to hospitalized coronavirus patients soon after they are admitted."[145]

Doctors across the globe took notice of the results and began organizing themselves so they could share knowledge and better understand how to treat their virus patients with HCQ. One of these groups called themselves America's Frontline Doctors. They came from different states across the country, from different medical specialties, and from different ethnic backgrounds and political affiliations. Their common ground was their common sense of purpose: "to always choose to do what's in the best interests of their patients."

On July 27th, 2020, America's Frontline Doctors traveled to Washington D.C. so they could "speak directly to the American people" and share what they had learned about treating the virus with HCQ. The video of their introductory press conference was the most watched video on social media accumulating over seventeen million views during the first eight hours it was hosted on Facebook. What happened next was both described and documented by Dr Simone Gold, the leader of America's Frontline Doctors as the events occurred between July 28th, and September 5th, 2020.

"The video was removed and banned from every major social media platform including Facebook, Twitter, Google, YouTube, and Vimeo."

"Twitter forced us to delete video testimonials from our physicians."

"The media smeared us by calling us 'fringe doctors' spouting dangerous falsehoods about HCQ as a COVID 19 wonder cure."

"Why are journalists claiming hydroxychloroquine is ineffective when there are numerous (over fifty) studies showcasing its efficacy against COVID-19?"

"Social media companies are censoring the opinions of trained physicians when it goes against their narrative."

"These actions are unprecedented and have never happened before in medicine."

All medical choices are made by weighing the risks vs. the potential gains. Decades of statistically significant safety and efficacy data provide one of the most valuable sources of information for any potential patient to consider as they assess whether the benefits of taking a drug like HCQ are worth the risks from its possible side effects. Learned knowledge of patterns provides our brains with options. When we have options we have freedom to choose between them. When our brains are denied freedom to learn knowledge of potentially life-saving options such as HCQ then we have no choice. Freedom of choice to learn knowledge of life-saving options is an inherently human right.

> *"Anyone who blocks use of this treatment*
> *is guilty of crimes against humanity."*
> Dr. Vladimir Zelenko

> *"Many or most of the 220,000 deaths in the United States to*
> *date could have been prevented by widespread HCQ use that*
> *the FDA blocked." Dr. Harvey Risch, M.D., Ph.D., Professor of*
> *Epidemiology at Yale School of Public Health. Oct. 20th, 2020*

> *"Those who cannot remember the past are*
> *condemned to repeat it." George Santayana*

With regards to HCQ, almost everything the corporate media told us during those critical first few weeks and months was either wrong or knowingly false.[146] As a result, our entire decision-making and problem-solving response to the virus: the lockdowns, the masks, the gloves, the fear of contaminated surfaces, the social distancing, the closing of nonessential businesses, the disastrous school closings, the destruction of our best-in-the-world economy, and the slaughter of thousands of our most frail senior citizens in nursing homes by authoritarian governors, were all based on the faulty premise that there was no known medication considered safe and effective enough to prevent and/or treat the virus.[147]

> *The dilemma of choice lies not so much on making the choice*
> *as the basis or foundation of knowledge upon which it stands.*
> *"Taking a stand," "Standing up for others," and "Standing*
> *our ground" are all timeless metaphors for choosing to do*
> *the "right thing." To do the right thing our brains require a*
> *strong structurally sound foundation of knowledge that can*
> *support the weight and gravity of the choices we make on it.*

If we can't learn from the past and present then we can't adapt to future contingencies. If we can't adapt we will perish. It doesn't matter whether your politics are left, right, center, or anywhere in between. The evolutionary crime of political partisanship, political correctness, and fake news, is that they impede, instead of enable, our freedom of choice and freedom of speech to learn from, adapt to, and make sense of what's going on around us so we can make sensible choices about what to do next.

Some of us may someday forgive the corporate media for the divisiveness they manufactured, the lawlessness and unnecessary deaths they contributed to, and the monumental betrayal of the trust we the people bestowed upon them. None of us should ever forget it. We've now seen it with our own eyes and heard it with our own ears and felt it in our hearts and souls. Thanks to what happened with HCQ during the pandemic of 2020 we don't have to wait for an imminent asteroid to learn this lesson as a species.

If we ignore the corporate media during the imminent asteroid contingency, how will we make sense of what's going on around us and sensible choices about what to do next?

The Way: There is no alternative source of information and knowledge. Do what the corporate media and your political party leaders tell you to do or else.

(Versus)

The Common Sense Way: We aren't helpless or dependent on the corporate media. Our secret weapon for understanding the world around us is our senses. Believe in and trust your senses. To engage them, all we have to do is take a couple long, full, deep breaths and pay attention to what's going on around us. Stay calm think. Like a cat searching for a mouse, look, listen, smell, touch, feel, then say out loud what you perceive and share it with others to see whether or not it makes sense.

"A physical theory must be based only on
primary sensory perceptions."

Once again, those critical first few days and weeks of the virus contingency (March 2020) provide us with a time-tested real world example we can learn from. How could we have made sense of what was going on around us during the first days and weeks of the virus contingency? The same way we humans have been making sense of contagious viruses and diseases for thousands of years previous. By paying attention to what modern day virologists refer to as the "canary in a coal mine" pattern. Canary in a coal mine refers to the former practice of taking caged canaries into coal mines to alert the miners of the presence of invisible poison gas. If the canary got sick or died it meant that deadly gas was present.

The canaries in a coal mine during the initial outbreak of a virus are the people who work in high human contact jobs such as: airline and airport employees, grocery store cashiers, package and mail delivery personnel, restaurant workers, healthcare workers, etc. When these human canaries get sick in larger numbers than the general population it's a good indicator that the virus is highly contagious. So what were our human canaries telling us in March of 2020?

During the first few days and weeks of the virus pandemic—before face-masks, social distancing, and Plexiglas barriers were required—airports were packed to capacity with people flying to get back home, while grocery stores had their highest customer traffic and inventory turnover. Despite maximum exposure to other people and minimum barriers to protect them, neither the airport workers nor the grocery store workers, nor any of the other high human contact "canaries" got sick at rates that were statistically different from the general population.[148, 149, 150] During those first few weeks and months our senses were telling us that we could avoid getting infected with the COVID-19 virus by following the same common sense cold & flu prevention guidelines we use to avoid getting infected from the yearly flu.[151] **Believe in and trust your senses.**

Technology and the corporate media haven't made believing in and trusting our senses obsolete. They've made it absolute. Follow the Mach principle: only believe what you can see, hear, smell, taste or feel with your senses and/or with self-controlled sense-enhancing devices (e.g. telescopes, microscopes, stethoscopes, etc.).

Back to the Asteroid: What if the deflection option that world leaders decide to pursue begins falling dangerously behind schedule and the President from the political party the corporate media despises happens to mention a previously unthought-of outside the box option for deflecting the asteroid (e.g. an old Apollo rocket with a laser cannon mounted on it, or a Ballistic missile that can be launched from a transport plane, etc.).

Similar to HCQ the outside the box deflection option has been used many times in the past, is well known to scientists and engineers, readily available, and time-tested safe and effective. Will the corporate media objectively report on the promising potential of this safe and sensible alternative asteroid deflection option? Or will they use their echo chamber of negative news to cast doubt and fear upon it? Will they take down videos of unsanctioned rocket scientists who say the alternative option has merit? Will they character assassinate those who speak up, out, or for the alternative option? Will they once again choose political partisanship over the safety, security, and survival of we, the people, and our planet?

On the national front, have our politicians and corporate leaders earned the trust and respect required to motivate inspire, and convince us (their constituents) to continue going about our daily business in order to ensure we hold our economic and social infrastructures together? Has the way our recent leaders led, organized, and treated us earned them the benefit of the doubt? Or has it bankrupted their credibility? *Trust can't be bought or borrowed, it must be built over time via the choices leaders make for the people, place, and purpose they were given the privilege to lead.*

As time marches on and the asteroid continues zeroing in on our planet can we count on our governors, our mayors, our city council members, and our police chiefs to maintain law and order and safeguard the rights of law-abiding citizens? Or will some State and local-level leaders repeat recent patterns of behavior that prioritize the rights of convicted criminals and opportunistic anarchists over the rights of law-abiding citizens instead?

What if you and your family aren't able to access the food, water, and/or life-sustaining medical supplies that you desperately need? As our neighborhood stores run out of life-sustaining supplies people will panic buy and flock to other stores that still have supplies until those stores run out too. On and on it goes until every store is out of everything.

Are we prepared? A study conducted by the Federal Emergency Management Agency (FEMA) noted that the majority of households have enough food in their kitchens to feed a family of four for five days. Most of us shop for food week to week or whenever we need something. One of modern society's least talked about, and most life-altering advancements, is just-in-time food production and distribution. The FEMA study includes an ominous warning:

> *"The day to day efficiency of modern day transportation and logistics has lulled society into a false sense of security that leads us to believe we don't need to worry about when, where, or how we'll find life sustaining survival items (food, water, medicine, gas, etc.)."*

The survival of mankind's most massive metropolises (e.g. Moscow, Mexico City, Tokyo, London, Beijing, New Delhi, Los Angeles, etc.) depend on just-in-time supply, production, and distribution of food, water, medicine, gas, and other key sustainment supplies. FEMA estimates global food supplies will last seventy-four days without replenishment.[152]

When our bodies are deprived of air, water, food, and/or warmth, our brains begin to shut down and revert to reptilian brain functions. Survivalists refer to the rule of threes for human survival limits: On average, we can go three minutes without air, three hours without shelter in bad conditions, three days without water, and three weeks without food. Recall the reptilian brain is responsible for our primal instincts and our most basic survival functions such as heart rate, breathing, metabolism, and body temperature. *Self*-preservation always has and always will take biologic precedence over all other behaviors. A starving human lives to eat.

The longer people have to go without food, water, and their habit-forming drugs the more reptilian their brains will get. Whenever this occurs food riots are common and people begin to behave somewhat similar to packs of animals fighting over scraps of meat*. Another way of looking at it is that seemingly stable societies such as those we see in all major cities all across the planet are really only three to five days away from deprivation-induced anarchy.

> *When populations of people are oppressed and/*
> *or denied their freedom to participate and have a*
> *say in their own destiny they will always inevitably*
> *rise up against the source of their oppression.*

When your governor and/or mayor uses their self-anointed Emergency Powers to dictate stay at home orders or get out of your home orders from the comfort of their well-stocked command bunker, will you trust that your governor and/or mayor knows what's best for you and comply?

Or will the senseless suffering of your family, friends, and fellow humans along with knowledge that the suffering is a direct result of your political leaders senseless restrictions make you rue the day you voted

for them solely because of their political, religious, sexual, and/or ethnic affiliation? Will you wish you had voted for a common sense leader instead?

Will leaders at all levels rise to the occasion and conduct themselves in a way future historians pinpoint as the Rubicon moment in the history of our Homo sapiens species? Or as impact day closes in and time begins to run out will we humans prove we're no smarter than the dinosaurs as we stand around shaking our heads in anger, frustration, and regret because we didn't change "the way" "we, the freedom loving people of the planet," are led and organized while we still had a chance?

To summarize, while we may be technologically prepared to deal with a life threatening asteroid, the bigger potential threat to the survival of our species is the way we, the people have currently chosen to lead and organize ourselves before and/or after it hits.

You can substitute any other natural or man-made disaster scenario (earthquake, pandemic, volcano, economic or nuclear meltdown, chemical contamination, and/or war) and ask the same questions: Do you feel comfortable with the current way leaders make decisions and solve problems? Do you trust the future of the planet, the future of your family, and the future of our species to the way we, the people, are currently led and organized? **If not, isn't it time we Asteroid "the way"?**

REFLECTIONS/LESSON LEARNED
The Way vs. the Common Sense Way

As the imminent asteroid thought experiment and current world events continue to reinforce, there is some urgency for creating conscious awareness of the Common Sense Way. Our future is not preordained. It's unfolding right here, right now, right in front of us.

The omniscience of communication and information technology has created a hyper-connected, hyper-sensitive, hair-trigger world where we're never more than a handful of mislead (fake news) and/or misguided (emotional) choices away from economic, military, or politically-inspired anarchy or Armageddon. The threat to freedom from within, in the form of extremism, bureaucratic bungling, and political corruption, is as significant as that from any anti-freedom of choice enemy around the globe.

We, the freedom-loving people of the planet, hold our destinies in our hands and in our heads. To survive, thrive, and evolve we must join together in a renaissance manner to change the way our countries, companies, schools, and species thinks about leading and organizing.

What's needed is an entirely new way. Not a way based on revisionist recommendations from super-rich CEO's, or a way based on academic theory, or consultant cut-and-pastes. We need a way that makes sense based on:

1. The way the real world going on around us works (e.g. the laws of nature, atoms, gravity, time, and DNA, etc.).

2. The way our DNA-enabled nervous systems are biologically hard-wired to learn from, adapt to, and make sense of the world around us and sensible choices about what to do next.

3. The evolutionary way our species got to where we are today: freedom of choice and freedom of speech to make sense of the world around us and sensible choices for the purpose, and the people we have the privilege to lead.

There is another way.

It's the Common Sense Way	
The Way	**The Common Sense Way**
• Process oriented	• Purpose oriented
• Do what you're told to do	• Do what makes sense
• Stay in your lane	• Learn to adapt to patterns
• Follow plans from the past	• Freedom to make sensible choices
• Orders, Commands	• Logic of Why it makes sense
• Strategy, Plans, Disconnected Chain-of-Command	• Foundational Logic of Why (FLOW)
• Wait to be told	• Develop the Situation/Go with the FLOW
• Organizational Structure	• Organize to learn
• Get along or get out	• Collaborate, Communicate, Reciprocate
• Teach them how to follow the process	• Teach them how to think
• Stay anchored to the chain	• Build learning-feedback loops not ladders
• Need to know	• Shared Reality
• Stoic/Not fun	• Humor/Creativity

Choosing the Common Sense Way isn't political or ideological. It's biological. Common sense leaders across the ages such as those that participated in the American Revolution of 1776, Poland's Solidarity uprising of 1980, Czechoslovakia's Velvet Revolution of 1989, and the Hong Kong Freedom Protests of 2019, instinctively rise up and band together whenever they perceive their leadership or governance is impeding, instead of enabling, their most inherently human right: freedom of choice and its verbal manifestation freedom of speech.

> *"We have it in our power to begin the world over again."*
> *"The cause of America (Freedom) is in great measure*
> *the cause of all of Mankind."* Thomas Paine

The Common Sense Revolution is upon us. Armed with knowledge of the new metaphors and timeless principles of the Common Sense Way we can collaborate, communicate, and reciprocate as common sense sentinels to change the way our countries, companies, schools, and species thinks about leading and organizing one human social system at a time. To accomplish our purpose we don't need a master strategy, plan, or step-by-step instructions from a disconnected chain of command. All we need is common ground on common sense:

> *"No one told us how to organize, so we self-organized. No*
> *one had to remind us of our purpose; our purpose was*
> *said out loud and shared by all. We didn't have a roster, or*
> *organizational structure, or a flag, or a chain-of-command.*
> *All we had was common ground on common sense."*

To put the Common Sense Way into practice, common sense leaders teach their people how to see themselves and those around them through the common lens and common language of common sense/ knowledge of patterns. There's no substitute for a prepared mind.

Common sense leaders prime their people's minds by saying the language of common sense out loud, sharing it with all, and constantly pressure testing it with everyday use. The more often you repeat a new pattern intentionally and precisely the same way, the faster it becomes a new routine. Over time, with feedback, our brains learn to adapt. It's the "Common Sense Way."

Patterns of evolutionary history such as walking upright, making stone tools, and speaking, reveal three things about the "Common Sense Way": it is unique to our Homo sapiens species, it's contagious, and it always prevails. We wouldn't be here today if it didn't. It doesn't take a lot from any of us, it only takes a little from a lot of us. **Stay calm. Breathe deep. Engage your Neocortex and let the Common Sense Revolution begin.**

NOTES

1. Pressfield, S. *Gates of Fire, 1999, Bantam. (One of greatest common sense leadership books ever written.)*

2. Predator is an un-manned aerial drone.

3. The Joint Chiefs of Staff is a cabinet of senior military officers within the United States Armed Forces who advise the Secretary of Defense and President on military matters.

4. The Coalition Provisional Authority (CPA) was a transitional government of Iraq following the invasion of the country on March 19, 2003. The Coalition consisted of the United States, the United Kingdom, Australia, Poland, and Spain. Ambassador Paul Bremer lead the CPA.

5. A lookout.

6. A current estimation of human total cell number calculated for a variety of organs and cell types is presented. These partial data correspond to a total number of 3.72×10^{13}. "An estimation of the number of cells in the human body," by Eva Bianconi, Allison Piovesan, Federica Facchin, Alina Beraudi, Raffaella Casadei, Flavia Frabetti, et al." Pages 463–471. Received 26 Sep 2012, Accepted 09 May 2013, Published online: 05 Jul 2013

7. Coen, E. PhD, *Cells to Civilizations: The Principles of Change That Shape Life, 2012, Princeton University Press,*

8. Lakoff, George, Johnson Mark, *Metaphors We Live By,* University of Chicago Press; 1st edition (December 19, 2008)

9. Weatherhead, L. D. *On Comradeship,*

10. In the context of foreign affairs, Inter-agency most commonly refers to interactions between agencies that are considered instruments of National power (e.g. Department of Defense, Department of State, the CIA, and the FBI).

11. Schroen, G. C. *First In: An Insider's Account of How the CIA Spearheaded the War on Terror in Afghanistan.* 2005. Presidio Press

12. SAD = Special Activity Division

13. IBID

14. The 9/11 Commission Report, New York, W.W. Norton and Company, 2004. 113, 120

15. Blaber, P.E. The Mission, The Men, And Me, Life Lessons of a Former Delta Force Commnder, Berkely, New York, pg 106

16. IBID

17. SAR is short for Search and Rescue, in this case it refers to dedicated helicopters, crews, and support staff that were capable of 24/7 medical support for the military personnel on the ground. This was a non-negotiable prerequisite for approval of any form of military participation. There was no such prerequisite for CIA personnel.

18. Schroen, 143

19. Although his full name is often spelled Osama bin Laden, "UBL" is the transliteration used by the U.S. Government and all U.S. military forces on the ground in Afghanistan

20. Berntsen, G. *Jawbreaker: The Attack on Bin Laden and Al-Qaeda: A Personal Account by the CIA's Key Field Commander. 2005. New York: Crown Publishers. 255–265.*

21. Donald Rumsfeld was Secretary of Defense from 1975–1977, and 2001–2006

22. French expression meaning "helper in the military camp." In the U.S. Military every General Officer has an aide-de-camp who accompanies them wherever they go and coordinates their schedules and communications for them.

23. Ability of a system to spontaneously arrange its components in a purposeful (non-random) manner without the direction of an external agent. Many natural systems such as cells, chemical compounds, galaxies, organisms and planets show this property. Self-organization is a process where some form of overall order or coordination emerges out of the local interactions between the individuals based on a common sense of purpose.

24. Amgen is a biotechnology company located in Southern California. The reason I chose it was because it was the first stock I ever purchased in 1994.

25. Approximately 300,000 years ago.

26. A for Adenine, C for Cytosine, G for Guanine and T for Thymine.

27. On June 26, 2000, Francis Collins and Craig Venter of the Human Genome Project jointly announced at the White House that human beings are 99.5 percent identical genetically.

28. The system of neurons, neurochemicals, and allied structures involved in receiving sensory stimuli, generating and coordinating responses, and controlling bodily activities: in vertebrates it includes the brain, spinal cord, nerves, and ganglia.

29. Hunt, M. *The Universe Within. 1982, Simon & Schuster*

30. IBID

31. Photo of Presidential Palace, Baghdad, Iraq, Photo by Staff Sgt. Michael Pryor, 2d Brigade, 82d Airborne Division Public Affairs. "The appearance of U.S. Department of Defense (DoD) visual information does not imply or constitute DoD endorsement."

32. Saturday is the Holy day for Muslims.

33. Pei, M. Kasper S. "Lessons from the Past: The American Record of Nation Building," Carnegie Endowment,

34. HESCO barriers are collapsible wire mesh containers with a heavy-duty fabric liner that are filled with sand, rock, and/or dirt, and used as temporary or semi-permanent fortifications against explosions and/or small-arms in both Iraq and Afghanistan.

35. Gordon, M. Trainer, B.E. *Cobra II, 2006. New York, Pantheon Books*

36. This reference to the history of leadership was inspired by an author of an Internet post that is no longer on-line.

37. Hunt, M., 160

38. Complexity science was pioneered by 'The Santa Fe Institute' which is a not-for-profit, independent research and education center where researchers come together to collaborate across disciplines, merging ideas and principles of many fields—e.g. biology, physics, mathematics, social sciences and the humanities—in pursuit of creative insights that improve our world

39. Buckingham, M. Coffman, C. *First, Break All the Rules: What the World's Greatest Managers Do Differently.* 2014. Gallup Press

40. *Age of Reason* (1794) continues the concepts of "Common Sense" and "Rights of Man" and asserts the individual's right to freedom of choice.

41. Employee Climate Surveys are used to provide a picture of an organization's strengths and weaknesses. The climate survey is a tool for gathering employee feedback on a variety of key issues such as leadership, communication, work environment, professional development, and retention.

42. The Corps of Discovery was a specially-established unit of the United States Army which formed the nucleus of the Lewis and Clark Expedition that took place between May 1804 and September 1806. The Corps was led jointly by Meriwether Lewis and William Clark. To create the Corps of Discovery and to maximize its potential for success, Lewis wanted to find the best possible men he could and recruit them to join his expedition. Men were expected to be excellent hunters and possess skills that would ensure their survival in the wilderness. He also

wanted men who were brave, unmarried, and healthy. Lewis entrusted recruitment to Clark. Clark went to Louisville, Kentucky where he found his first recruits who became known as the "Nine Young Men from Kentucky": William Bratton, John Colter, Joseph Field, Reubin Field, Charles Floyd, George Gibson, Nathaniel Pryor, George Shannon, and John Shields. **In total almost a third of the party's permanent members were highly experienced Frontiersmen who possessed survival skills and wilderness acumen that few other men on the planet could equal at the time.** Sacagawea and her knowledge of plants, weather, and Indian language was the final piece of the puzzle that made The Corps of Discovery one of the most highly skilled and well-prepared teams in human history

43. John Maynard Smith, Naturalist, from Sussex England.

44. In 1959 Robert W. White wrote a classic article for *Psychological Review* titled, *"Motivation Reconsidered: The Concept of Competence."*

45. Conklin, J. PhD, *Wicked Problems and Fragmentation,* 2001, pg. 6

46. On June 26, 2000, Francis Collins and Craig Venter of the Human Genome Project jointly announced at the White House that human beings are 99.5 percent identical genetically.

47. Rosenberg, N. Pritchard, J.K. Weber, J.L. Cann, H.M. Kidd, K.K. Zhivotovsky, Z.V. Feldman, m.w. (2002) "Genetic Structure of Human Populations," Science 298: 2381–2385.

48. IBID

49. All DNA analysis vendors struggle to separate ethnicity clusters within continents, in particular, within Europe. Which is why ethnicity estimates are generally only accurate to the continent level.

50. http://www.newsweek.com/there-no-such-thing-race-283123 11/8/14

51. Andreasen, R.O. (2000). Race, Biologic Reality or Social Construct? Philosophy oof Science, 76, 653–665

52. Mevorach, Katya Gibel (2007). "Race, racism, and academic complicity". American Ethnologist. *34* (2): 238–41. doi:10.1525/ae.2007.34.2.238.

53. Marks, Jonathan (1996). Science and Race. American Behavioral Scientist. 40, 123–133.

54. "Unraveling the Human Genome: Six Molecular Milestones," Stephanie Pappas January 23, 2013, *Live Science.*

55. Gordon, M. M. (1964). Assimilation in American Life: The Role of Race, Religion, and National Origins. Oxford: Oxford University Press. ISBN 978-0-19-500896-8.

56. Barnshaw, John (2008). *"Race".* In Schaefer, Richard T. (ed.).

Encyclopedia of Race, Ethnicity, and Society, Volume 1. SAGE
Publications. pp. 1091–3. *ISBN 978-1-45-226586-5.*

57. The epistemological moment where the modern concept of race was
    invented and rationalized lies somewhere between 1730 and 1790.
    Bancel, Nicolas; David, Thomas; Thomas, Dominic, eds. (23 May
    2019). "Introduction: The Invention of Race: Scientific and Popular
    Representations of Race from Linnaeus to the Ethnic Shows". The
    Invention of Race: Scientific and Popular Representations. Routledge. p.
    11. *ISBN 978-0367208646.* "The Invention of Race" has assisted us in the
    process of locating the "epistemological moment," somewhere between
    1730 and 1790, when the concept of race was invented and rationalized.
    A "moment" that was accompanied by a revolution in the way in
    which the human body was studied and observed in order to formulate
    scientific conclusions relating to human variability.

58. Harvard Magazine, May–June 2008. *Race in a Genetic World.*
    https://harvardmagazine.com/2008/05/race-in-a-genetic-world-html

59. IBID

60. IBID

61. Morgan Freeman is an American actor, director and narrator.

62. https://blog.hubspot.com/sales/why-we-hate-meetings-so-much

63. https://www.nobelprize.org/nobel_prizes/medicine/laureates/
    2004/press.html

64. "Bear" is used throughout the book as the universal metaphor for
    caution and/or a real-world danger

65. Thomas, A. *Harnessing The Windmills Of The Mind.* 2016.Body and Soul
    Books. 146–149

66. Olfactory refers to our **"olfactory** nerves," the nerves that pass from the
    nose to the brain and contain the receptors that make smelling possible.

67. Neuroscience doesn't agree on how many total senses humans have,
    they do agree on the five primary senses.

68. Dawkins, R. *The Blind Watchmaker: Why the Evidence of Evolution
    Reveals a Universe without Design.* 1986. W.W. Norton

69. Wolfram Alpha DNA Facts: If we uncoiled a single strand of our DNA it
    would be approximately 6 feet long. That's 1.8 billion feet of DNA in our
    neocortex alone. Enough to stretch from your body to the moon and
    part of the way back. (**225,623 miles away at its closest, (x) 5,280 ft per
    mile = 1,191,289,440 If you include the DNA contained in the rest of
    your body's 33 trillion (+) cells it would stretch from Earth to Pluto and
    back…12 times.

70. The term "algorithm" is most often associated with computers; when used to describe the brain it's not to imply....

71. Thomas, A. 148

72. IBID. 220

73. Thomas, A. 147

74. Someone whose sarcastic, wisecracking, or humorous manner is delivered in an offensive, obnoxious, or cocky way. https://www.merriam-webster.com/dictionary/smart%20aleck

75. Many years later I learned that Saint Vitus is considered the patron saint of actors, comedians, dancers, and epileptics.

76. The triune brain model suggests the Reptilian or Primal Brain evolved first and is thought to be in charge of our primal instincts, followed by the Mammalian or Emotional brain that's in charge of our emotions, and finally our newest brain the neocortex or "thinking" brain which is responsible for rational or logical thought. Some dismiss the triune brain model as an oversimplification, which of course it is because any discussion of the human brain at this time in human history is an oversimplification of the most complex organism yet discovered in our Universe.

77. It is important to recognize that the functions of this part of the brain have to take precedence over other brain activity. For example, if you try to hold your breath (a neocortex initiated activity), you will find that as carbon dioxide builds up in your bloodstream the reptilian brain is going to respond with panic and anxiety in order to regain control and make you breathe again. By strengthening your neocortex (stay calm and sing a song) you can increase your resistance to the basic urge to breathe for three-plus minutes. However, inevitably, eventually, your biology will force you to give in and take a breath. To hack in and take control of your nervous system, I highly recommend WimHoff.com. I've been doing the Wim Hoff breathing routine in the morning since 2016: thirty deep breaths, exhale and hold breath for three-plus minutes; exhale, hold another fifteen seconds. Repeat thirty deep breaths, exhale and hold while doing as many push-ups as possible.

78. Lamia, M.C. *Emotions!: Making Sense of Your Feelings*. 2012. Magination Press

79. http://humanorigins.si.edu/education/introduction-human-evolution

80. Thomas, A. 105.

81. Hunt, M. *The Universe Within. 1982, Simon & Schuster*

82. Trevena, J. Miller, J. (2010). "Brain preparation before a voluntary action: Evidence against unconscious movement initiation". Consciousness and Cognition. 19 (1): 447–56.

83. https://www.psychologytoday.com/us/blog/understanding-the-anxious-mind/201912/the-3-parts-anxiety-thoughts- emotions-and-behaviors, (Schlenker & others, 1994; Tice, 1992)

84. Hof, W. De Jong, K. Itzler, J. *The Way of The Iceman: How The Wim Hof Method Creates Radiant Longterm Health—Using The Science and Secrets of Breath Control, Cold-Training and Commitment. 2016.* Dragon Door Publications. This was a life changing book for me. Though Wim Hoff does not talk about the neocortex specifically, he reinforces the life-saving importance of a strong neocortex when faced with the harshest of physical survival challenges. By controlling your breathing and strengthening your neocortex you not only strengthen your body you also enable your mind to override your instinctive reactions to cold and wet survival situations (think of falling in the icy waters engulfing the Titanic and having the ability to swim to a raft.) I do Wim Hoff's morning routine of deep breathing, holding my breath for 3:10, then another round of deep breathing before doing 80 push-ups while holding my breath. Wim Hoff teaches you how to strengthen your neocortex to control your nervous system.

85. Gonzales, L. *Deep Survival: Who Lives, Who Dies, and Why. 2003.* W. W. Norton & Company

86. Halo = High Altitude Low Opening Parachute

87. https://www.lockheedmartin.com/en-us/products/c130/history.html.

88. Photo by Staff Sgt. Jonathan A. Guzman, U.S. Air Force. "The appearance of U.S. Department of Defense (DoD) visual information does not imply or constitute DoD endorsement."

89. Photo by Tech. Sgt. Jason Robertson United States Air Forces Central. "The appearance of U.S. Department of Defense (DoD) visual information does not imply or constitute DoD endorsement."

90. Coen, E. PhD, *Cells to Civilizations: The Principles of Change That Shape Life, 2012, Princeton University Press.*

91. https://www.livescience.com/33895-human-eye.html

92. Rosenau, J.N. The Study of World Politics and theoretical and methodological challenges, Vol I, pg. 116, Routledge, New York, 2006.

93. Peterson, J.B. 12 Rules for Life: An Antidote to Chaos. 2018. Random House Canada.

94. Newberg, A. Waldman, M.R. 2012. *Words Can Change Your Brain: 12 Conversation Strategies to Build Trust, Resolve Conflict, and Increase Intimacy.* Avery Publishing.

95. Photo by Staff Sgt. Billy J. Nelson, Jr., Combat Camera Afghanistan. "The appearance of U.S. Department of Defense (DoD) visual information does not imply or constitute DoD endorsement."

96. Eid al-Adha (Festival of the Sacrifice), also called the "Sacrifice Feast" or "Bakr-Eid," is the second of two Muslim holidays celebrated worldwide each year and considered the holier of the two.

97. Thirteen hours total. At the time, the longest AC-130 combat mission ever.

98. A burka is a long, loose fitting garment usually blue in color that covers a woman's entire body from head to feet.

99. As we were loading the aircraft in preparation for takeoff, a staff officer from our Higher Headquarters ran up to me and said "we're adding a Navy Fighter Pilot to the other AC-130 for this mission." I was momentarily speechless, "there's already an LNO on that aircraft and adding a non-operational person who didn't participate in any of the rehearsals is something you never do in training and don't even think about doing for a combat mission…" The staff officer cut me off mid-protest, "the chief-of-staff wants him up there in case the ground guys need help with close-air support." I quickly explained that I was Air Force certified to control any type of close air support aircraft." "What if your aircraft goes down? We have to have redundancy, the decision is final." I knew it didn't make sense but the fact that the AC-130's engines were running and we only had thirty minutes to get situated before taxiing for takeoff, meant I didn't have the time to get to a phone and call the "chief of staff" to protest. Nor did I have the time to comprehend the down-stream implications of the decision. Like 9/11 and the U.S. election of 2020, I failed to imagine the potential for catastrophe and chaos, in this case from what a last-minute addition to a back-up aircraft could cause once we were over the target. In this regard I also believe I was complicit.

100. "Feelings Into Words: Contributions of Language to Exposure Therapy," Katharina Kircanski, Matthew D. Lieberman, and Michelle G. Craske, UCLA, https://www.scn.ucla.edu/pdf/Kircanski(inpress)PsychSci.pdf

101. Thomas, A. 160

102. Peterson, J.B. Introduction

103. Blaber, P.E. *The Mission, the Men, and Me, 2008, Berkley*

104. Photo by Sgt. Jonathan Thomas, U.S. Air Force. "The appearance of U.S. Department of Defense (DoD) visual information does not imply or constitute DoD endorsement."

105. Pashtu is the common language spoken in Kandahar and most of southern and eastern Afghanistan.

106. Actual grid coordinates redacted for operational security reasons.

107. VTC" stands for Video Tele-Conference

108. Photo taken by my friend and fellow AFO Operator, Mike aka "Goody." In 2020. Mike died as he lived, in service to his country and protecting those he loved. His memory and his sacrifices for freedom live on with all of us.

109. Those were the exact words he said to me and exactly the way we shared it with each of the teams.

110. Winning hearts and minds is a term born out of cold way colonialism. It started from the premise that every conflict was a conflict between Communism and Democracy. If one side does more for the host country than the other side then they will "win" their hearts and minds. Reality says you can't "win" people's hearts and minds unless you live with them and are subject to the same hardships as them. No expeditionary army in recorded history has ever won the hearts and minds of the local populace. You can accomplish your purpose without "winning" the hearts and minds, however it will be almost impossible to succeed if you lose the hearts and minds of the locals. .

111. R-O-E governs the conditions under which members of the military are authorized to use force during combat operations

112. Actual grid redacted for operational security reasons.

113. https://www.merriam-webster.com/dictionary/why

114. Hunt, M., 112

115. Thomas, A. 155

116. We called it "Foundational Logic" in 2002.

117. Biology 2.0

118. Neolithic Settlement. Illustration by Zdeněk Burian

119. John Nash's Nobel Prize winning "Strategic Gaming Theory proved that a reciprocal, or "tit-for-tat," strategy results in a consistently positive overall outcome for any group/team. In a "reciprocal" strategy the first person "communicates" their willingness to "collaborate" and then practices "reciprocity" in all subsequent interactions. If the second person continues to reciprocate then they *both* continue collaborating and communicating until they accomplish their purpose. If the initial offer of collaboration is rejected, met with hostility, or competition, then the person who made the offer reciprocates accordingly. To collaborate, our brains instinctively communicate and reciprocate. Even when we're not consciously aware of it.

120. Hackworth, D.H. *About Face; the Odyssey of an American Warrior. 1989.* Simon & Schuster

121. 'Drone' is a term used by military personnel to describe a state of mind that occurs when an individual is physically exhausted and sleep deprived. A 'drone-fest' occurs when most everyone is 'droning'.

122. A patrol base is a location (usually in the woods) that a platoon uses as a base of operations from which to launch patrols. It's primarily used so the platoon can rest, reorganize, or ready mission-essential equipment and personnel for a follow-on operation.

123. Standard operating procedure for map checks during hours of limited visibility is to stop, take a knee, and put a poncho over your head to ensure the enemy won't inadvertently see your light.

124. Hand railing is a land navigation term that describes the technique of using a linear terrain feature such as a road, a ridge, or a river as a navigation "handrail" to guide you to your destination.

125. Lt. Gen. Walter Ulmer, 1986

126. Moore, H. G. Galloway, J.L. *We Were Soldiers Once And Young.* 1992. Random House

127. Coen, E. PhD, *Cells to Civilizations: The Principles of Change That Shape Life, 2012,* Princeton University Press, pg 2673

128. In 2002, while still at NASA, Lu co-founded the B612 Foundation, dedicated to protecting the Earth from asteroid strikes. As of 2020, he is its Executive Director. (https://b612foundation.org/our-team/#hash_filters=leadership)

129. https://www.nasa.gov/planetarydefense/overview

130. As of 2020 NASA/JPL NEO offered a "Deflection App" that was available for free download. https://cneos.jpl.nasa.gov/nda/: Although this app was not designed to be an operational tool for actual mission planning, it provides the same tools that astrophysicists use to calculate how to deflect an asteroid.

131. This scenario is part of the actual NASA "war-game" conducted in 2019. https:www.nasa.com

132. According to Noam Chomsky, the "Mainstream Media" in the U.S. includes cable and national networks, CNN, MSNBC, CBS, ABC, FOX, as well as most of the biggest newspapers: NYT, Washington Post, USA Today, LA Times, etc. All of these "media corporations" are owned, funded, and controlled by an interconnected network of large profit-motivated conglomerates.

133. "Big Tech" includes Google, Apple, Facebook, Microsoft, Twitter, etc.

134. https://www.projectveritas.com/news/google-election-influence-exposed-senior-google-executive-ashwin-agrawal/

135. https://www.thegatewaypundit.com/2020/08/broadcast-coverage-trump-95-negative-new-study-says/ https://www.investors.com/politics/editorials/media-bias-left-study/ A recent report from *Wired* magazine states that almost ninety-five percent of donations from employees working at Silicon Valley tech giants such as Alphabet, Amazon, Apple, Facebook, Microsoft, and Oracle went to Democratic presidential nominee Joe Biden over President Donald Trump. Wired reports that employees from the tech firms have contributed twenty times as much money to Biden as to Trump since the start of 2019. https://www.journalism.org/2017/10/02/covering-president-trump-in-a-polarized-media-environment/pj_2017-10-02_trump-first-100-days_c-16.

136. "Hydroxychloroquine Sulfate Monograph for Professionals". The American Society of Health-System Pharmacists. 20 March 2020. *Archived* from the original on 20 March 2020. Retrieved March 20, 2020.

137. Statement made by Department of Veterans Affairs Secretary Robert Wilkie on May, 21, 2020

138. World Health Organization (2019). World Health Organization model list of essential medicines: 21st list 2019. Geneva: World Health Organization. *hdl:10665/325771*. WHO/MVP/EMP/IAU/2019.06. License: CC BY-NC-SA 3.0 IGO. https://apps.who.int/iris/bitstream/handle/10665/325771/WHO-MVP-EMP-IAU-2019.06-eng.pdf?ua=1

139. "Hydroxychloroquine Sulfate—Drug Usage Statistics". ClinCalc. Retrieved April 7, 2020

140. Severe acute respiratory syndrome (SARS) is a viral respiratory illness caused by a coronavirus, called SARS-associated coronavirus (SARS-CoV). SARS was first reported in Asia in February 2003. Over the next few months, the illness spread to more than two-dozen countries in North America, South America, Europe, and Asia before the SARS global outbreak of 2003. https://www.cdc.gov/sars/about/fs-sars.html

141. CDC.com; Costedoat-Chalumeau N, Amoura Z, Duhaut P, et al. Safety of hydroxychloroquine in pregnant patients with connective tissue diseases. *Arthritis Rheumatism*. 2003;48:3207-3211.

142. Aspirin is associated with a risk of Reye's syndrome in children. Therefore, you should not give aspirin to a child or teen unless specifically directed by a doctor. Generally, aspirin isn't recommended during pregnancy unless you have certain medical conditions. (Source: https://www.mayoclinic.org/healthy-lifestyle/pregnancy)

143. Note: HCQ and other corticosteroids do not kill the virus. They work by preventing the body's autoimmune system from overreacting (aka a "cytokine storm") and attacking the body instead of the virus. Susceptibility to this type of overreaction increases with age. It is the

resulting inflammation that is the primary cause of COVID deaths. When the cytokine storm reaction is controlled, antibodies that kill the virus are produced normally. HCQ is most effective when administered early before severe symptoms develop.

144. Dr. Zelenko made this statement during an interview on The Dennis Prager radio show of July 10, 2020:

145. https://detroit.cbslocal.com/2020/07/06/henry-ford-health-system-study-hydroxychloroquine-lowers-covid-19-death-rate/

146. https://humanevents.com/2021/03/13/bad-optics-on-pseudo-events-and-pseudo-democracy/. By Adam Ellwanger, March 13, 2021

147. Lifson, T., www.americanthinker.com, 2020

148. Justin Blackburn, Constantin T Yiannoutsos, Aaron E Carroll, Infection Fatality Ratios for COVID-19 Among Noninstitutionalized Persons 12 and Older: Results of a Random-Sample Prevalence Study. Annals of Internal Medicine, Jan 2021

149. Scott Atlas US Senate Testimony, May 6, 2020, https://www.hsgac.senate.gov/imo/media/doc/Testimony-Atlas-2020-05-06.pdf

150. John Ioannidis US Senate Testimony, May 6, 2020, https://www.hsgac.senate.gov/imo/media/doc/Testimony-Ioannidis-2020-05-06.pdf

151. Keep your hands clean, avoid touching your eyes and nose, stay home if you feel sick, and practice good health habits (get plenty of sleep, be physically active, manage your stress, drink plenty of fluids, and eat nutritious food).

152. https://www.fema.gov/

Made in the USA
Las Vegas, NV
09 September 2023

77299252R00152